ORDINARY

John Rowan in Vice-President of the European Association for Humanistic Psychology, a board member of the Association of Humanistic Psychology Practitioners, review editor of *Self and Society*, and on the editorial board of the *Journal of Humanistic Psychology*. He works in private practice as a psychotherapist and organizational consultant, and teaches at the Institute of Psychotherapy and Society Studies in London. John Rowan's previous books include *The Reality Game* (1983) and *The Horned God* (1987), both published by Routledge & Kegan Paul.

ORDINARY ECSTASY

HUMANISTIC PSYCHOLOGY IN ACTION
(Second edition)

JOHN ROWAN

ROUTLEDGE

LONDON AND NEW YORK

First published in 1976
This edition first published in 1988 by
Routledge
11 New Fetter Lane, London EC4P 4EE

Published in the USA by
Routledge
in association with Methuen Inc.
29 West 35th Street, New York, NY 10001

Set in 10 on 12 point Times Roman
by Columns of Reading
and printed in Great Britain
by The Guernsey Press Co. Ltd.,
Guernsey, Channel Islands

Library of Congress Cataloging in Publication Data

Rowan, John.
Ordinary ecstasy.

Bibliography: p.
Includes index.
1. Humanistic psychology.   I. Title.
[DNLM: 1. Humanism.   2. Psychology.
BF 204 R877o]
BF204.R68   1988   150.19′2   87–23455

British Library CIP Data also available
ISBN 0–415–00190–0

THIS BOOK IS FOR SUE
WHO DID SO MUCH

CONTENTS

vii

CONTENTS

CONTENTS

INTRODUCTION

IN INTRODUCING a second edition, I thought at first that it would only be necessary to say that the intention of the first edition was maintained. I said in the introduction to that edition that this was a book either for people who have heard of humanistic psychology and want to know more about it, or for people who have been to an encounter group (or co-counselling, or meditation, or any of the other activities mentioned in this book) and want to understand more about what they have been doing.

This book, I said then, was intended to tell such people something of the spirit of humanistic psychology, its scope and limits, where it came from, what it actually does in each field, and how it might develop in the future.

But whereas in the first edition it was sufficient to say that humanistic psychology existed and was an exciting new field – because very little literature had been available in Britain about it – now, eleven years later we have to be much tougher and more specific. In the first edition I said:

> It is not intended as a book of academic scholarship, but rather as a pointing finger, showing some definite directions. It is not totally balanced, not totally complete, not totally detached. I am personally involved in humanistic psychology, and biased in favour of it. I haven't done elaborate research in writing this book, but have simply written of what I know best. There is a lot of me in this book.

But now that is not enough. We have to answer the

criticisms which have been made of humanistic psychology; we have to deal with the further ramifications which have emerged; we have to be aware of the different historical and economic situation we are living in now.

Although this book is addressed to the general reader, it does try to satisfy the proper academic conscience which says – How do you know this? What right have you got to say this? I have tried, by giving rather full references for further reading, to leave the way open for the reader to do properly scholarly checking. The advanced theory is all there, the empirical research is all there, for the reader who is curious enough to check these references.

In revising it I have tried to keep to the spirit of the original, and to change as little as possible. The main changes come in three areas – the advent of primal integration therapy, which I did not come across until 1977, and which puts together many of the separate approaches to therapy which had been developed up to that time in one coherent framework; the theoretical work of Alvin Mahrer, which only appeared in 1978 and onwards, and which shows how the best insights of the existential thinkers can be translated into practical action; and the success of Ken Wilber, from 1977 onwards, in integrating the whole process of psychospiritual development into one coherent map. Many smaller details have changed a great deal too, in the years between, and those who are familiar with the old book may find it substantially changed.

But the main thrust remains constant. Humanistic psychology is interested in personal growth, existential choice and the fulfilment of human potential. It is on the side of healthy change, and against alienation and human diminution. If you want to know what this means, read on.

PART ONE

WHAT IS HUMANISTIC PSYCHOLOGY?

CHAPTER ONE

―――――――――=❦❦❦=―――――――――

THE WESTERN ORIGINS

HUMANISTIC psychology is not just a new brand of psychology to set side by side on the shelves with all the old brands. It is a whole different way of looking at psychological science. It is a way of doing science which includes love, involvement and spontaneity, instead of systematically excluding them. And the object of this science is not the prediction and control of people's behaviour, but the liberation of people from the bonds of neurotic control, whether this comes from outside (in the structures of our society) or from inside.

Most of us have felt, at some time or other, that we were less free than we wanted to be. Perhaps the limitation seemed to come from the family situation, perhaps it seemed to come from the job, or the lack of one; or perhaps it seemed to come from our own inability to get things together, to overcome the problems inside ourselves. Often it is not clear precisely where the main problem does lie.

If we want to get to the heart of this mystery (how many of our difficulties come from outside and how many from inside) one of the best places to start may be the small group. In a group, we have the external pressures and the internal conflicts all present and actually operating in some form. Even if what is there is not precisely the same as in our natural situation, there may be enough similarities at least to give us some hints.

GROUP DYNAMICS

In 1946 an extraordinary incident happened, which suddenly threw a flood of light on this subject. A number of people had been working with Kurt Lewin (Marrow 1969) on various semi-political approaches to the study of groups, particularly focusing on the question of how to use groups to develop more democratic attitudes within the participants. (Lewin as someone who had left Nazi Germany had a particular interest in fighting fascism.) It had become obvious, because of the Nazi and fascist propaganda during the war, that authoritarian attitudes were strongly favourable to, and tied in with, extreme right-wing politics. And a lot of evidence had accumulated that rigidly hierarchical organization, where all power is concentrated at the top, and carefully delegated downwards, encouraged authoritarian attitudes, and diminished democratic attitudes. As soon as one said this kind of thing, however, people had immediately accused Lewin of wanting to subvert all authority, and assumed that if you did away with rigid hierarchies, you did away with order as such – and this could only lead to chaos. But Lewin and his co-workers in social psychology then did a series of experiments which were later repeated many times, showing that there was such a thing as democratic leadership (aiming at cooperation and participation) and that it actually worked better (in Western cultures at least) than autocratic leadership. This had led to a whole series of training courses led by people close to Lewin, in which people were taught the skills of democratic leadership. And because of the success of these courses, people came from all over the world to observe such training groups.

What happened on this occasion in 1946 was that the observers of one training group arranged to have a meeting with the group trainers one evening to discuss what had been going on in the group that day. The trainees asked if they could attend that meeting. This was unheard of at the time, and was clearly risky, introducing a completely untried element into the course, which could conceivably upset the trainees and be more than they could cope with. It could also expose the trainers to criticism in front of the trainees, which felt like a dangerous thing to do. How would it affect them?

There are two things I want to underline about this: first, the pressure came from the bottom, from the people who were affected most, and second, there was genuine risk-taking on the part of those in charge, as it was agreed to, and the meeting duly took place. The interaction became emotional, involving, almost explosive, but was a fantastic learning experience for those who took part. The meeting went on into the early hours, and became the first occasion when the principle of feedback (telling people honestly how their actions come across to you) was used on such a scale.

It may seem crazy to us now, that Lewin and the others had for so long tried to teach democratic attitudes through the process of a *leader* giving *lectures*, even though there was some practice and working-through allowed, often in the form of role-playing. But without theory and without planning, the principle of feedback was discovered.

In other fields, feedback was already important. What was now being discovered was that certain kinds of feedback could also help to make human beings more self-controlled, more in charge of their own lives.

This, then, was the origin of what is now known as the T-group (Bradford et al. 1964) – T stands for Training – which has been used a great deal by organizations which are trying to move over from an autocratic to a more participative style of management. The aim is to produce a person who is sure enough of herself not to need to push others around or restrict their freedom.

The process by which a person becomes so sure and self-aware has been called by Maslow 'self-actualization' (Maslow 1970). It means becoming that self which you truly are. It means realizing all of what you have it in you to be. It has been said that there can only be self-actualizing people, probably never any self-actualized people. It seems to be not a state but a process – a process of continually laying oneself on the line and being open to experience, so that one can genuinely meet it. Mahrer (1978) later clarified this a good deal by distinguishing between integration and actualization.

More recently (Rowan 1983a) I have worked on the question of what exactly Maslow meant by self-actualization, and it appears that he had a two-stage version of it. Stage one was basic self-actualization in existential terms (we shall be looking at this later in this chapter), and stage two was self-actualization with peak experiences, or in other words a more transcendent, or spiritual, or mystical experience: we shall come back to this in Chapter 9.

Maslow was working at about the same time as Lewin, and he did not know how well his ideas were to fit in at what became the National Training Laboratories in Maine. Maslow (1970) had got the idea of studying people who seemed to have gone a long way down the line of self-actualization – who seemed more healthy and more truly human than the average. What he found was that these people had a number of things in common – a very clear perception of reality (as distinct from the social lie, or what is supposed to be the case), a simple acceptance of themselves and others, a high degree of spontaneity, and so on.

Abraham Maslow is a very important pioneer figure in humanistic psychology. His theory of human needs and human development says that there is a normal process of growth which applies to all people. We start with purely physiological needs, which have to be satisfied. Once these are satisfied to an acceptable extent, security needs appear, and we want a fixed framework for our world – something firm to hang on to and believe in. Once we have this to an acceptable extent, effectance needs appear (this step was added by David Wright (1973) but I think Maslow would have accepted it), and we want to achieve some kind of mastery of our own bodies and the world around us; at this stage it is seen in rather rigid terms, on a kind of horse-trading, win/lose basis, in the short term. This marks the end of what Alderfer (1972) calls the Existence phase of development.

Once we have this feeling of mastery to an acceptable extent, needs for love and belongingness appear, and we seek general social approval – we like to be liked. Once these needs are satisfied to an acceptable extent, we go on to the need to win esteem from others – we want to measure up and be accepted for our performance in some specific role; it becomes very important to know where we stand. This marks the end of what Alderfer (1972) calls the Relatedness phase of development.

Once these needs are satisfied to an acceptable extent, our own self-esteem needs begin to appear, but are often suppressed or find the way blocked. However, difficult or not, at this point our own self-respect becomes the most important thing; we set our own standards, rather than taking them from others. And once this need is satisfied to an acceptable extent, the full self-actualization needs appear, and we start to seek to realize our full potential, to raise our sense of what is possible, to explore our own creativity, our need to know and understand, our need for beauty, and so on (see Table 1). This marks the end of what Alderfer (1972) calls the Growth phase of development.

This theory of development or maturation became very acceptable to the people involved with following up Lewin's work, and it made a lot of sense when applied to the problems found in organizations, as we shall see in later chapters. Later it was strongly supported by quite independent work on moral development (Kohlberg 1969) and ego development (Loevinger 1976) – hard research carried out in several countries.

Now it was Maslow who actually took the main initiatives in starting up the movement now known as humanistic psychology. In the spring of 1949 he and Anthony Sutich met for the first time. Out of their discussions emerged an agreement to work together on developing a psychology which would get away from the then current emphasis on less-than-fully-human behaviour. Maslow had already published his first paper on self-actualization, and Sutich had written one on growth experiences, which was published soon after.

In 1954 Maslow organized a mailing list for the purpose of circulating duplicated copies of articles that could no longer be published in the official journals because of the

Table 1 Staging posts on the developmental spiral. After David L. Wright (1974). Omitting lowest level of Maslow (physiological) and of Loevinger (pre-social, symbiotic).

	MASLOW	KOHLBERG	LOEVINGER	PIAGET	ALDERFER	REICH
6	**Self-actualisation** Being that self which I truly am. Bring all that I have it in me to be. A fully-functioning person.	**Individual principles** True personal conscience. Universal principles fully internalised. Genuinely autonomous. Selfishness B.	**Autonomous: integrated** Flexible and creative. Internal conflicts are faced and recognised. Tolerance of ambiguity. Respect for autonomy. Feelings expressed.	**Dielectical operations** (Riegel 1973)	Growth	Consciousness III
5	**Self-esteem 2** Goals founded on self-evaluated standards. Self-confidence. Self-respect.	**Social contract** Utilitarian law-making. Principles of general welfare. Long-term goals.	**Conscientious** Bound by self-imposed rules. Differentiated thinking. Self-aware.	**Formal operations** Substage 3: Systematic isolation of variables. deductive hypothesis-testing. True formal thought.		
4	**Self-esteem 1** Respect from others. Social status. Recognition.	**Law and order** Authority maintenance. Fixed social rules. Find duty and do it.	**Conformist 2** Seeking general rules of social conformity. Justifying conformity.	**Formal operations** Substage 2: Capacity to order triads of propositions or relations.	Relatedness	Consciousness II

				Existence	Consciousness 1
3	**Love and belongingness** Wish for affection, for a place in the group, tenderness, etc.	**Personal concordance** Good-boy morality. Seeking social approval. Liking to be liked. Majority is right.	**Conformist 1** Going along with the crowd. Anxiety about rejection. Need for support.	**Formal operations** Substage 1: Relations involving the inverse of the reciprocal. Capacity to form negative classes.	
2	**Effectance** Mastery. Personal power. Imposed control. Blame and retaliation. Domination.	**Instrumental hedonism** Naïve egocentrism. Horse-trading approach. Profit-and-loss calculation. Selfishness A.	**Self-protective manipulative.** Wary, exploitative. People are means to ends. Competitive stance. Fear of being caught. Many stereotypes.	**Concrete operations** Substage 2: Reversible concrete thought. Relations of invariance.	
1	**Safety** Defence against danger. Fight or flight. Fear—world is a scary place.	**Obedience/punishment** Deference to superior power. Rules are external and eternal.	**Impulsive** Domination by immediate cue, body feelings. No reflection. Retaliation fears.	**Concrete operations** Substage 1: Categorical classification.	

commitment of these journals to the behaviourist orthodoxy, or, on the other wing, to the psychoanalytic orthodoxy. The papers dealt with the wider possibilities of the human person, with areas like creativity and autonomy, and with topics like love and growth.

In the summer of 1957 Maslow and Sutich agreed that the time had come to launch a journal. What should its title be? Suggestions included: *Journal of Growth Psychology*, *Journal of Ortho-Psychology* (one meaning of 'ortho' is 'to grow or cause to grow') and *Journal of Self Psychology*. Carl Rogers suggested *Journal of the Human Person*; Herbert Marcuse proposed the name *Journal of Human Studies*.

It took until 1961 before the first issue of the *Journal of Humanistic Psychology* appeared. It was sponsored by Brandeis University, who helped with the costs. Within three months, more than 150 letters had come in, suggesting that an Association be formed. A committee on organization was set up, and took a year to drum up possible members, write a constitution and organize a founding meeting, which took place in 1963. The Association, whose first President was Jim Bugental, began as a subsidiary of the journal and was directly responsible to the editors. This enabled Brandeis University to help again with the expenses.

In 1964 the Old Saybrook conference took place, where about 25 people founded an independent Association for Humanistic Psychology. The people at this conference, where the whole case for humanistic psychology was really laid down firmly for the first time, were a varied lot, and made it clear that the AHP was never just a psychologists' club. Jacques Barzun was there, and René Dubos, and Floyd Matson, as well as Gardner Murphy, Gordon Allport and Clark Moustakas. And of course Carl Rogers, Rollo May and Abe Maslow, as well as Charlotte Buhler and Norma Lyman.

In 1965 the Association severed its link with Brandeis and became a charity, and in 1969 the control of the journal was transferred to the Association for Humanistic Psychology (AHP), which in the same year dropped the word American from its title, and became an international organization, some more of whose story is given in Chapter 12.

Going back now to the late 1940s, besides the twin streams of Lewin and the NTL, and Maslow and self-actualization, Carl Rogers (1942) was also doing research on his own approach to psychotherapy. His approach was essentially based on the idea that the 'neurotic' or 'mentally sick' patient was basically all right, and made sense. By simply paying attention to the patient – or client, as Rogers preferred to call her – and taking her speech and actions seriously, the person's own basic health would begin to work and produce a cure.

This brings out one of the thoughts which all these approaches have in common – people are all right as they are. There is nothing extra which they need in order to be whole – all that is necessary is for them to take down the shutters and the blinkers, and let the sun shine in. As Rogers (1961) puts it:

> One of the most revolutionary concepts to grow out of our clinical experience is the growing recognition that the innermost core of man's nature, the deepest layers of his personality, the base of his 'animal nature', is positive in nature – is basically socialized, forward-moving, rational and realistic . . . We do not need to ask who will socialize him, for one of his own deepest needs is for affiliation and communication with others . . . He is realistically able to control himself, and he is incorrigibly socialized in his desires. There is no beast in man. There is only man in man . . .

This outlook distinguishes humanistic psychology from the other two main streams in psychology today. Both behaviourism and psychoanalysis have a pessimistic, 'bad-animal' view of human nature, and therefore an exaggerated respect for the needs and powers of society to socialize and tame the child, and to keep the adult socialized and tamed. (Cognitive psychology in its own way betrays a lack of trust in the person, and is no better in this regard.) It is for this reason that humanistic psychology is sometimes called the Third Force (see the fuller account of this in Chapter 15).

Rogers links with Maslow in that his theory of the person also holds that people tend naturally and of themselves to grow into fully functioning people, though they can hold themselves back from that in many different ways and for many different reasons. There is again one great force which drives through people and pushes them on, though they may resist or be prevented by others from going all the way. (This is not to be regarded as a humanistic orthodoxy, however, because of the emphasis on existentialism, which we shall be dealing with shortly.)

The three strands in humanistic psychology which we have been following – democratic training, research into healthy people and psychotherapy – all converged in the early 1950s. Ever since then, humanistic psychology has been particularly strong in organizational theory and practice; in research and other academic work on human potential; and in psychotherapy. This has given it a three-legged base which is very stable, even more so because of the advent of the Esalen Institute in 1961 (the first growth centre) which took psychotherapy, married it with art, drama, Eastern philosophy and various other ingredients, and turned it into a discipline which could help anyone who wanted to understand themselves better and relate better to other people. This made psychotherapy (and particularly group therapy) into something which was much less frightening and much less peculiar, as we shall see in later chapters.

But now we must look at a second and quite distinct series of sources for what we now call humanistic psychology, because it is far from being true that it only has one origin.

EXISTENTIALISM

In France in the 1940s Jean-Paul Sartre (1969) aroused a whole new spate of interest in existentialism. And one of the people most influenced by him, and by the existential psychiatry of Binswanger (1975), Medard Boss (in Rollo May et al. 1958) and others, was Ronald Laing (see for example Laing & Cooper 1964). Orthodox psychiatry speaks in terms of adjustment, of curing the patient and returning her to the uncriticized environment. Existential psychiatry speaks in very different terms. It denies the whole concept of mental illness, as if there were some kind of disease entity, something like a germ, which had got into a person and made her no longer responsible for her actions. Laing is not concerned with disordered perception of external reality, but with the falsification of the self. To an existential psychiatrist the purpose of therapy is to allow the person to recover a sense of self and personal authenticity. Not competence in dealing with the normal environment, not a reduction of the discomfort of fear, and not adjustment to the family setting – although these things may certainly happen – but self-awareness and access to the full range of feelings from despair to ecstasy, together with the courage and strength to be open to experience.

This sounds very much like the approach of the others we have met already, but it includes two new elements. The first is the greater acknowledgment of the dark side of experience. Maslow, Rogers and some of the other Americans always manage to sound optimistic and sometimes a little bland (though this is often a misjudgment when one goes in for a closer look), but the existentialists have a much greater sense of the pain of awareness, the anguish of human existence. There is in fact a whole American tradition of boundless optimism, which has never been transplantable – many religions and other cults which have been enormously successful in America have been quite unsuccessful in Europe, particularly when they had this strong emphasis on perfectibility.

More specifically, the existentialists do not hold that there is one great escalator on which we are all travelling (though we may stop off or be pushed off at times), and in fact they quite explicitly deny this. People who are very central to humanistic psychology, like Rollo May (1967) and Alvin Mahrer (1978) say that there is no inevitable process of growth – there is only choice. We may choose to grow, to stagnate or to decline; and in a world where there is little encouragement to grow, most of us may not do it very much or at all.

The second difference is the greater political awareness of

13

the existential psychiatrists. Sartre became a kind of Marxist, Laing (1967) wrote *The Politics of Experience* – which turned out to be an accurate label for the women's movement a year or two later – Cooper's work is often explicitly political (Cooper 1971), May (1974) has much of value to say about social questions, Mahrer (1978) has a long and explicit chapter relating his psychological ideas to social matters, and so on. Society is seen as systematically producing mental distress because of being arranged in certain ways – if these social arrangements could be changed, perhaps much mental distress would not arise at all, or would not be defined as disorder or illness. One of the most disastrous of these arrangements is the nuclear family – a conclusion which again was also arrived at by the women's movement quite independently – because it forms a teaching situation in which men learn how to put down women, and both men and women learn how to put down children.

This 'putting down' is the precise process which the human potential movement seeks to reverse, a process in which human beings are diminished and reduced to fractions of what they could be, as many writers have shown. Unfortunately, what the family does is reinforced by the school, by the place of work, by the political system, by the media, by most of what goes on in the culture, so that there is hardly any escape from it. Consequently, alienation becomes a normal state of affairs. (See Chapter 14 for more on this question.)

The existentialist view, then, agrees very much with that of the men we have met so far in its positive aims, but has a much more pessimistic view of how difficult it is to achieve them. It is not just a case of helping people to become more self-aware, as if it were something they had just forgotten or not known about, but which they could now easily pick up; it is more a case of helping people to turn to face an enormous and implacable enemy, which is much bigger than they are, in the knowledge that that is the only way to live, if one wants to be fully human.

This is the well-known existentialist demand for authenticity. David Wood (1971) says that authenticity consists of

14

two related achievements, self-respect and self-enactment:

Self-respect: • Awareness of subjectivity.

• Awareness of freedom.

• Acceptance of self-responsibility.

Self-enactment: • One acts consistently.

• One enacts what one believes.

• One avows or owns one's actions.

By 'subjectivity', Wood means that we are active origins, not passive pawns. We are sources and not just focuses of meaning. We are subjects and not merely objects. And this applies to others too. We treat another person as a 'You personally' over against our own 'I personally', rather than as one role interacting with another.

The other points are, I believe, quite clear as they stand. They will be very familiar to anyone who has been to an encounter group. They seem very obvious, certainly to the young, yet it seems that they are not universally observed. And this is because of the alienation which has already been mentioned – we are split off from ourselves – we do not own ourselves. So we do not 'own up'. This alienation is even more obvious and more hard-edged now in the late 1980s than it was in the late 1970s when this book first appeared.

Much of humanistic psychology is devoted to a study of how to enable people to fight their alienation and become more authentic. The T-group developed into the encounter group; Rogerian therapy became an ally of Fritz Perls's Gestalt therapy and Lowen's bioenergetics; Maslow's (1968) emphasis on peak experiences became realized in psychosynthesis and meditation techniques, as we shall see in later chapters. All these are ways of personal growth, which do produce people who are more like Rogers's 'fully functioning person'.

And it can be seen that there are ethical implications here. If you believe that you and the others are free subjects, fully self-responsible, upfront in their actions and speech, you will be unlikely to tell them what to do, or assume that what has been good for you will necessarily be good for them. You will let them find their own way, in the confidence that it is better than any way you give them or show them. In the words of 1960s slang – 'You can't lay your trip on someone else.'

MIND-EXPANDING DRUGS

But this important ethical truth actually came out of yet a third origin of today's humanistic psychology – the psychedelic experience. If what we want to do is, as we said earlier, to take down the shutters and the blinkers, then LSD and the other psychedelics offered a new way of doing this.

The effects of LSD differ from person to person, and within the same person from time to time, but always, it seems, it takes away many of the blocks to experience (Solomon 1964). The feeling of intensity of experience is tremendously increased, and ecstasy becomes quite common. Many people have a kind of vision of oneness with the universe – a picture of the whole universe as having a pattern and a sense which is *one's own*. This is the opposite of alienation (Stafford & Golightly 1967).

The LSD experience is so different from what we normally encounter in our lives that it has often been called a trip. On a trip, we leave one domain and enter another, live there for a while, and come back with refreshment, new information, a new vision or whatever. On an LSD trip there is, in addition, this tremendous sense of truth – that the experience, be it horrible or marvellous, is absolutely authentic. And of course our constant temptation, with the truth, is to tell it to someone else. However, the LSD trip is also immensely personal – it turns out that when we try to give it to someone else, they reject it for them, while accepting that it is true for us. We find that we literally cannot lay it on someone else. And this rejection becomes in itself a much more general revelation: much of our thinking, our beliefs, our theories, turn out to be our fantasy to just the same extent and in much the same way.

Gestalt therapy tunes in to this thought, and urges the person to take responsibility for her own fantasies as fantasies. This turns out to be very liberating, in quite a surprising way.

We shall be returning to psychedelia in Chapter 9, but let it suffice here to say two things about these drugs. The first is that they are illegal, so that what is said must not be taken as an invitation to use them. And the second is that any experience which can be obtained with drugs can be obtained without them.

It is, however, an historical fact that these drugs did make a big impact in the late 1960s, by giving people a direct demonstration that there were such things as transcendental and ecstatic experiences, and that they did have important effects in giving people insights about themselves and their relationship to the world – in particular convincing people that they were much more creative than they had given themselves credit for. (For an interesting discussion of this whole area see Bakalar (1985).) Once the drug had made the point, there were many other ways of getting there, as we shall see in later chapters. Why is creativity important? Maslow (1973) gives one answer:

> It seems to me that we are at a point in history unlike anything that has ever been before . . . To put it bluntly, we need a different kind of human being . . . What some professors at MIT have done, I understand, is to give up the teaching of the tried and true methods of the past, in favour of trying to create a new kind of human being who is comfortable with change, who enjoys change, who is able to improvise, who is able to face with confidence, strength and courage a situation of which he has absolutely no forewarning . . . The society which can turn out such people will survive; the societies which cannot turn out such people will die.

It turns out, then, that the transpersonal stuff is not so far removed from everyday life as one might at first have supposed.

THE PARADIGMS

At the heart of humanistic psychology what I find is not a model, a theory, a form of words, but a set of key experiences (what are sometimes called paradigms).

1 The experience of paradox. Dialectics as a felt experience. What Maslow calls dichotomy-transcendence: that is, going through and beyond our conventional splits into a kind of wholeness. This can be approached in a number of ways, but for many of us it came through a deep and intense group experience; some kind of insight or breakthrough in a group. Exactly what this is like will come through in later chapters.

2 The experience of contacting the real self, the existential self, the unified bodymind self, leading to the existential experience of being totally alone and totally responsible – there are no excuses and no evasions – we have to act as if what we did meant something, even while knowing that our projects are going to be twisted and distorted in a social system which is denying, in layer upon layer, our free existence.

3 The ecstatic peak experience, which can be approached in many ways and have many different contents, but one of the most characteristic features is a sense of glimpsing for a moment the pattern and unity – or better, the constant patterning and unifying – of every thing and every person in the universe.

For me it is the first and third of these which give me the courage to face the second. I know that the structures of society seem very hard and definite and rigid, but that this is an illusion: it is all moving and changing. You push, and sometimes it gives, and sometimes it does not; you can only find out by trying.

And this is another great underlying emphasis of

humanistic psychology – something it shares with science generally – the emphasis on experience. You don't know till you try – let's experiment – let's do it and see. Hence the institutions which most clearly express humanistic psychology in action tend to be institutions where people are doing things, rather than just reading books. Maybe what it says in the books was true last year, but is it true this year? And all the time there is an emphasis on the body. The body is always seen as integral with the mind, rather than as separated from it. Intentional action does not just use the body – it intimately involves the body all the way along. It is this emphasis on unity and integration that makes it possible to be truly present at each moment. All the time we are on this existential edge, where we are systematically trying to reduce our expectations and increase our involvement. More of me, and less of my fixed frameworks. More wholeness and less separation.

In a way, this book is an embarrassment, because it suggests that humanistic psychology can be completely understood through books. This is not so. No one can fully appreciate humanistic psychology, whether to support or oppose it, unless she is willing to try some of the key experiences mentioned in these pages. Humanistic psychology is about human change and growth, about the realization of human potential, and about being an origin rather than a pawn. This means that the reader is always challenged to change and grow, to realize her potential, to become more of an origin and less of a pawn. But to do this needs certain specific kinds of paradigm experiences, not just the reading of books.

And do not imagine that any of this is being offered as an optimistic panacea. The realization of human potential is not the same as achieving happiness, or a plateau of perfection. Allen Wheelis (1972), in a deep and moving essay, says this:

The surprise we feel when a 'well analysed' person breaks down derives from the wish to view man as a machine. Very delicate and complicated, to be sure, like a fine watch, and liable therefore to subtle, tricky problems of adjustment which may require the lengthy services of an expert; but when finally we get rid of all the bugs we may expect smooth and reliable function. Such an image of man is at odds with what we know life to be. If we seriously regard our private thought and feeling, our visions at night when the wind blows, when rain falls on a deserted island, then – though fine adjustments have been made by a great watchmaker – we find so much conflict, misery, confusion that we know we are never through and never safe. The suffering and the danger cannot be left behind. They are what we are.

In the West, we need such warnings. But in the East, everything looks slightly different. Humanistic psychology today contains many things which came originally from the East, and it is time now to look at these.

CHAPTER TWO

THE EASTERN ORIGINS

AT THE same time that the Western foundations were being laid by Rogers, Maslow, May and the rest, a great wave of Eastern interest was sweeping over an important part of the literary world. The so-called Beat Generation included poets like Ginsberg, Ferlinghetti and Corso, and novelists like Kerouac and Burroughs. They were all deeply taken by Eastern philosophy and religion, and in particular by one aspect of it – the emphasis on spontaneity and mistrust of the intellect as a controller. But the crucial thing was that these people did not just read Suzuki and the Tao-te-Ching – they acted on what they found there.

This was quite new. For many years cultured people had appreciated Eastern art and metaphysics, and had occasionally joined some official Buddhist cult – but to go right to the heart of Taoism and act out what one found there – that was different. Of course the established intelligentsia reacted with scorn: these young people didn't really understand what they were doing, they were immature and shallow, and besides it was dangerous. The young poets and artists reacted with equal scorn (Lipton 1960) –

'She's a square' the young man told me afterward.
'She *knows* all about it – up here – ' tapping his forehead – but she doesn't dig it, man. Like you got to swing *with* it or you get hung up on the *numbers* man, on the little black dots and all that corn, and you *never* make it.'

There is an important truth here, hidden behind the dated slang. It is clear in Rogers's approach to therapy that the therapist or counsellor may or may not have a great deal of knowledge or experience behind her, but the important thing is that she should leave it all behind when she is in the actual therapy session with a client. (This is not really very different from the practice of the best psychoanalysts, such as Bion, as Bergantino (1981) makes clear.) In that session she must be all here now, totally present to the client. If she can really listen to the client, and go with the client, that is the best she can do. And this means letting go of her knowledge, her theory, even her experience of similar cases. Rogers actually gives this quote from a film-maker (Flaherty 1968):

> What you have to do is to let go, let go every thought of your own, wipe your mind clean, fresh, innocent, newborn, sensitive as unexposed film to take up the impressions round you, and let what will come in. This is the pregnant void, the fertile state of no-mind. This is non-preconception, the beginning of discovery.

In terms of our social stereotypes, this approach is much more feminine than masculine. This is an important theme which we shall return to again and again. To the extent that we can actually live and work in this way, we begin to exemplify a quality which the Chinese call *tzu-jan* (spontaneity, nature). Another example would be the artist painting a picture who accidentally splashes paint on to her canvas, and instead of rubbing it out or covering it up, makes it into an integral part of the finished painting. This is taking responsibility for our actions. It is my mistake, which I made; I do not blame an external clumsiness, or an external brush, or an external self who wanted something else. I take it into my whole situation as a part of that situation, neither minimizing it nor exaggerating it. It is there, and has its own meaning, which I must now take into account.

This is opposed to a theory of painting which holds that the artist has a picture in her imagination which she then puts on to canvas as accurately as possible, and still more to a theory of painting which holds that the artist is there to represent as accurately as possible what is out there in the world. But these theories of painting are not held by many artists today, though they are held by many non-artists who want artists to conform to them. In fact, many artists are very much influenced by the Taoist approach which is also found in Zen and some of Tantra. As the six precepts of Tilopa (Watts 1957) put it:

> No thought, no reflection, no analysis,
> No cultivation, no intention;
> Let it settle itself.

It seems easy enough to see how this approach could be used in art – and it is interesting to see here how rock music fulfils all the demands more than most other art forms – but less easy to see how it could be used in science.

Maslow (1966) says that the usual conception of science is to approach objects by manipulating them, poking at them, to see what happens; taking them apart, etc.

> If you do this to human beings, you *won't* get to know them. They won't *want* you to know them. They won't *let* you know them . . . Real receptivity of the Taoistic sort is a difficult achievement. To be able to listen – really, wholly, passively, self-effacingly listen – without presupposing, classifying, improving, controverting, evaluating, approving or disapproving, without dueling with what is said, without rehearsing the rebuttal in advance, without free-associating to portions of what is being said so that succeeding portions are not heard at all – such listening is rare.

This more Taoistic approach is very characteristic of humanistic psychologists, as we shall see in the chapters which follow, and especially in Chapter 15, where we consider research specifically. It is possible, in fact, to carry out scientific investigation in a more feminine way, and in the spirit of Zen.

ZEN

Zen is all about letting go. One of the key terms is *wu-wei* (non-action, non-making, non-doing, non-striving, non-straining, non-busyness) which is in some ways not all that far from the Western idea of 'not pulling up the roots to see how the plant is getting on'.

One of our characteristic and very masculine beliefs in the West is that if we have a problem, the correct thing to do is to face it, grapple with it and deal with it. In this way we do two new things: we turn the problem into a thing (usually giving it a name, which helps considerably in this) and a dangerous thing at that; and we raise up an opponent of some kind, which becomes equally real and hard and definite. Medicine is an excellent example of this, as Inglis (1964) has spelt out in some detail. This almost invariably has the same result – the problem and its opponent become institutionalized and permanent.

In psychology this happens all the time. A problem arises, like the reliability of a battery of questions. It is found that reliability can be increased by adding items to the battery. Now we have so many items that the battery can only be used on very special occasions; also the meaning of the words keeps changing with time, and so on.

The Zen approach is to let go of your problems, rather than tackling them. Does the word 'reliability' make sense? Does the whole idea of giving the 'same' test to two different people make sense? It would be convenient if human beings were like machines, because we know how to handle machines, and 'we' want to handle human beings in the same way. But do we? Who is the 'we' who want to predict and control human beings? Do you want to be predicted and controlled?

If we can ask enough of these simple Zen questions we can perhaps start to let go of some of our psychological assumptions.

In recent years the word Zen has become rather too popular for its own good, and we have even had books like *Zen and the Art of Motor Cycle Maintenance* which are not about Zen at all, and are even quite opposed to Zen. One of the classics remains Reps (1961), which is beautiful and unpretentious. I also liked Watts (1957), because of its explanation of the Chinese characters. Kapleau (1967) is very helpful and explicit. And it seems to me, in spite of all the controversy, that *Roots and Wings* (Rajneesh 1979) goes to the heart of the matter.

TAO

One of the assumptions often made in psychology is that we have to concentrate the powers of our intellect upon the things we want to study. We have to see them clearly and distinctly, and talk about them unambiguously. Only in this way can we prove them true or false.

There is a whole other approach which we find in the Tao (Rawson & Legeza 1973). This is that we can only start getting close to something when we unfocus our eyes. As long as we stay focused and single-minded, we are limited by the categories which our intellect (or someone else's, in really bad cases) has already set up. We are at the mercy of old knowledge, which has become fixed and inflexible. When we unfocus, we let in the object, and we let out our other faculties – feeling, intuition, remote associations, creativity.

The *I Ching* (Baynes 1968) is the classic Taoist way of demonstrating this. If we want to make a difficult decision, we prepare ourselves to throw the coins or stalks, ask the question while casting the objects, and then interpret the pattern set up, referring to the traditional wisdom on the subject. If we can do this in an intuitive and centred way, an answer either comes or it does not. If it comes, it is probably the best decision we could have made, because our whole self is involved, and not just one cut-off part of ourself. If it does not come, we are not ready to make that decision yet; and that is important too.

Many of us have had a similar experience when doing crosswords, particularly the more difficult ones. If we laboriously puzzle over each clue, trying to make logical sense of it, nothing much happens. But if we unfocus, and let the words play around in our minds in an intuitive way, this is often much more productive, particularly if we are familiar with that specific series of puzzles.

I mentioned the word 'centred' earlier, and this is a crucial word in Taoism. Mary Richards (1969) writes movingly about how centring in the person is like centring in pottery:

> As I grow quiet, the clay centres. For example, I used to grieve because I could not make reliably a close-fitting lid for a canister, a teapot, a casserole. Sometimes the lid fitted, sometimes it didn't. But I wanted it to fit. And I was full of aggravation. Then a GI friend of mine who was stationed in Korea sent me an ancient Korean pot, about a thousand years old. I loved it at once, and then he wrote that he thought I might like it because it looked like something I might have made. Its lid didn't fit at all! Yet it was a museum piece, so to speak. Why, I mused, do I require of myself what I do not require of this pot? Its lid does not fit, but it inspires my spirit when I look at it and handle it. So I stopped worrying. Now I have very little trouble making lids that fit.

In Taoism centring has a very precise meaning. In the body there are three 'crucibles' where energy is processed, and they run down the centre of the body. The function of Taoist meditation is to connect up these three crucibles (*tan-t'ien*) so that the energy may flow freely and produce a state of ecstasy.

The discipline of T'ai Chi is a moving meditation which is deeply wound into Taoist philosophy and practice. It is carried out every morning by many thousands of people in China today. It is often taught as a fixed series of exercises which have to be learned and practised exactly until the pupil matches the master. But as Ma-Tsu said many years ago (Huang 1973):

> The Tao has nothing to do with discipline. If you say that it is attained by discipline, finishing the discipline turns out to be losing the Tao . . . If you say there is no discipline, this is to be the same as ordinary people.

26

Note carefully what this is saying. It is not saying that the Tao is attained by discipline, and it is not saying that the Tao can be attained without discipline. The collateral Indian phrase is *neti neti* (not this, not that) and this expresses an important truth about the Tao – it escapes all opposites. Maslow talks in various places about 'dichotomy-transcendence' and this is another way of putting it. In philosophical terms, we are talking about a dialectical approach to the world, which can do equal justice to the masculine and to the feminine, and which is not taken in by apparent opposition and contrast. This is symbolized in the well-known *yin-yang* symbol:

The two shapes are contrasted and unified at the same time. Nothing could be more different, nothing could be more similar. As Hegel (1892) says:

> Thus essentially relative to *another*, *somewhat* is virtually an other against it: and since what is passed into is quite the same as what passes over, since both have one and the same attribute, viz. to be an other, it follows that something in its passage into other only joins with itself. To be thus self-related in the passage, and in the other, is the genuine Infinity.

This may sound difficult, but what he is saying is that the old idea of infinity, where something just goes on for ever, is a bad infinity – it can never really be infinite, because it excludes the finite, and the finite therefore limits it forever. But when one thing – or one person – finds itself in another, that is the good infinity. And this is really a statement about love rather than about mathematics. If I meet another person, and instead of finding alienation find myself, that is the true infinity, or true love. If I meet another person, and find that the more of myself I give away, the more I get back, that is the true infinity – which may also be ecstatic. (And this is actually the philosophical background to the idea of synergy, which we shall meet further on.)

So the *yin-yang* symbol can be very powerful in what it suggests, once we are able to look at it with the kind of insight which dialectics gives us. It is also extremely simple, as Huang (1973) makes clear.

In recent years Tao has again become very popular, and we have had such titles as the Tao of Physics and even the Tao of Pooh. Wilber (1982) has an excellent critique of such attempts to use the Tao for illegitimate purposes, as for example where he says:

> Reduce all things to material particles, then discover the particles are holoarchic, then claim that the holoarchy is the Tao.

This sort of thing is nothing much to do with the Tao at all, and Wilber goes on to criticise many of the New Age thinkers who are actually very one-sided, whereas the whole essence of the Tao is not to be one-sided.

TANTRA

But there was also another current from the East which went into humanistic psychology. This was the Tantric tradition, running through various Hindu centres, strong in Tibet, and found in other forms among the Hopi Indians, the Sufis, the Theosophists and Rosicrucians. The best-known form is the Kundalini system.

The essence of the Tantric approach is its experimentalism. There is little or no emphasis on learning the correct theories and reading the correct books – the important thing is to do it. And there are tremendous numbers of things which can be done, all with the aim of rousing and using the energy which is there in the body. This energy is not just something which is postulated and understood – it is felt physically (Rawson 1973).

There are seven *chakras*, or centres, in the body, and the energy passes through them. It is important to understand that these *chakras* are not just nodes or points – they are locations of the person. It is as if the person had seven brains, instead of one; or as if there were seven sub-personalities which had to be contended with (see Chapters 9 and 13 for more about this); or seven ego-states which could be entered into.

And it seems that we cannot enter into the higher ego-states until we have dealt properly with the lower ones. Here is the order in which they stand. There are many versions of this, but this is the one which makes most sense in my experience:

Chakra	Meaning	Location
7	Cosmic consciousness, bliss	Top of head
6	Intuition	Level of pineal body, 3rd eye
5	Communication, expression	Level of throat
4	Affection, love	Level of heart
3	Assertiveness, anger, aggression	Level of navel, solar plexus or spleen
2	Sexual energy	Level of genitals
1	Primitive energy, grand potential	Base of spine

Here is an example to show how this schema can actually be used in group work. Schutz (1971) says:

A man in an encounter group is having difficulty establishing a love relationship (fourth chakra) with a woman in the group. She reports that she feels some phoniness in his approach and feeling. What frequently results is that he has a sexual desire (second chakra) for her and is not acknowledging that this issue must be dealt with first. Or sometimes he has great hostility toward women (third chakra) that he is also not dealing with.

Schutz feels that the general principle that one cannot skip over chakras at will has been extraordinarily illuminating for him. Certainly it gives much food for thought to anyone who is seriously concerned with communication: we are continually trying to communicate (fifth chakra) without entering into any real relationship with the other person – as I am doing now, for example.

In the work of healing, the chakras can be very important, but that area lies rather outside the scope of this book.

What is also important, however, is the vision that all these centres are part of one process – they are not (or need not be) separate and isolated. When the serpent power of the base rises to the thousand-petalled lotus at the top, all the centres are working as one, and the energy released can be fearful if the person is not properly prepared. If she is prepared, ecstasy can result (Gunther 1978).

However, it is also important to realise that Tantra is not just about the chakras – it is a deep and wide-ranging discipline which has made a special study of all the forms of meditation. This is made clear in such books as Rajneesh (1977), which deals with the 112 forms of meditation ascribed to Lord Shiva.

MYSTICAL EXPERIENCES

All these Eastern approaches talk of ecstasy, sometimes calling it *samadhi*, sometimes *satori*, sometimes *fana*, sometimes simply as the absolute Tao experience. The Western mystical tradition also says much of this (Maloney 1979). To most of us, ecstasy means either a very high sensual experience, such as we might get from sex or music or Nature; or else it means something religious, with which we may be unfamiliar and for which we may feel suspicion as something vague and supernatural.

It is important to understand it aright, because it has always been one of the concerns of humanistic psychology. George Leonard (1968) wrote a book called *Education and Ecstasy*, and this title is incomprehensible unless we understand how ecstasy is something ordinary as well as extraordinary, how ecstasy – nothing less – is the birthright of every one of us. Maslow (1970a) went deeply into the study of peak experiences (his name for ecstasy and the other Eastern terms) and came to the conclusion that a peak experience could be the most important event in a person's life. A single moment of ecstasy could change the way a person lived. I have examined the whole of this area in detail elsewhere (Rowan 1983a), and found that there are at least seven different mystical experiences:

1 *The peak experience* This is quite common, and in surveys it is found that about one third of the population has had something like this. Horne (1978) calls it casual extraverted mysticism.

2 *Pure energy* This is a sense of being in touch with energy or power as such. It is not the same as the kind of energy met with in bioenergetics or in biofeedback. It is a subtle form of energy which is spiritual in nature. The Yoga people have been very discriminating in this area (Chaudhuri 1975) and pay a lot of attention to different qualities of energy flow.

3 *Real self* The feeling of getting in touch with my own centre, my identity, my true self – the self that lies behind or beyond all self-images or self-concepts. It comes in step-jump rather than in in gradual form (Pedler & Boydell 1981). It brings with it an experience of authenticity.

4 *Higher, deeper or greater self* The sense of being in touch with my transpersonal self, or inner teacher. At first this usually appears to be outside us, in the form of a guru, a spirit guide, a guardian angel, a high archetype, a goddess – some symbolic representation of the divine. A very much accentuated ability to use symbols comes with such an experience.

31

5 *Deity as substance* This is the sense of being in touch with the Deity, considered as the power behind or beyond the universe, the One creator and sustainer of all life and being. One's picture of the Deity may be personal, symbolic or abstract. But idolatry is ruled out at this stage, and symbols are regarded as highly questionable and probably misleading.

6 *Deity as process* A sense of being in touch with the Deity as process, rather than as subject or object, no matter how fine or abstract. Hegel (1895) is the person who does most justice to our experience of this stage, but Moltmann (1981) is more accessible and up to date, and Maloney (1979) is more friendly and open.

7 *The ultimate* This is the sense of having fallen into the Void, into the Absolute, of being everything and nothing at the same time. Wilber (1977) has a great deal to say about this.

Now many of these experiences are beyond anything that most of us have been through ourselves. But the fact that they have been so well described and distinguished is an important indication that they are not reducible to one another. Continually in this field we find people using what I have called the 'one-two-three-infinity' model of spirituality: one is the body, two is the emotions, three is the intellect, and anything beyond that is just a uniform 'spirituality' with no structure other than that. But in reality, spirituality is a world just as large and just as complex as the world of psychology, and there is just as much to learn in it. But at the more accessible end it overlaps with psychology, and particularly with humanistic psychology.

Coming now back to Maslow and peak experiences, he was also interested in the question of exactly what happened in a peak experience, and how exactly it worked. And he found that the usual way we have of knowing the world – reducing it to serve our purposes and needs – gets changed in the peak experience to another way of knowing the world, based on abundance rather than deficiency.

Instead of grasping the world 'with my intelligence pre-hensile, exactly like a monkey's tail', we *allow* the world to come in to us, so that we can then flow out and become that world, losing our usual boundaries. Instead of focused perception, we have what Krishnamurti called desireless awareness, or choiceless awareness. One key phrase which we can use to enter this state is to say – 'I want nothing' (see also Chapter 15).

Maslow (1973) later expanded on this further, and outlined nineteen specific differences between B-cognition (the way of knowing the world which occurs in the peak experience) and D-cognition (our ordinary way of knowing) which make a great deal of sense. The basic thing he found, however, was that in the peak experiences we naturally feel all the things which Taoism, Zen, Tantra and the Western mystics speak of at such length and in such a precise way. It happens by itself.

And this is of course crucially important. If it is true that when we experience ecstasy we inevitably fall into the way of seeing things and talking about them that Tao and Zen teach, this makes the Eastern doctrine far more than just a fad which we can pick up one year and lay down the next. It makes it something which we have to understand if we are to understand our own experience.

At the heart of this is a view of the self. As the *Maitreyana Upanishad* puts it: 'Having realized his own self as the Self, a man becomes selfless. . . . This is the highest mystery.' It is impossible to talk of the self without paradox and self-contradiction, because in the peak experience one sees quite easily how the self can be individual and universal at the same time, and how the historical 'self' (personality, mental ego, persona), which is the repository of all the roles we have ever played, and which is the mask which everyone knows us by, is the most misleading and unreal of all. (See Chapter 13 for more on this.) Outside the peak experience, one can't describe the self, even internally. And so one sage finds a form of words which is meaningful to her, and the next sage shows how absurd it is to take it literally; and the next sage tries again, and the next one pushes her off her pedestal. The sage who is pushed off her pedestal laughs, if she is any good, because it is not about the words, but about the experience which the words can never do full justice to.

So when Maslow talks about 'self'-actualization, he is being consciously paradoxical and provocative. This is not always appreciated by the earnest management psychologists who sometimes study him. Maslow was very much influenced by the Taoist way of looking at things, and this must never be forgotten.

THE NOW

Another thing which is clear in any of the mystical experiences is the now. In the moment of ecstasy, we just know that 'now' is all there is. It is not narrow, it is as wide as it needs to be. It is not static, it moves with enormous complexity and amazing simplicity, and I am part of it. It seems just as likely that the future causes the present as that the past causes it – both seem pretty irrelevant. The now is nothing like the past – it has a different structure from that. When we have this experience of the now, it turns out to be just like eternity. In eternity the concept of time either disappears or becomes a series of paradoxes, and so it does in the now. In eternity we have a feeling of being unlimited, and so we do in the now. Eternity belongs to Deity, and induces a sense of awe – and this is also one way of looking at the now. Laughter is another.

This works the other way round too: the now is just ordinary, it is just what is happening – and so is eternity. The now is with us all the time, wherever we are; and eternity is there too. As the ancient monk Yeno said

This very 'moment' is not subject to birth-and-death and therefore there is no going beyond it as long as we live in this present moment. Here is absolute tranquillity which is no other than the present moment. Bliss lies in the timelessness of this present moment. There is here no particular recipient of this bliss and, therefore, every one of us is blessed with eternal bliss.

This again is easy to understand from inside the peak experience, but impossible from outside it – it just sounds like nonsense, or playing with words. But at least it must be clear that when we say something about living in the now, we are not saying something either trivial or impossible – we are saying something important and very real. The Eastern writers make it clear, too, that few people can live in the now all the time – it is more often a matter of being able to draw on this experience when we need to, as an essential part of our whole centring.

SECULAR HUMANISM

There has been no attempt here to do justice to all that the East has to say about psychology, philosophy or life; all that we have done is to look at some of the elements of Eastern thinking which have been taken over and used by humanistic psychology. Perhaps the main feeling which comes out of it all is effortlessness.

This even applies to the peak experience. Over and over again we are warned that the attempt to push and hustle for mystical experiences is not the way to get them – they are not a commodity to be demanded. It is true that we can set up circumstances in which they are likely to come, but in the end we are surprised by joy – it is never exactly what we expected or wanted.

There are two important cautions we may need to offer about the Eastern approaches we have been considering. One is that, in spite of the emphasis on the ordinariness of the Tao, there is a persistent tendency to elevate mystical experience to some kind of superhuman elevation – a tendency to see the spiritual as in some way superior to the material. Relations with the infinite are somehow seen as more important than relations with one's spouse or friends. But a Zen monk once said – 'Now I'm enlightened, I'm just as miserable as ever.'

The other defect is that if we see everything as perfect as it is, we may be inclined to quietism and retreatism in political terms. We may be hard to control – and that is good as far as it goes – but unlikely to get together or innovate. In a fast-changing society like our own, this seems far from what is needed.

If we can keep a suspicious eye on these two dangers (which we shall return to again) it seems that we can take a great deal from these Eastern approaches. These dangers are only tendencies which emerge in practice – they do not seem to be inherent in the notions themselves. It depends on us what we make of them – we have our own choices to make and our own sense to construct. But looking at all these matters makes us much clearer about one thing at least.

There have been a number of pronouncements by important people recently about secular humanism, saying that it is a dead end, a spiritual disaster, a false doctrine and the gospel of materialism.

However true or false these accusations may be – and others like them – our withers are unwrung. We do not have to concern ourselves about them one way or another. because humanistic psychologists are not secular humanists. How could they be, if what we have seen in this chapter is true? But it is one of the oldest confusions in the business. I remember when I first went to an AHP event in Kentish Town, the caretaker told me it was the humanist meeting, and I thought at the time that it was run by some humanist group.

But in fact the two things are like chalk and cheese. The main plank in humanistic psychology is the integration of body, feelings, intellect and spirit, and it says so very clearly in all the introductory leaflets put out by AHP affiliates in various countries around the world. This integration is the key to what we call self-actualization, and all our workshops touch on it in some way. The secular humanists, on the other hand, are often not much interested in the body or in feelings, and actively deny any existence to the spiritual or transpersonal aspects of our life.

I actually joined the British Humanist Association at one time, to see whether any links could be made, but I found the people involved in it to be aridly intellectual, unawarely sexist and very narrow, spending a lot of their time and energy knocking Christianity, and some of the rest on issues like abortion and euthanasia. I lasted a year and walked out in protest at the sexism expressed at the Annual General Meeting.

Now it may well be that secular humanism should not be judged by the activities of the BHA (or the National Secular Society, which it much resembles) because humanism is itself a much wider philosophy. Nevertheless, the BHA are trying to represent it, and there must be some connection somewhere.

The name 'humanistic psychology' was first put forward by Maslow's son-in-law at the breakfast table, and Maslow liked it and pushed it, and it was later adopted by everyone. But neither then or now did he or any of us take up the position of secular humanism. There was always a recognition of the spiritual side of human beings, particularly in the work of Abraham Maslow, who as we have seen was more than any one other single person responsible for the founding of the Association for Humanistic Psychology.

The message then is not to worry about anything that might be said about secular humanism. As we have seen in this chapter, some of the key elements which have gone into humanistic psychology have been spiritual in the purest sense.

CHAPTER THREE

THE JOINING OF THE STREAMS

IN THE 1960s these things came together more and more. The National Training Laboratories introduced a whole new programme of groups devoted to personal growth. Teachers of art, drama and dance started to use their skills to foster the development not just of the art form, but the self-concept of the participants – often moving into mental hospitals to do so. Instead of talking about frustration in the home or at work, people acted it out, or expressed it in clay or movement, and found it beneficial (Kahn 1973).

And the Esalen Institute was founded as a growth centre, where in the idyllic surroundings of Big Sur on the Pacific coast those who wanted to develop and experiment with these new ideas could live and work. The first seminar was held there in 1962: it was led by William Harman and was entitled *The Expanding Vision: A review of the current conceptual revolution in psychology*. It was quite academic and had a booklist and lectures.

In December 1963 a five-day conference was advertised there under the title *Education of the Imagination*. It was organized by Gene Sagan, and featured Fritz Perls, Will Schutz and Charlotte Selver, among others. So few people signed up for it that it was cancelled, but Sagan put on a cut-rate version of it anyway, though some of the leaders, including Schutz, dropped out. Those who did come got only $100 each for the five days: they included Mike Murphy and Dick Price, the two founders of Esalen; Perls, the father of gestalt therapy; Sagan, who for years had been using art, music and pscyhodrama in his therapeutic practice; Bernard Gunther, a young patient of Perls from Los Angeles, who had studied yoga and massage; and Charlotte Selver, who, with her husband, Charles Brooks, taught sensory awareness (Anderson 1983).

Several things happened as a direct result of this conference. One was that Selver and Brooks were soon invited back to lead more workshops, and Big Sur soon became the west coast headquarters of sensory-awareness training. Another was that Bernard Gunther got the idea that he would like to learn more about sensory awareness and get a job at Esalen. The third, which would utterly transform the institute and its reputation, was Fritz Perls's decision to take up residence.

But one of the most influential leaders at Esalen became Will Schutz, and in a way he joined together most of these influences.

WILL SCHUTZ

At Esalen he had been able to develop from a very interesting theorist specializing in group work (he had written a book on this in 1958 which is still in use today) into a group leader with an appreciation of therapy, human relations training, dance and drama, Eastern and existential philosophy. And he had found that groups could not only lead to self-understanding; they could also lead to ecstasy. His best-selling book, *Joy* (1967) was written in a single weekend (that is the first draft – it was added to and tidied up later) and it summed up ten years of work drawing together the influences we have already looked at.

In a Schutz group (to which he gave the name of 'open encounter') one of the main values expressed is openness or honesty. People are encouraged to say what they really feel, and really feel what it is they are saying or hearing or doing, and generally to experience and share their own reality. This is very risky for most of us – we fear rejection, partly because there is so much of us that we reject in advance. If we have parts of ourselves that we reject and want to disown, it is no wonder that we do not want to tell others about them. But the extraordinary thing is that if we take the risk, and do it properly and thoroughly, going where it leads, we find that it can make us feel much better about ourselves, not only in the group, but in our life generally. This is what Schutz (1971) actually says:

> These seem to be the important features of honesty in an intimate relationship. Total honesty should be experienced first, because a judgement about what areas the couple wants to keep open and what areas they agree to keep closed cannot be made soundly without their having had the first-hand experience of the full openness. After that the choice of areas can be made jointly. The mutual decision is vital. If one person makes it for the other's own good it is almost certainly defensive and will lead to difficulty. Agreeing that the closed area can always be opened up again is essential and gives confidence that the relationship will not slip back . . . In general, most couples profit from more honesty than they think they can handle, with a resulting increase of energy, spontaneity and closeness.

So Schutz is very strong, but also very reasonable, about this honesty business. It is always a matter for negotiation and agreement, not something to be forced on someone who does not want it.

One of the symbols for honesty is nakedness, and in a Schutz group it often seemed to happen that it became appropriate to take one's clothes off. Contrary to some of the expectations which might be aroused by this, it was not an excuse for sexual titillation or even voyeurism, but simply an expression of this high valuation of openness and lack of pretence. This can be seen quite clearly in the film also entitled *Here Comes Everybody*, in which one of Schutz's groups is followed through its life. One of the most moving incidents is where a housewife, stuck in the feeling that her body is ugly, comes to a realization of the fact that it is not ugly at all; the look on her face, and the whole way she carries her body, changes to express this new vision of herself. As Schutz (1971) says:

As a person is able to face his real feelings about his body and deal with them, the reality of his body is almost always far better than his private image and he begins to accept his body more. This is reflected in holding the body more proudly, relaxing formerly unwanted parts, breathing more deeply, and often feeling so much better about his body that better dieting and exercising result as a sign of caring.

So in one of these groups, the body, the emotions and the mind all get involved, and the interplay between them becomes much more vigorous and alive.

In 1973 Schutz put together all his knowledge about encounter groups into a more formal book, *Elements of Encounter*. It makes clear that in addition to the influences we have already mentioned, three others were also crucial to the development of his type of encounter group. These were the contributions of Wilhelm Reich, Jacob Moreno and Roberto Assagioli, and we shall be meeting each of these people shortly.

But Schutz then went away from the complexity of adding more and more new techniques to the encounter group, and started to see how he could reduce all his ideas and discoveries to a much more stripped-down statement. This he did in his 1979 book *Profound Simplicity*. This is a disturbingly simple book, which is quite deceptive in its sophistication. It takes up an uncompromisingly holistic position, recognizing the existence of 'an organism who manifests through thinking, feeling, sensing and moving, and who has a spiritual aspect', and the need for integration of all this into a functioning unity.

In this book Schutz recognizes the importance of sexist pronouns and the he/man convention, and overcomes it in a rather elegant way. He uses 'I' for the universal self and 'you' for the universal other. It is surprising how well this works, and it gives an example which others might well follow. Schutz is still in the forefront of humanistic exploration and development.

CHARLES HAMPDEN-TURNER

Someone else who has done a great deal to bring the strands together, though in a completely different way, is Charles Hampden-Turner, an Englishman who trained at the Harvard Business School. He takes as his focus the application of the principles of humanistic psychology throughout the whole society.

In his first major work (Hampden-Turner 1971) he starts by making very explicit the point which Maslow starts from – that there is a process of human development which moves from a position of alienation or anomie to a position of creativity and spontaneity. This is just the process of development which the Schutz group is designed to hasten and encourage. At one end of the scale we have human diminution, where people use each other as means, put each other down, score points off each other and so on, while at the other end of the scale we have full humanness, where people treat each other as ends in themselves.

What Hampden-Turner says is that this can be seen as a spiral of experience, such that at any one time we are either moving up the spiral toward full humanness or down the spiral towards alienation and anomie. The assumptions we make, the relationships we set up, the organizations we produce, all help in some way to move us up or move us down the spiral. And the one thing which is most important in enabling us to move up the spiral is authentic human interaction. As we saw in Chapter 1, this is the existentialist insight; and Hampden-Turner is very much in the existentialist tradition. He would agree with Laing (1967), another person working in this tradition, that:

> Personal action can either open out possibilities of enriched experience or it can shut off possibilities. Personal action is either predominantly validating, confirming, encouraging, supporting, enhancing, or it is invalidating, disconfirming, undermining and constricting. Personal action can be creative or destructive. In a world where the normal condition is one of alienation, most

personal action must be destructive both of one's own experience and of that of the other. (Laing 1967)

But what Hampden-Turner does is to document this with a mass of evidence, marshalled with immense care and thoroughness, and applied to every aspect of our society. For example, he shows that most of our organizations (whether industrial, governmental or whatever), most of the time, are driving people down the spiral into anomie and alienation, rather than up the spiral into autonomy and moral insight. Such organizations act as if it is good for people to be put down, because that way they learn to be tough and impervious, and that is necessary in a tough world. But this is just the kind of action to create the horror world it purports to deal with.

The other way, where we open up to the other person, treating her as an equal suffering human being, helps to create instead someone who is strong and vulnerable at the same time. And this is a partial description of full humanness.

But Hampden-Turner also shows how organizations can be changed in such a way as to move people up the spiral, through genuine participation and real industrial democracy. He shows that many companies and other organizations have actually done this. It is not a remote Utopia which can be safely postponed until 'after the revolution', but something we can start doing now (see Chapter 8).

As soon as we see the implications of personal growth in these social terms, we become to some extent political, and Hampden-Turner is not afraid to grasp this nettle. He actually called his book *Radical Man*, because he became convinced that those above a certain level on the spiral would be seen by others as radical even though they themselves might not so describe themselves. And he has a discussion of radicalism, in which he shows that the student radicals of the late 1960s were in fact operating from a higher point on the spiral than their conservative opponents.

The areas which Hampden-Turner shows to be most important, and which recur over and over again in his analysis, are these:

Existence People exist freely. The further up the spiral an individual is, the more he or she acknowledges this.

Perception The world has contradictions in every area, and clear perception sees this.

Identity Awareness of one's own body, one's own experience, one's own self – a refusal to cut out or block off any of these things. Self-acceptance.

Competence Owning and allowing one's own ability. Refusal to cripple oneself.

Authentic Investing oneself intensely in human relationships, not holding back or seeing things in terms of the past or future. Acting as a whole person.

Risk A willingness to suspend one's existing understanding, and open up to a new possibility. Flexibility involves constant self-questioning, and ultimately taking nothing for granted.

Bridging distances The higher up the spiral, the bigger the gap which can be bridged between oneself and another person. This distance may be physical, psychological or social.

Impact One can meet another person in such a way that it is at the same time self-confirming and self-transcending. This is particularly important when meeting people in authority.

Dialectic If a meeting is genuine, a higher synergy can come out of it. A real meeting of differences is creative. But this means not suppressing the differences, and doing justice to them.

Integration By taking real notice of the feedback from one's encounters, one's own mental structures become richer and more complex, thus

> enabling a deeper understanding to take
> place. This is an expansion of consciousness.

Obviously a great deal could be written about each of these points, and this is just what Hampden-Turner has done in his book. They are mentioned here merely in order to suggest that these are all points which are within the scope of each one of us. What Hampden-Turner says is that working on each of these helps each of the others – they are connected in a very precise way, such that each one on the list facilitates the one following, and the last one on the list facilitates the first.

What Hampden-Turner has given us, then, is a well worked-out theory of human development in the social field, which can be used for our own personal growth, or to change the organizations we work in, or to change the way our whole society works. It enables us to see through the pretensions of most of the psychology that is taught in our universities and other halls of learning, which merely serves to uphold the existing order for the benefit of those who run it.

Since *Radical Man* was written, David Wright has written a number of papers which seem to show that Hampden-Turner's general case makes a lot of sense from a sociological point of view. The many research studies by Lawrence Kohlberg (1969) and Jane Loevinger (1976) are brought together and shown to be consistent with Maslow's theory. David Wright (1974) points to a gap between the lower levels and the higher levels on the spiral (see chart in Chapter 1), and says

> The transition between [these] levels [4 and 5] marks a significant watershed in terms of the *nature* of the possible bases of social order . . . [After it] people can consciously and intentionally construct and maintain a social order of their own choice.

In other words, so long as we are operating at low levels of development we are liable to be pushed around by external forces or our own internal rigidities, or to find ourselves competing with others for scarce resources. At the higher levels, the possibilities open out, and we no longer see problems in the same way. We start to see how to cooperate with others in a non-exploitative way, a way of using power in such a fashion that the more power we give away, the more we have. This is called synergy, which is sometimes referred to as the $2 + 2 = 5$ principle. (Some more on synergy in Chapter 8.)

This makes it possible to believe that our present time of troubles is actually a transition period to a person-centred society, where the industrial system would be subservient to, and responsible to, the larger purposes of the society. The overall goal would be the cultivation and enrichment of all human beings, in all their diversity, complexity and depth (see Chapter 14). Nowadays more and more people are saying the same thing, notably Marilyn Ferguson (1982), Frijthof Capra (1983) and Murray Bookchin (1986).

The more recent work of Hampden-Turner (1981, 1983) shows how important dialectical thinking is for humanistic psychology. In the first of these two books he shows it can link many separate fields of psychology and philosophy together and illuminate them all. And in the second of the books mentioned, he also shows how helpful catastrophe theory is as an adjunct to this. My own essay (1979) on Hegel makes the links between pure dialectical thinking and what Hampden-Turner calls being fully human. Hegel (1971) says that there are three levels of mind – the Primary level, the Social level and the Self-actualizing level (actually he says Soul, Consciousness and Mind, but I prefer my version). Self development consists in moving up the levels from the Primary level, through the Social level, to the Self-actualizing level. And each of these three levels contradicts the previous one, so that we have to reject one to go on to the next. The Primary level has to do with one-sided subjectivity, the Social level is to do with one-sided objectivity, and the Self-actualizing level is subjectivity on a higher level – a new kind of subjectivity which includes but surpasses one-sided objectivity – an objective subjectivity, in fact. Rationality (as redefined by Hegel) runs through all the levels. My own view is that most people involved in humanistic psychology do not realize how much they need and use and depend on dialectical thinking in their work.

SIDNEY JOURARD

Schutz developed the encounter group, Hampden-Turner developed a general dialectical theory, but Jourard (1964) actually did some research. Psychology has traditionally, and in some ways quite rightly, valued research as the key to its whole endeavour. After all, without research we do not know which of our ideas are true and which are false. It is only research which can give us any answers to our questions about empirical fact. (But see Chapter 15 for some important qualifications to this.)

We have already seen that for both Schutz and Hampden-Turner openness and honesty are extremely important. One of the implications of this is that it would make a great deal of difference to any human interaction if one of the parties would reveal herself to the other person. If she held back all information about herself, and talked only about neutral matters, that would be one extreme; and if she talked about nothing but herself that would be the other.

What Jourard did was to check this out systematically, over a period of about ten years, in a whole series of experiments. And what he found was that if you want somebody to tell you about themselves, there is no better way of getting this information than to tell that person the same sort of thing about yourself. There seems to be a certain matching quality about questions and answers of this kind, particularly if the subject-matter is intimate and personal.

In one experiment, (Jourard 1968) for example, carried out by Lee Reifel, a series of questions were printed on cards, and the experimental subject had the choice of answering the question in detail, answering it minimally, or refusing to answer. The questions in this study were similar to these, which were used in another piece of research:

What features do you most dislike in your mother?

How much money do you get each month?

What do you feel most ashamed of in your past?

47

What is the most serious lie you have ever told?

Have you been arrested or fined for breaking any law?

Do you approve of segregation of Negroes?

What features of your appearance do you consider most attractive to the opposite sex?

How much money have you saved?

Have you ever been drunk?

Have you ever been tempted to kill yourself?

Is there any particular person you wish would be attracted to you? Who?

What is the subject of your most frequent daydreams?

What is your nickname? Do you like it?

It can be seen that these are indeed questions of some degree of intimacy and rather personal. Jourard (1971) found that people were fairly willing to answer questions on work, tastes and interest, attitudes and opinions; but were much less willing to answer questions about money, their bodies and their personalities. However, if the experimenter answered questions or volunteered information in the 'difficult' areas, this made a great difference to the experimental subject doing likewise, affecting both the proportion of questions answered and the extent and depth of the answers.

In a later experiment, Sermat & Smyth (1974) set up four experimental conditions. In Group 1 the experimenter matched in intimacy what the subject said about herself, and kept his questions at the same level. In Group 2 the experimenter disclosed more intimate information about himself than did the subject, but did not ask intimate questions. In Group 3 the experimenter asked more intimate questions than the subject's current level of self-disclosure but did not exceed the subject's intimacy in his own self-revelations. In Group 4 the experimenter both disclosed more intimate information about himself than the subject did and asked for increasingly intimate self-disclosure from the subject. As predicted, the highest level of self-disclosure was obtained in Group 4, and the lowest in Group 1, with the other two falling about equally in between.

Now supposing that these experiments are all properly conducted and do show what they purport to show, what emerges from them? One thing which comes out is that if someone predicted that too much self-disclosure would put people off, they would be wrong. One of the fears about self-disclosure, and one of the things which makes it seem risky, is that the other person might be embarrassed by our revelations. Well, the research makes it clear that this does not happen. What happens is that the relationship develops and deepens. And this is not just an American phenomenon; John Davis did some of this type of work and found the same thing to hold true in Britain.

Another thing is that self-disclosure is a cure for loneliness. The need to express one's most important thoughts and feelings to an intimate friend, without fear of being misunderstood or rejected, was found by Sermat (quoted in Middlebrook 1974) to be one of the most important needs mentioned by a broad cross-section of people. In line with what we should expect from our knowledge of Schutz and Hampden-Turner, an I-Thou encounter with another person is actually a deep human need. If we do not get it, we miss so much. And the main reason why we miss it is that we fear to take the risk of getting to know another person. So perhaps it is a question of waiting until we have a fairly good morning, when we begin to feel some of things Hampden-Turner talks about, and then using that little bit of strength to reach out, and take that risk, and bridge some distance, and talk to another person about the things that matter most to us.

A third thing to say is that in self-disclosure we actually learn something about ourselves. Jourard put it very strongly:

Through my self-disclosure, I let others know my soul. They can know it, really know it, only as I make it known. In fact, I am beginning to suspect that I can't even know my own soul except as I disclose it. I suspect that I will know myself *for real* at the exact moment that I have succeeded in making it known through my disclosure to another person. (Jourard 1964)

If the word 'soul' bothers you, as it did me at first, substitute the word 'self'. We shall come back to this later on. But in any case the statement is quite a clear one: we get to know ourselves better in the process of opening ourselves up to another person. And Hampden-Turner explains why this should be. Our own identity is tied into the same spiral on which we find the relationship with the other person. The process embraces both moments in the dialectic.

So Jourard's experiments are an important contribution, in that they represent an attempt to check out, in the hard-nosed statistical language of experimental science, the insights of humanistic psychology.

The three men we have met in this chapter represent for me the three aspects of humanistic psychology which it is so important not to let get separated. The innovative practice, the wide-ranging theory and the highly specific research are all important to humanistic psychology. Only by cultivating all these three ways of working can humanistic psychology save itself from the fate of narrowness and aridity which has befallen behaviourism and the cognitive approach, and the fate of woolliness and uncheckability which has befallen psychoanalysis.

ALVIN MAHRER

But there is one man who has worked in all three of these ways, and in doing so has made, in my opinion, the greatest contribution to humanistic psychology since Maslow died. This is a Canadian therapist, theorist and researcher named Alvin Mahrer. He had been writing for years about research in psychotherapy, but in 1978 he produced a remarkable book called *Experiencing*, which was in effect a manifesto for a whole new look at psychology and psychotherapy. In it he says that we have to talk, if we want to make sense of human beings, in terms of their deeper potentials. These deeper potentials are always OK, but they may be defined by the person who has them as bad or dangerous, for reasons which may be very complex and under many influences. All the psychopathology of the person can be traced to the nature of her relationship (integrative or disintegrative) with these deeper potentials; and all therapy must be essentially concerned with enabling the person to meet and to come to terms with them.

He went on to write two more books (1983, 1986) about the actual practice of psychotherapy, exposing the very central nerve of what goes on in the process of therapy between the two parties involved, and showing that most of what is done in the name of therapy is anything but therapeutic. He is indignantly critical of many different approaches:

> Virtually every helping approach assists the person in achieving the above goals [of avoiding real change] by shifting to another operating potential, and thereby helping the person maintain his self, reduce the burgeoning bad feelings, and push back down the rising deeper potential. These are the aims of supportive therapies, crisis therapies, suicide prevention centres, and the whole enterprise of chemotherapeutic drugs and pills. These are the aims of custodial treatment, behaviour therapies, ego therapies, milieu therapies and social therapies. Nearly every approach which aims for insight and understanding joins the person in achieving these goals. Programs of desensitization and token economy and deconditioning are the allies of the person in working effectively toward these goals. The war cry of all these approaches is the same: control those impulses, push down the insides, reduce the bad feelings, stop the threat, maintain the ego, push away the threat to the self, deaden the tension, guard against the instincts. (1978, p.367)

In his more recent book (1986) he has mellowed a great deal, finding something good even in behaviour therapy,

51

but the contrast still remains between therapy which fulfils the humanistic paradigm, as we have seen it so far, and other therapies which do not. So his work on psychotherapy is radical and challenging, no matter how mellow the manner of its presentation.

A very similar critique has been put forward by Gendlin (1979) who also calls what he does experiential psychotherapy. Gendlin makes it clear that the felt experience of the client is central to all forms of psychotherapy, no matter what the labels. And he uses research very well to point this up.

Mahrer (1985) has actually written a complete book on research in psychotherapy, saying radical and far-reaching things such as that all the existing research on outcomes is misconceived and illusory. But this is not a negative statement for him, merely the obvious implication of his strongly argued view that the only legitimate way of doing research in psychotherapy is to examine the outcomes which take place in each individual therapy session. Some of the vignettes he uses to illustrate this are some of the most moving and highly charged incidents that I have ever seen in a book on therapy. Such moments are visible and can be examined in minute detail through the use of recordings, and analysis of them can lead to actual improvements in therapeutic practice. Such research is of actual use to practitioners. It is an extraordinary but little-known fact that the existing research, massive though it is (Garfield & Bergin 1978, Brown & Lent 1984), has never been of the slightest use to practitioners.

We shall come back to the question of research in Chapter 15, but enough has been said to show what a unique and massive contribution has been made by Mahrer over the past few years, in the mainstream of development of humanistic psychology.

But having now seen how these individuals have put together the three factors of practice, theory and research, it is now time to go on to see how the basic principles which we have now examined are used in practice.

PART TWO

APPLICATIONS OF HUMANISTIC PSYCHOLOGY

CHAPTER FOUR

PERSONAL GROWTH

IN THIS part of the book we shall look at eight different areas where humanistic psychology has been applied. The first of these, and possibly the best known, is personal growth. The term seems to have arisen in California during the late 1950s: in the early 1960s the term was applied by John and Joyce Weir to groups they were running for the National Training Laboratories. All through the 1960s growth centres sprang up, mostly following in some way the model of the Esalen Institute. In 1968 the list compiled by the Association for Humanistic Psychology had 32 growth centres on it: in 1970 this had risen to 121 entries; and in 1973 to 265, in 9 different countries. Since then more countries have opened up growth centres, though in the United States each centre has tended to become more specialised. In Great Britain there are a few growth centres, but more common are more specialized centres devoted to just one or two of the possible approaches. But the idea of a growth centre is still important, as underlining the basic point that we do not have to be unhealthy, or have mental problems, before going to a group or consulting with an individual practitioner. We may simply want to be more than we are, to be more of what we could be.

What is a growth centre? It is just a place where people can go to grow, in the sense of allowing themselves to encounter other people, and work on themselves, in the kind of open ways we have already noticed. In this way they hope to change from people who want safety at all costs (but do not seem able to obtain it) to people who are able to see themselves, and the world, as they really are, and to take some risks in the world. This brings about the expansion of consciousness which Hampden-Turner and the others talked about. Let us just take four of the things which are often offered as means of personal growth, and look at them.

GESTALT AWARENESS PRACTICE

The first of these is Gestalt therapy. It should really be called Gestalt awareness practice, because it is much more than just a therapy, but since it is usually called Gestalt therapy, we may as well give in to this usage. Gestalt is used probably more than any other method in growth centres, either on its own or in combination with other approaches. It originated in the work of Fritz Perls, who was one of the most creative therapists of the Esalen era. He was always at the centre of controversy, and as Gaines (1979) has shown, was a very interesting, if often infuriating man.

Gestalt therapy can be carried out on a one-to-one basis, or in a group. But even in a group, it is usually one person who is the focus of attention, and the therapist is usually working with one person at a time. The attempt is made to get the person to be aware and in contact with her world, instead of suppressing most of what is going on. Perls says that rather than try to change, stop, or avoid something that you don't like in yourself, it is much more effective to experience it fully and become more deeply aware of it. You can't improve on your own functioning, you can only interfere with it, distort it and disguise it. When you really get in touch with your own experiencing, you will find that change takes place by itself, without your effort or planning.

There are two things which Perls warns against, and two which he favours. He warns against 'shouldism' and 'aboutism', and is in favour of the 'how' and the 'now'. 'Shouldism' he calls 'the self-torture game':

I'm sure that you are very familiar with this game. One

part of you talks to the other part and says, 'You should be better, you should not be this way, you should not do that, you shouldn't be what you are, you should be what you are not.' (Perls 1970)

He says that we grow up completely surrounded by demands of this kind, and that we spend much of our time playing this game in adult life. But it is a non-productive game – it does not actually produce any action – and in Gestalt therapy one learns how to give it up.

'Aboutism' is the attempt to keep any real awareness or contact at arm's length by an intellectual process which is often called scientific, though as many people have pointed out (Reason & Rowan 1981), this is actually a mistaken understanding of science. It produces the kind of reification which, as we have already seen, is not countenanced by humanistic psychology:

> Talking about things, or ourselves and others as though we were things, keeps out any emotional responses or other genuine involvement. In therapy, aboutism is found in rationalization and intellectualization, and in the 'interpretation game' where the therapist says, 'This is what your difficulties are about.' This approach is based on noninvolvement. (Perls 1970)

In relation to people, Perls sometimes calls this 'gossip'. When we talk about someone's problem, even if the person is there, and even if we are highly trained professionals, and call it a 'case conference', it is still gossip.

The 'how' is what Perls invites the people involved in therapy to attend to. How are you stopping yourself doing what you really want and need to do? 'Gestalt therapy is being in touch with the obvious.' How are you sitting, how are you breathing, what are your hands doing, where are your eyes looking – all these things are part of who you are and how you are living your life. By becoming aware of these things, and enabling them to speak to us, Gestalt therapy opens up a whole wide window on our functioning, and starts off a process of change towards greater integration of mind and body:

So if you find out how you prevent yourself from growing, from using your potential, you have a way of increasing this, making life richer, making you more and more capable of mobilizing yourself. And our potential is based upon a very peculiar attitude: to live and review every second afresh. (Perls 1969)

And this brings us to the second positive principle, the 'now'. The 'now' is both very easy and very difficult to grasp, as we have already seen in Chapter 2. It can only be fully understood in or after a peak experience. But one of the things which Gestalt therapy aims at is just this peak experience. As Perls (1969) says:

The task of all deep religions – especially Zen Buddhism – or of really good therapy, is the *satori*, the great awakening, the coming to one's senses, waking up from one's dream . . . When we come to our senses, we start to *see*, to *feel*, to *experience* our needs and satisfactions, instead of playing roles and needing such a lot of props for that – houses, motor cars, dozens and dozens of costumes. . . .

So by trying to assume that we are in the now already, we may actually get there. Many of the techniques of Gestalt therapy – the role reversal, the turning of questions into statements, the importance of saying 'I' instead of 'it', the use of fantasy and present-tense dreams – stem from this resolve to act as if we were fully in the now.

There is a superb book of readings on Gestalt therapy, which covers many aspects of this approach and the various ways and contexts in which it can be used, edited by Fagan & Shepherd (1970). The work of Barry Stevens (1970) shows what it would be like to live this way all the time, instead of just using it during therapy sessions. And if you want to see Fritz Perls in action, there are several films and a book called *Gestalt Therapy Verbatim* (1969).

ENCOUNTER

The second of these ways of cultivating personal growth is encounter. This is an approach which is almost always carried out in a group setting, though the principles are equally applicable to individual work. There are actually three types of encounter group which need to be distinguished from one another, and also a fourth thing called a microlab which is often confused with an encounter group.

The first kind of encounter group is called the basic encounter group, developed by Carl Rogers and his associates in Chicago. Rogers (1970) has described it very well, and I have also experienced it at first hand. There are two or three films available, which show at least something of what the process is like. The participants usually sit in a circle throughout, and there is little or no physical interaction. The leader (who is called a facilitator) offers no techniques, and does not have to adopt any particular role, except that of an open participant, ready to reveal her feelings and show interest, care and involvement in the talk and actions of the other group members. She may also share her intuitions or fantasies about other members of the group, not as truths about the other person, but as truths about what is going on in her.

Rogers has formalized his expectations for the group leader in terms of three main requirements: that she shall show acceptance of other people and the way they are, not judging or evaluating them; that she shall cultivate accurate empathy – hopefully being able to sense feelings that are just below the surface and sometimes help them to come out; and that she shall be genuine, in the sense of being aware of what is going on in her and doing justice to that. As he says:

> I seem to function best in a group when my 'owned' feelings – positive or negative – are in immediate inter-action with those of a participant. To me this means that we are communicating on a deep level of personal

meaning. It is the closest I get to an I-Thou relationship. (Rogers 1961)

The Rogerian group tends to be very slow, but very sure – whatever happens, be it little or much, is very real. There is no space, as it were, for phoniness to creep in.

This basic encounter is very good as a starting experience for someone who has never been to an encounter group before. No one will push one into extreme experiences before one is ready, and one can progress at one's own pace. It is true, however, that because of the slowness of the process, it is advisable to go in for a fortnight's group, or at least a week, rather than the weekend or one-day experience which is sometimes offered. And an ongoing group, which is always a good idea, becomes very much so in this case.

The second kind of encounter group is called the open encounter group, and it was developed by Schutz (1973) and others at Esalen. It differs from Rogers's basic encounter in a number of important ways.

First, it is more body-oriented. It is emphasized that people interact with their bodies even when they do not mean to – emotions and reactions register in all sorts of ways in my body, and if I can become aware of that it gives me a whole lot of new knowledge about myself. The leader often works directly with the body in a physical way. For this reason, chairs are not used (we sit on the floor on cushions) and shoes are removed; this makes movement and interaction easier, and takes away barriers. There is often some emphasis on breathing, because shallow or stopped breathing are seen as ways of holding in emotion.

Second, the leader is much more active. She will sometimes start the group off with a set of breathing or interaction exercises (Lewis & Streitfeld 1972), in order to skip the first two or three stages described by Rogers. The leader takes responsibility for setting the basic group norms – what is or is not appropriate behaviour in the group – and for getting the group off the ground. This tends to make open encounter a more intensive experience, quicker than basic encounter – in fact a basic encounter group, because it sets its own norms, may set them much too restrictively, and never get very far. It is because the open encounter is so much more intensive that leaders of this persuasion will never allow their groups to be compulsory, and always insist on them being voluntary. The people who come must be people who feel that they are ready for this sort of headlong plunge into openness and honesty.

Unfortunately, this important proviso was ignored by the most ambitious piece of research carried out on the encounter group (Lieberman, Yalom & Miles 1973), where people were assigned to eighteen different types of group at random, thus producing a very high drop-out rate in some of the groups. I have criticised this at length elsewhere (Rowan 1975), and so have others (Schutz 1975, Smith 1975). But even in this flawed piece of research there is evidence to show that what people get out of a group is very much determined by their readiness for it.

The honesty of these groups is crucial, but often misunderstood, as we saw in the previous chapter. What is central is honesty with oneself, openness to oneself, and this is what is encouraged. What to say to another person is then a real decision, taken with that full awareness. The main message of the encounter group, if there is one, is 'you don't need to be afraid of yourself'. And so you don't need to be defensive with yourself.

Third, there is a great emphasis on energy. The open encounter leader does not take words very seriously – it is the energy behind the words or actions which matters, and she sees her job as enabling that spontaneous energy to flow as freely as possible. Jerome Liss (1974) has written very well about this. He says that one of the main things which can happen in groups is the release of stuck feelings. A simple exercise which can be used, for example is, 'Relax, deep-breathe, focus on a persistent area of tension or discomfort in the body, and imagine a body action involving this area directed toward another person.' This will often lead to emotional discharge or catharsis, with the right kind of encouragement. The emotional discharge – crying, laughing, angry shouting, trembling with fear, etc. – clears the stuck feelings. Usually a sequence of feelings appears, rather than just the one; unpleasant distress transforms into pleasurable warmth; and the person's life energy intensifies.

Fourth, there is a general adoption of the outlook of Gestalt therapy. One of the most characteristic points here is the emphasis on spontaneous flow as opposed to neurotic control. As Caroline Sherwood (1973) has said:

> One of the most significant things about control is its link with dishonesty. When I am in control I have ceased to be open and accessible and am imposing a false rigidity on myself; or I am attempting to limit other people or situations in which I find myself. This dishonesty springs from self-distrust – a fear of my inadequacy to cope as I am.

This links very much with Sartre's notion of bad faith – which can also be translated as self-deception. The open encounter leader attempts to set up a situation in which the participants can learn to trust themselves enough to let go of their usual roles, rigidities and patterns of behaviour. 'Don't push the river; it flows by itself' as Barry Stevens (1970) beautifully explains in her book of this title. And one of the ways the leader can do this is to focus on the words or actions of one group member – always asking if the person wants to work on this particular thing – using some dramatic device to allow the person to experience at first hand the nature of some self-defeating pattern, and then to work on it to achieve some kind of resolution.

For example, in one group a woman said to her husband – 'I feel I can't depend on you.' The husband denied this. The leader suggested that the woman literally depend on her husband by hanging round his neck with her feet off the floor. They did this only for a moment, and then he drooped and let her fall. He was rather thin, and she was quite big, and this might have seemed reason enough. But there was another woman in the group, lively and attractive, and about the same size and weight as his wife. She came over and put her arms round his neck, and took her feet off the floor. He held her up successfully for some while, and then walked round the room, with her still hanging on him. This little bit of action said more about the relationship than any amount of words. Some further work was done on this, but some time afterwards, this couple decided to split up. Happy endings are not always guaranteed.

So the open encounter does not look like a number of people sitting round and talking – it looks like a rather slow-moving dramatic performance, with people getting up, moving round the group, meeting one another in different formations, going back to their places, perhaps screaming, perhaps arm-wrestling, but always in an atmosphere which is basically healing and caring. This atmosphere is so incredibly nice, particularly towards the end of the group, that people often feel let down when the group is over. The glow lasts maybe for a matter of days, and then the rude world breaks in. But perhaps this is good. At least one knows now what good social relationships feel like. Perhaps then we can try to create them in our places of work, in our homes, in the everyday world. This is certainly what Schutz wants.

The aims and outcomes of open encounter are not very different from those of basic encounter, though they are closer to therapy groups, in the sense that someone could bring up something which was a very particular personal problem more readily in an open encounter group, because the leader is willing to offer a great variety of techniques. See Haigh (1968) for a very good example of this process in action, Shaffer & Galinsky (1974) for a good academic account, and Ernst & Goodison (1981) for the way in which encounter can be used in self-help groups.

The third kind of encounter group is Synanon encounter (Yablonsky 1965). This started with Chuck Dederich, who found a way of working with ex-drug-addicts in California. It went through various changes, and much of it got handed on down through Phoenix House and other places for ex-addicts, in the UK and elsewhere, which used some of the same approaches. Then it got used in various ways in growth centres.

The essence of the Synanon approach is direct aggressive

confrontation of one group member by one or more other members. The attacking members use emotion and intuition rather than reasoned criticism, and are not in the least afraid of projecting their own problems on to the focal person. (Projection is the defence mechanism by which we find our own faults out there for all to see, in other people. If I experience someone as hostile, as giving me dirty looks, as slighting me, as giving me the cold shoulder, it may well be my own hostility which I am perceiving – only I am putting it in the wrong place. Instead of being aware of it, and owning up to it, I am shutting off my own self-awareness because it would be inconvenient to admit I were hostile – maybe there is no good reason to be – it is more convenient for my good image of myself to see it in the other person. Then – and this is the cleverest part – if I do feel angry at the other person, it is justified after all, because she started it by being hostile to me!)

This is unlike the other two approaches; in both of them the emphasis is all the time on taking back your projections, on owning your fantasies, on taking responsibility for yourself, and not laying your trip on someone else. But with this third approach, it seems that it is most valuable when it is used by people who also know each other outside the group. They can then confront each other about behaviour in the group or outside it, and relate the one to the other – this makes it the most real-life of the three, where this happens. There is a very good description by Hampden-Turner (1977) of a similar set-up in the Delancey Street Foundation. This approach is unsuitable for most of the work done in growth centres, which is of a short-term nature, and done mainly with strangers. But it can fit in with some of the longer term programmes, where the same group stays together for three, six or nine months.

Of the three approaches which have been mentioned – basic encounter, open encounter and Synanon encounter – open encounter is the most flexible and varied, and depends most upon the personality and experience of the group leader.

A microlab is a set of exercises, derived from the encounter group experience, which can be put on for a large group as an introduction to some of the ways of exploring each person's feelings and responses in an experiential way. It is a very good way of giving a lot of people a revealing and sometimes quite intense experience in a short time.

It is perhaps worth saying that all forms of personal growth work, whatever their orientation, find themselves working a great deal of the time with childhood material. No matter how much we may disagree with Freud – and most of us have some very severe disagreements – we all seem to find that he was right in saying that many of our personal difficulties can be traced back to things that went wrong in some way very far back in our lives. Wilber (1984) has now written a long essay in which he explains rather clearly and fully why this should be so, and why it doesn't seem to matter very much whether we want to get into such material, or whether our theory tells us that or something quite different. It is even reported (Kapleau 1967) that when people first go to a Zen monastery and practise meditation, they often go to the *roshi* and say – 'I expected to receive enlightenment, but all I get is all this childhood stuff!'

BODY WORK

This is certainly true of body work, which represents another important aspect of the work which can be done in personal growth. The main tradition here starts with Reich (Boadella 1985), though Lowen and Rolf have made some major additions to the armoury of what can be done.

Reich's basic insight was to acknowledge that our defensive patterns, brought into being for what seemed like good reasons at the time, and then later resorted to whether appropriate or not, affect not only our minds, but are also registered and held in our bodies. We do not just use our bodies – we *hold* them in certain ways. We permit certain movements and stop others, and these stopped movements form up into rigidities and tensions. They are there to stop the natural movement of our own sexual energy, which has been defined by others, and by ourselves later, as being

65

dangerous instead of pleasurable. It is these rigidities and tensions which we call our character. In terms of the body, we wear a suit of 'character armour', which effectively shuts out a great deal of our experience, and robs us of naturalness and spontaneity. The idea that character *is* neurosis is a challenging one.

Alexander Lowen (1970) has written a book called *Pleasure* which states the case for body work in a readable and convincing way. By simply working on the body tensions – the therapist moving her hands over the body of the person being treated, in a way that might look at first like massage but which is in fact quite different – very strong, pre-verbal, infantile experiences can be evoked. Or vivid memories of traumatic experiences may come back. Or a kind of emotional release which does not seem to be attached to any one thing may come about. In all these cases, the experience tends to be quite frightening the first time it happens, because it is an example of the spontaneous flow we have been spending all that energy holding back, in a quite unnecessary way. And even though it may have been unnecessary, we have still got used to doing it, and to let go seems dangerous and difficult. So what the therapist does is to encourage the person to stay with the experience, and go with it, and accept it as *one's own* experience, which one is entitled to, and can be identified with.

Body work can also use another way of going about things, which is to use the voice to get energy flowing. Often some simple phrase will be used, such as 'No!' for opposition, or 'I want it' for positive assertion, and the person will be encouraged to say it louder and louder, until it turns into a scream. This, too, can lead to a whole sequence of emotional releases, particularly if it is combined with some movement which adds tension or meaning to the exercise.

The best book on the actual techniques of bioenergetics is Lowen & Lowen (1977) which gives full details of exactly how the various exercises are carried out and used.

These kinds of body work are very effective in bringing out answers to very deep-seated problems, because they by-pass the intellect and cut through the games which the person may use to avoid dealing with the real world and her real self. But they do need a skilled therapist to be present, and are best done on a one-to-one basis, so that they are expensive. Also they represent a 'heavy' approach, as against the 'light' approach of co-counselling; the person is very much in the hands of the therapist, and not in control of their own progress. This means, in my view, that a person would be unwise to go to a bioenergetic group, or for individual therapy using these methods, as the very first step in fostering their own personal growth. It would seem to be better to get in touch with some unconscious material in a gentler way first.

However, it is true that these methods can produce the most beautiful sensations if they are carried out to the end. The strong and frightening emotions are genuinely dealt with and worked through, and then what Reich calls the 'streamings' may be felt – pleasurable sensations running through the body, like a continuous orgasm. This is the natural energy of the body, flowing without blocks or hindrances.

It will be clear by now that all these forms of personal growth involve catharsis – the process by which emotional discharge leads to a sequence of changes ending in peace, joy or even ecstasy. As John Heider (1974) puts it:

> Frequently in the course of an encounter group, participants experience a cathartic release of pent-up emotions or tension followed by an unusual, even ecstatic, sense of well-being – a feeling of having been cleansed or reborn. In this postcathartic state, conditions for healing, growth and transcendence exist to an unusual degree: psychosomatic symptoms fall away, insights into personal behaviour come easily and naturally, and a transcendent sense of union with cosmic order is common.

In his early days, Freud noticed the value of catharsis, and used it; but later gave it up, because it did not last, and seemed to him illusory for that reason. The symptoms returned, and the amazing experience seemed less amazing because of this. But this need cause disappointment only if we over-value catharsis in the first place. It is beautiful, and so is the cherry-blossom. We can learn from all these things, and the insight from a peak experience is no less real because we remain the person we always were. The moral which Heider draws from this is that catharsis needs to be integrated into an ongoing experience if it is to have the maximum effect.

But body work is not just about bioenergetics or biosynthesis (Boadella, in press) – it is also about touch. One of the distinctive features of the humanistic approach is its friendliness to human touch:

> In the evolution of the senses the sense of touch was undoubtedly the first to come into being. Touch is the parent of our eyes, ears, nose and mouth. It is the sense which became differentiated into the others, a fact that seems to be recognised in the age-old evaluation of touch as 'the mother of the senses'. (Montagu 1978)

In a humanistic group devoted to personal growth there will almost always be some touch, for reassurance, for sensual pleasure, for parental comforting, for support, as a form of meditation, or in any other of the many ways in which touch is used in normal human interaction.

One of the most important uses of touch is in Sensory Awareness, pioneered by Charlotte Selver and Charles Brooks (1974) at Esalen in the early 1960s and popularized by Bernie Gunther (1969). This is a very beautiful approach, with a lot of emphasis on breathing and naturalness and the wisdom of the body.

We used to be very unaware about this politically, but since Nancy Henley (1977) opened our eyes, we realise that touch can represent power. In her research she showed that people of higher status can touch people of lower status, but people of lower status cannot touch people of higher status. She has some suggestions for women which are well worth mentioning here:

> *Women can stop*: smiling unless they are happy; lowering or averting their eyes when stared at; getting out of men's way in public; allowing interruption; restraining their body postures; accepting unwanted touch.
>
> *Women can start*: staring people in the eye; addressing

them by first name; being more relaxed in demeanour (seeing it's more related to status than morality); touching when it feels appropriate.

She adds that there is an especially important thing women can do – support other women nonverbally. She also has some hints for men along similar lines:

> *Men can stop*: invading women's personal space; touching them excessively; interrupting; taking up extra space; sending dominance signals to each other; staring.
> *Men can start*: smiling; losing their cool, displaying emotion; sending gestures of support; being honest when they are unsure of something; condensing their bodies.

By becoming more aware of such matters, people in groups can avoid unnecessary dominance and submission, and relate more as equal members of the group. So the whole question of touch and body language has many different aspects to it. We need to work at a number of different levels at the same time if we are to get the most out of personal growth.

JEAN HOUSTON

Someone who has taken this idea to the furthest extreme is Jean Houston (1982) who has really tried to put all the levels together, from the body right through to the spiritual, in one connected series of workshops. She is a most inspiring leader, teacher and public speaker, and her book can be used to open a person up to much of her potential in many different areas. Subtitled *A Course in Enhancing Your Physical, Mental and Creative Abilities*, that is exactly what it is.

Anyone who wants to know what personal growth is really all about needs to get hold of this book, or better still, go to one of Jean Houston's workshops, which are sometimes held in Europe.

If we are going to take personal growth seriously, we need some ongoing discipline, as well as the one-off groups we may want to try. The obvious way of doing this is to go in for long-term counselling or psychotherapy on a one-to-one basis, and more people seem to be doing this nowadays as humanistic practitioners get better known. But other ways can be used too: T'ai Chi can be very good if taught in the right way; as also can Aikido (if taught in a way which emphasizes the spiritual aspect). Meditation (particularly perhaps mindfulness meditation) is another way, and so is Hatha Yoga. Another way is regular dream sharing, as Shohet (1985) has urged with persuasive force; dream work can in fact be one of the best ways of getting to know one's internal world, which is so immense and rich. The most important thing is that it be a regular practice, conducted in the spirit of personal growth, and aimed at self-actualization.

CHAPTER FIVE

COUNSELLING

THERE ARE many varieties of counselling, and it is a term which is used rather loosely. One recent book distinguished counselling from psychotherapy by saying: 'Again this usually involves a one-to-one relationship of professional worker and client. Here the aim is usually to give a more practical kind of advice about personal, work or emotional problems.' But humanistic psychology has quite a different view of counselling, derived from the work of Carl Rogers. And in recent years this has been added to by the work of Harvey Jackins and the people who have followed him.

PERSON-CENTRED COUNSELLING

It was in the early 1940s that Rogers (1942) started to put forward his ideas about counselling, and in the next ten to fifteen years his views became very widely accepted (Rogers 1951). Nowadays probably most of the courses on counselling in this country are based on Rogerian principles – or as he preferred to have them known, person-centred principles. He said in conversation in 1981 that he hoped the name 'Rogerian' would go down the drain.

People come for counselling – whether to school counsellors, marriage guidance counsellors or whatever – with a variety of problems. Usually the problem has to do with a conflict of some kind. And resolving the conflict is not easy; if it were easy, one would not consult a counsellor. And usually the reason it is not easy is that the person's rigidities or fixed patterns of behaviour have become involved, either with each other or with another person. So working on this one problem may mean working on these long-standing patterns, or at least giving the person some space and time to see what is really involved.

Perhaps the essence of the matter is that the humanistic counsellor genuinely believes that the client has the answer, and can find the answer given the time and space to do so. And so the person-centred counsellor refuses to help, and does not see her role as one of taking any kind of responsibility for the client's problems. What the counsellor does instead is to facilitate the client's own self-searching, in such a way that the client feels understood, and believed-in, and basically capable. As Rogers (1961) says:

> One brief way of describing the change which has taken place in me is to say that in my early professional years I was asking the question, How can I treat, or cure, or change this person? Now I would phrase the question in this way: How can I provide a relationship which this person may use for his own personal growth?
>
> It is as I have come to put the question in this second way that I realize that whatever I have learned is applicable to all of my relationships, not just to working with clients with problems.

So what is the secret of this relationship which Rogers tried to build up, and which he found to be so fruitful and healing?

A few years ago, you might have read that Rogers's technique was one of reflection – mirroring the client's responses back at her. This was never, in fact, true. And in recent years Rogers has taken great pains to make it clear that this is not what he is saying at all. What he is saying is that in so far as the counsellor can be genuinely *there* in the relationship, the client will feel genuinely listened to and taken seriously; and will start to take herself seriously. Now it is surprisingly difficult to be genuinely there, in that sense; listening is a hard task, for reasons which John Enright (1970) outlines very clearly:

I am quite serious in asserting that most of us . . . are . . . not fully aware of our actual present. Much of the content of our consciousness is remembering, speculating, planning ('rehearsing' for our next interpersonal performance), or carrying on a busy inner dialogue (or monologue). More specifically, we professionals sitting with a patient may be diagnosing, 'prognosing', planning our next intervention, wondering what time it's getting to be, etc. – we are only too rarely being really open to our experience of self and other.

So asking the counsellor to be genuine, and to be there, and to be listening, is asking a lot. It seems clear that the counsellor cannot in fact do this unless she has done some work on her own personal growth, sufficient to open up perception to the point where the outer world is let in rather than kept out. Enright continues:

> Those of us who are not seriously mentally ill remain sufficiently in touch with the actual environment to move through it reasonably effectively . . . but miss so many nuances that our experience of the world and the other is often pale and our memories of it, therefore, weak. Engaged as we are with our own phantoms, we attend only sketchily to the other. Since he then seems rather pale and incomplete, we fill him out with our own projections and react vigorously to these. The resulting encounter often gives a convincing show of life and involvement where, in fact, there is little.

So person-centred counselling always implies that the counsellor is willing to undergo the same discipline which she is urging on the client. The person-centred counsellor is not someone who has undergone training and is now an expert – she is someone who is continually working on herself to be more aware of potential sources of bias, partiality and general inattention. Let us then look, with this much understood, at the three conditions which we touched on briefly before, which Rogers says are necessary to his kind of counselling.

The first is genuineness. At times Rogers has used the

term 'congruence' to clarify what he means by this. The counsellor is, as near as possible, completely open to her own feelings – she is able to live these feelings, be them, and be able to communicate them if appropriate. Note that Rogers, like Schutz, is not advocating that the counsellor should blurt out her feelings at all times, but simply that she should be aware of them, and allow the whole situation to determine whether they are uttered or not, and if so, how. The important thing, Rogers (1961) says, is to be real. 'The more genuine and congruent the [counsellor] in the relationship, the more probability there is that change in personality in the client will occur.' In case the last line causes some raised eyebrows, it may be worth noting here that Rogers distinguishes between the personality of a person, as something on the surface, something that the person *presents* to the world, and the self, which is more basic; and the organism, which is more basic still (see Chapter 13). What Rogers is aiming at is the ultimate integration of the organism, with all its sensory and visceral experiences, with the self, in a consistent and harmonious way.

For this to happen, the second requirement of the counselling relationship is non-possessive warmth. This has sometimes been put by Rogers as a demand for 'unconditional positive regard', which seems hard to achieve. But like genuineness, this is a limiting case, something to aim at. It is easier if the counsellor accepts herself first – again it cuts both ways, and again it is not easy.

It involves . . . genuine willingness for the client to be whatever feeling is going on in him at that moment – fear, confusion, pain, pride, anger, hatred, love, courage or awe. It means that the [counsellor] cares for the client, in a non-possessive way . . . By this I mean that he does not simply accept the client when he is behaving in certain ways, and disapprove of him when he behaves in other ways. (Rogers 1961)

This attitude by the counsellor was phrased by someone else as 'I care, but I don't mind.' That is, I care about you, but when you do something bad, wrong, or stupid, it doesn't hurt me, it doesn't make me suffer – I won't add my evaluations to your burdens. And this comes out of the basic outlook we found in Chapter 1 – that each human being, deep down underneath it all, is *all right*. There is a basic lively health and intelligence there which we can believe in and rely on.

The third requirement is empathic understanding. It is not enough for the counsellor to be genuine and accepting and warm – there must be some demonstration that this is all working. And if it is working, the client will feel understood. When someone understands how it feels and seems to be me, without wanting to analyse me or judge me, than I can blossom and grow in that climate. Rogers (1967) puts it like this:

> Acceptance does not mean much until it involves understanding. It is only as I *understand* the feelings and thoughts which seem so horrible to you, or so weak, or so sentimental, or so bizarre – it is only as I see them as you see them, and accept them and you, that you feel really free to explore all the hidden nooks and frightening crannies of your inner and often buried experience.

But it seems to Rogers that empathy can never actually put ourselves into someone else's world. Only that person can really experience her own world. So all we can do is continually check it out with the person – 'I heard you say you felt left out. Does that mean you felt weak and helpless, or was it something a bit different from that?' If we keep doing this in the early stages, we may eventually get on to the person's wavelength, and be able to sense things which are just beneath the surface. It means cultivating our intuition, and helping our intuition by giving it good materials to work on. But ultimately we can never be as empathic with another person as we can be congruent with ourself, according to Rogers.

Now Rogers does not simply say that these three requirements are good – he has undertaken and stimulated a great deal of research to check them out empirically. The book which he co-edited with Rosalind Dymond (1954) is a superb example of how research can be used to discover a great deal about what actually goes on in the process of counselling.

Three years later, Rogers (1961) outlined a seven-stage process which has been used in subsequent research, and which I think helps a great deal in understanding what his form of counselling is all about. It is based on analysis of many recorded interviews, and details seven stages which the client may go through in sorting out her problems.

First stage: Communication is only about externals. There is no desire to change. Much blockage of internal communication. Sees the present in terms of the past.

Second Stage: Feelings may be shown, but are not recognized as such or owned. No sense of responsibility in problems. Experience is held at arm's length.

Third Stage: Some talk about the self, but only as an object. Description of past feelings. But very little acceptance of feelings – they are usually seen as unacceptable.

Fourth Stage: More intense feelings may be described from the past. Some recognition that there may be more than one way of looking at things. Some awareness of contradictions in self.

Fifth Stage: Feelings are expressed freely in the present. More differentiation of experience – more precision, more self-responsibility. But some fear of what bubbles up through.

Sixth stage: A breakthrough stage, where feelings come through, are experienced now, and accepted. Physiological loosening takes place, and also a mental loosening of previous ways of seeing the world and self.

Seventh Stage: New feelings are experienced and accepted. The person trusts her own process. No need to pin things down finally. Strong feelings of being able to choose and be self-responsible.

Rogers says that any change down this list is desirable and worth working for. A full traverse from beginning to end would probably take years rather than weeks or months.

One of the great strengths of Rogers's approach has always been his interest in research, and the Garfield & Bergin (1978) handbook gives much of it, showing that his approach does actually bring people along the path which he has set.

One question of terminology may not be out of place here. We have talked about personal growth, and about counselling, and in the next chapter we talk about therapy. In my view these are all the same thing – and indeed some forms of learning and some forms of attitude change are the same thing too. In all these cases we are referring to movement up Hampden-Turner's spiral, or through Rogers's stages, or up Maslow's levels, away from alienation and anomie towards full humanness. But the great advantage of Rogers's approach is that is does not push the client into any special techniques or assumptions. It takes the client right where she is, and takes that seriously. And so it is an approach which has very wide application – we can even use it informally in our ordinary social contacts and personal relationships. But if we do, it is important to do it our own way, and not to think to ourselves – 'How would Carl Rogers do it?' You can't be genuine, and be Carl Rogers, at the same time – unless, of course, you actually are Carl Rogers.

Someone who has taken Rogers's ideas further in his own way is Eugene Gendlin, who we shall meet again in the next chapter. Gendlin (1979) has emphasized the importance of listening, and again has used research to show how important it is to pay attention to the whole felt experience of the client and not just her words.

Counselling of this and closely allied types is now very

common in Britain, and there is an organization, the British Association for Counselling, which brings together the various approaches and organizations offering counselling under one umbrella.

CO-COUNSELLING

It would be a mistake, however, to think that this is the only way of carrying out the process of counselling. One of the most powerful influences of recent years has been the rise of peer counselling networks quite outside the orbit of the growth centres, and outside the practice of professional counselling.

The basic idea of peer counselling is this: after proper training, which ensures the presence of shared assumptions and techniques, two people meet once a week (or as often as suits them) for two hours (or whatever time suits them). Then for one hour the first person is the client and the second the counsellor; and for the second hour they swap roles. Thus each person gets counselling and gives counselling equally.

The role relationship is quite formal: the counsellor is not to comment, or give advice, or sympathize, or share experiences; but only to listen, to assist the client to get into emotional discharge, and to allow the client to control the interaction at every point. The counsellor has a few simple techniques to offer – repetition of key phrases, contradiction of self-deprecatory statements, role-playing and a few others – but nothing elaborate and nothing mystifying, because the client knows and can use all the same techniques, too. It then becomes crystal clear what is mystified in most other forms of therapy, and may take years to discover – that it is the client who has to do the work. Only the client knows what she is ready to work on, and how deep she is ready to go. So the client remains in charge of her own therapy from the beginning to the end.

It is also very cheap. The 40-hour course costs between £40 and £115 at 1986 prices, depending on where you do it, which includes the necessary literature. It can sometimes be obtained much more cheaply through local educational authority classes. And from then on (unless you go for extra training courses or want to become a teacher of the method) it is free. The training for teachers of the method takes somewhat longer, and some care is taken to ensure that no one teaches co-counselling without formal approval from the community, except on a one-to-one basis. One-to-one teaching – sharing your skills with another person – is very much encouraged for all co-counsellors. And so it spreads.

As the counselling goes on over the weeks, what may happen is that, after having started on a superficial level, each person starts to get into deeper material which often involves childhood incidents and relationships. You may begin to discover that your childhood self created many rules and decisions about how you should live your life which your adult self knew nothing about, but was acting on just the same. But now that you know about this – on an emotional level – you can in effect go back and re-evaluate that decision or those rules in the light of your new knowledge. As this process goes on, you find your moods changing for the better, your fixed patterns of behaviour becoming more flexible, and your abilities coming out and being expressed more often. You are moving up the spiral.

This obviously gets the benefit of the findings of Jourard on self-disclosure, which we saw in Chapter 3. And consequently, it does appear to be a particularly effective technique for fostering personal growth. It has the further benefit that the practice has grown up of giving each person who is trained in the method the names and addresses and phone numbers of all those who have ever been on similar training courses, so that there is a network or community of people who can be called on in case of urgent need.

This system was started by Harvey Jackins (1965) in Seattle, and spread to Britain largely by the efforts of Tom Scheff. The organization grew fast, but friction started to grow over the amount of control exercised from Seattle, and the amount of autonomy wanted in Britain. This led to the British representative, John Heron, seceding from the main body and starting up his own organization, which became part of Co-counselling International, a rival group.

And John Southgate started up his Dialectical Peer Counselling network, later better known as the Barefoot Psychoanalyst group (Southgate & Randall 1978), bringing in a heady mixture of Marxism, Karen Horney and other approaches. Glyn Seaborn Jones started his own system, called Reciport, mainly for people already in his network of therapy and group work. In spite of all this variation, the basic principles have remained the same, and this seems to be a very stable and well-organized area of work.

The basic theory of co-counselling is not so very different from that of Carl Rogers. Deep down, people are OK: they are possessed of a creative and flexible human intelligence. But when they are hurt (physically or mentally) this intelligence stops functioning, and feelings of distress take its place. If the upsetting feelings aroused by any incident are not discharged (given full expression) immediately or at a later point, the upset does not just go away, but rather remains locked up within one. So the residue of emotional tension stays after the hurting event and so does the fragmentation of thinking due to blocked expression. This affects our present experience in various ways: one is that patterns of defence get built up, which may get too efficient at keeping experience out; and another is that the residue, seeking discharge, may be evoked by new situations bearing some similarity to the original distressing events. This is called 're-stimulation' by Harvey Jackins (1970). When we are 'cut to the quick' by a remark which may seem quite innocent to everybody else, we may suspect the presence of re-stimulation. Madison (1969) has some very interesting examples of this, under the heading of what he calls 'reintegration', in his book on student personality.

Jackins has said that the one-point programme of his form of counselling is 'to recover one's occluded intelligence and to assist others to do the same'. This can only be done, of course, on this analysis, by breaking down or loosening in some way the blocks we have set up to deal with hurt. And since the original fault was in not expressing the emotion, so the answer is to 'go back', as it were, re-experience the situation, discharge the emotion relating to it, and re-evaluate the situation in the new light thus made available.

What this means, in effect, is that Jackins is aiming directly at the sixth stage which Carl Rogers has described. He is aiming very directly at emotional discharge and catharsis. And so, in his form of counselling, the client is made aware of the importance of emotional discharge; the counsellor holds the client's hands and looks into her eyes all the time; sometimes the client is encouraged to 'act into' an emotion to encourage it to break through, and so on. Co-counselling uses up a lot of Kleenex.

And the process does seem to work. Experienced counsellors find that they can get to the real work on a problem much quicker using these methods, than by sticking to the more naturalistic Rogerian conversation. The client can still spend time walking all round the problem if she wants to, but there is no longer any need to disguise, mystify or ignore the real aim of the counselling session, which is to get into this opened-up state which Rogers describes as his sixth stage, and where the real work of breaking down the body-mind patterns can take place most effectively.

One of the key differences between the co-counselling approach and the Rogerian approach comes in the treatment of self-denigration – the times when a client starts labelling herself as bad or inadequate or dangerous, or when a client goes in for a great deal of self-blame. The Rogerian approach is well stated in the book by Audrey Newsome (1973) and her colleagues at Keele:

> Clearly it is often painful to listen to a person denigrating himself or spelling out in detail the extent of his anguish or self-rejection but this must be endured if authentic growth is to take place later. It is usually the case that only when negative feelings have been fully explored can faint and hesitant expressions of positive impulses be voiced.

The Jackins view, however, is that putting oneself down is usually a distress pattern in itself, and has been reinforced down the years by parents, teachers, peers and others. It is therefore self-perpetuating, and very difficult to come out of. Furthermore, while one is 'sunk in the depths' of one's bad feelings, one has very little free attention available to see what is going on, and use one's intelligence to change it. According to Jackins, the key essential to good counselling is a 'balance of attention' on the part of the client, such that she is poised between the freshly experienced distress and the real situation (the presence of the counsellor, the outside realities, and so on). So what the counsellor must do, on this reasoning, is to lighten the darkness of self-criticism by contradiction and validation.

In contradiction, the counsellor asks the client to try saying the exact opposite of the statement just made, or sometimes to say the same thing, but in an expansive way, or a cute way, or a silly way – anything to break the pattern and let in an altered perspective. And this contradiction may often come out as a self-validating statement – a statement about how good or right or marvellous one is. What happens after this is very interesting and often very valuable; the client starts laughing. And if the counsellor can look a bit quizzical, the laughter can go on and on for quite a while; it may then switch into tears, because it is felt to be so untrue after all; then anger may come, at the unfairness of it all; and then perhaps fear. This fear is interesting, because it is a very deep and primitive fear of our own OK-ness. It is as if somehow it was wrong or dangerous to be healthy and happy and strong and good. For example, I went through this whole sequence using the phrase – 'I just want my own real strength'. And after the fear, when I had gone right into that, came laughter – the laughter which says – 'Yes! It is true!'

There is, of course, no guarantee that this sequence will follow always or even often, but almost always some change comes in the way the problem is seen. Somehow the breaking of the pattern allows some chink of light into a black situation, and enables one to be less *identified* with that problem. These assertions of one's own OK-ness are called positive directions, and are regarded as very important to the whole co-counselling method. Indeed, it is sometimes thought to be desirable to attend a group meeting simply to repeat the positive directions obtained from one-to-one sessions, in order to get even more out of them. So discharge, re-evaluation, positive directions are all key concepts; and a fourth is goal-setting. Goal-setting is used at the end of a session to take charge of one's environment and way of life, to apply humanistic principles progressively in diverse aspects of daily living as part of an ongoing commitment to social change (Jackins 1973).

The group associated with John Heron (Evison & Horobin 1983) have added such techniques as non-verbal interaction; guided fantasy; good parent and bad parent; regression techniques, possibly leading into a primal (briefly described as a deliberate regression to an early stage where one re-experiences the intense pain of the infant); and transpersonal directions. All these will be described later on – they come from a variety of disciplines, and some of them go away from the principle that the client shall be in charge. There is no way, for example, in which the client can be in charge during a primal (Janov 1970), or even a 'mini-primal', as Heron reassuringly but perhaps misleadingly calls it. As Evison & Horobin (1983) say:

> [When working in the primal area] it is also a good idea to work with an experienced counsellor, since you are bypassing the usual safeguards which in co-counselling usually ensure that you do not get any further into distress than you can handle. You need to know that your counsellor can fish you out of deep distress if you get caught in it.

The addition of the transpersonal is also perhaps worth a word, since it does seem very consistent with the basic discipline of co-counselling. Transpersonal psychology deals with altered states of consciousness – meditation, trance states, expanded awareness – all the things which we looked at in Chapter 2, and will come back to in Chapter 9. It says that these things can be studied and understood in the same way as any other aspect of human experience.

Now if anything like this is true, the methods of co-counselling are well designed for dealing with such matters. As Heron (1974) has suggested, the 'positive directions' could now include things like – 'I am'; or – 'I am one with all things'; or – 'I am one with creation'. Not all people's problems are mundane – some of them have to do with the orientation of one's whole life, and one's relation to spiritual realities. Why should counselling not deal with these areas too?

Another set of additions to the basic co-counselling armoury comes from the other breakaway group, associated with John Southgate (Southgate & Randall 1978). They have added Gestalt therapy, guided fantasy, some ideas from Karen Horney (1942) and again regression leading to primals in the Janov (1970) manner. There is also a whole new theoretical rationale, based on the dialectical thinking of Marx and Hegel, which in my own view is very interesting, and I became a teacher of this method for a year or two. But today the group exists no more, and the book remains on its own as a still valuable monument which can be used by people who want to work on themselves without spending more than the price of the book itself.

Some of the same reservations obviously apply as in the case of the Heron additions – the client not being in charge during regression, and so on. Gestalt therapy can, it seems to me, be either compatibile or incompatible, depending on how much it is used.

An issue which is raised by John Southgate more than the others, however, is the question of how self-improvement or self-development relates to the wider society. By adopting a dialectical point of view, he makes it clear that there is an historical element which most of the other approaches ignore. Our counselling or other practices have effects which depend not only on what they *want* to be or do, but also on the part they play in the social change processes which are going on in contradictory ways. In other words, co-counselling is on someone's side, whether it wants to be or not.

And while in some ways it is on the side of social change, because it tends to produce more autonomous people, who can say 'No!' to the injustices and unfairnesses they find around them and inside themselves, in other ways it is on the side of those who want things to stay the same, so that they can hang on to their privileges – it can remove burning anger, and turn it into understanding adjustment.

This is an important point to be aware of; it is not for

nothing that people in Left groups often call social workers (who use counselling techniques a great deal) the 'soft cops'. In the past, social workers have often played this role, of controlling by helping. So it seems that John Southgate is raising very real issues here.

To do them justice, both Jackins and Heron do in fact stress that co-counselling does not begin and end with the individual client. They see the wider community as very much a part of the whole operation, and are concerned about relationships between the sexes, treatment of the handicapped, the problems of teachers in schools and other organizations, etc. They have published a number of magazine articles and books in these areas. They are also consistent in urging that co-counselling should carry on over into the way relationships are conducted generally – for example, that we could be much more aware of the way we invalidate others, especialy children and those weaker than ourselves. But it still seems to me that Southgate has a better sense of history.

Dreams

One area which is not given much direct attention either in personal growth work or in counselling, yet which really belongs there very firmly, is the realm of dreams.

The great thing about working with dreams is that we can do it at many different levels and in many different ways (Wilber 1986). Hence almost any approach to therapy or counselling can gain from working with dreams.

There are four main ways of working with dreams. One is to treat them as information about the past (Freud 1975). They can be looked at for clues about internal conflicts stemming from childhood traumas or decisions. They can give a great deal of news about the unconscious mind and what is going on there. And obviously this will be helpful in analysing one's life and one's problems.

The second way is to treat them as information about the present. We can see a dream, as Perls (1969) used to say, as an existential message from you to you. One way of using this approach is to take up the role of each person and each thing in the dream, to find out what it is trying to say. This, too, can be productive and useful.

A third way is to treat them as information about the future (Mahoney 1972). Not simply as precognition – though this can certainly happen – but more as information about where you need to go next. This kind of prospective approach, pioneered by Jung, is very popular in the transpersonal approaches.

And the fourth way is not to interpret the dream at all, but to let it be a guide to the inner world. This is the approach of Hillman (1979), who says that the dream world is a world of its own, needing to be understood on its own terms, and not needing to be translated into some other terms.

All these approaches are possible because dreams are symbolic, and like all symbols, can be taken in various ways (Faraday 1976). For example, a cross is a symbol which, in various contexts, can mean a crossroad, a kiss, a Christian emblem, an addition, a hospital or ambulance, a flag of St George and so on. It is hopeless to say that a pistol always stands for this, or an oven for that, as old-fashioned dreams books try to do.

Most forms of therapy encourage people to remember and work with dreams (Garfield 1976), and it is worthwhile to keep a dream diary. To remember a dream, write it down in the same position as that in which you dream it, preferably without putting on the light. Then change position and see if more details come. Write down the specifics as much as possible, including any unusual words or phrases that seem to be remembered.

It is possible to set up informal dream-sharing groups, and this can be very interesting, even if you are not in any process of therapy or counselling (Shohet 1985). There is a saying that an unremembered dream is like an unopened letter. We owe it to ourselves to get access to the whole dream country in our minds. And this peer-counselling approach is a good way of doing it.

CHAPTER SIX

PSYCHOTHERAPY

HUMANISTIC PSYCHOLOGY does not attach very much importance to diagnostic categories, and does not see mental distress as a medical problem. So, as was hinted in the previous chapter, no great dividing line is drawn between 'normal', 'neurotic' and 'psychotic' people. Every technique which is used in personal growth and in counselling is also used in psychotherapy, and vice versa. Probably most humanistic professionals would go along with the statement made by Friedenberg (1973) in his book about Laing:

> To an existential psychiatrist the purpose of therapeutic intervention is to support and re-establish a sense of self and personal authenticity. Not mastery of the objective environment; not effective functioning within social institutions; not freedom from the suffering caused by anxiety – though any or all of these may be concomitant outcomes of successful therapy – but personal awareness, depth of real feeling, and, above all, the conviction that one can use one's full powers, that one has the courage to be and use all one's essence in the praxis of being.

This word 'praxis' is an unusual one, and deserves some explanation. It means the way a person acts intentionally – that conduct which is informed by her own projects. Such action cannot be reduced to determination from outside – it is that person's *own* action, for which she is responsible. It is possible for psychologists either to help the person be more self-determining, by validating people, respecting their praxis, and confirming their reality as persons; or to hinder it by intentionally or unthinkingly reinforcing the rigidities which stem from the general alienation of society. Keith Paton (1971) puts it very well:

> People like being treated as persons, and they know and hate it when they are treated as things. Wherever *praxis* is reduced to *process* we can speak of *reification*: thingification, reducing a person to the level of a dumb animal or a thing . . . When your parents said – 'Oh, you're just going through a phase', you probably protested and said – 'I can decide for myself. When I need your advice I'll ask for it. For goodness sake, *stop treating me like a child.*' In our society, 'being treated like a child' *means* being reified, having our praxis denied, being explained out of existence, in short – NOT being treated like a PERSON.

So the humanistic therapist does not treat the person like a child, but with the full respect due to a person. And she actually objects to the attempts of other supposed therapists who do reduce people to the status of a patient. As Scheff (1966) and Szasz (1961) have shown, psychiatric classification is less like medical diagnosis, and more like a subtle way to invalidate the experience of a human being.

PRIMAL INTEGRATION

One of the most interesting recent developments in humanistic psychotherapy is the advent of primal integration therapy, which was not included at all in the first edition of this book.

Primal integration is a form of therapy brought over to Britain by Bill Swartley, although it was also pioneered here by Frank Lake. It lays the major emphasis upon early trauma as the basic cause of neurosis, and enables people to regress back to the point in time where the trouble began, and to relive it there. This often involves a cathartic experience called 'a primal'. But some people using this approach do not like this language, and instead call what they do regression-integration therapy. It is strongly influenced by the research of Stanislav Grof (1975), who pointed particularly to the deep traumas often associated with the experience of birth.

Catharsis is sometimes referred to as the ventilation of emotion. But in the kind of work which is done in therapy it seems better to be more specific, and to say with Pierce et al. (1983) that catharsis is the vigorous expression of feelings about experiences which had been previously unavailable to consciousness. This lays more emphasis upon the necessity for the emergence of unconscious material.

What Swartley, Lake, Grof and others did was to bring together the idea of catharsis and the emphasis on getting down to the origins of disturbance with another very important question – the transpersonal and the whole area of spirituality. (These terms are explained in Chapter 9.) This means that primal integration therapy can deal with the major part of the whole psychospiritual spectrum mapped out by Ken Wilber (1980). I believe it is unique in this, except possibly for the holonomic approach recently described by Grof (1985).

It will be clear from what has been said that primal integration is a syncretic approach which brings together the extremes of therapy: it goes far back into what Wilber (1983) calls the pre-personal realm and deeply into the internal conflicts of the individual; and it goes far into the transpersonal realms of symbols, intuition and the deeper self. It is this combination of extremes which makes it so flexible in practice.

In primal integration therapy the practitioner uses techniques taken from body therapies, feeling therapies, analytic therapies and transpersonal therapies in a very imaginative way, because a lot of stress is laid on the unity of body, feelings, thought and spirituality. As Shorr (1983) says, the intensive use of imagery in therapy leads to much more involvement and much more exciting sessions.

Because of the emphasis of primal integration on early trauma, people sometimes think it is going to put all neurosis down to one trauma, happening just once in one's life. But of course traumas are seldom as dramatic as this.

The commonest causes of neurosis are simply the common experiences of childhood – all the ways in which our child needs are unmet or frustrated. Hoffman (1979) has spoken eloquently about the problem of negative love. Because of the prevalence of neurosis and psychosis vast numbers of parents are unable to give love to their children. Hoffman says:

> When one adopts the negative traits, moods or admonitions (silent or overt) of either or both parents, one relates to them in negative love. It is illogical logic, nonsensical sense and insane sanity, yet the pursuit of the love they never received in childhood is the reason people persist in behaving in these destructive patterns. 'See, Mom and Dad, if I am just like you, will you love me?' is the ongoing subliminal query.

This is not necessarily a single trauma, in the sense of a one-off event – that is much too simplistic a view. Rather would we say with Balint (1968) that the trauma may come from a situation of some duration, where the same painful lack of 'fit' between needs and supplies is continued.

The goal of primal integration is very simple and straightforward, and can be stated in one sentence. It is to contact and release the real self. Once that has been done, enormously useful work can be done in enabling the person to work through the implications of that, and to support the person through any life-changes that may result. But until the real self has been contacted, the process of working to release it will continue (see Rowan 1983, Chapter 5).

But there is one aspect which we must not miss out, and which is crucially important. This is that the primal integration therapist feels it very important to be authentic. If the aim of the therapy is that the client should be enabled to contact the real self, as we have said above, then it is important for the therapist to model that, and to be a living example of a real human being.

So this gives us the paradox of primal integration therapy relying at one and the same time on authenticity and tricks. At first sight these two things seem simply contradictory. How can I be real and at the same time be using techniques, which must inevitably be artificial? I think Bergantino (1981) puts his finger on the answer when he says:

> Being tricky and authentic can be two sides of the same coin. Being an authentic trickster will not destroy the patient's confidence if the therapist's heart is in the right place. (p.53)

A very similar point is made by Alan Watts (1951), who tells us that in Eastern religious disciplines the learner is often tricked by the teacher into some insight or break-through or awakening. The tricks (*upaya*) which are used are an expression of spiritual truth. In primal integration, we may use massage, or painting, or guided fantasy, or hitting cushions, or reliving birth, all in the interests of enabling reality to dawn.

Obviously the main technique is regression – that is, taking the person back to the trauma on which their neurosis is based. Laing (1983) has argued that we should also talk about recession – the move from the outer to the inner world. And Mahrer (1986) makes a similar point. Going back is no use unless at the same time we are going deeper in to our own experience. Primal integration finds that recession and regression go very well together. One of the clearest statements of the case for doing this comes from Grof (1975) when he talks about the COEX system. A COEX is a syndrome of trauma-based experiences which hang together emotionally. It is a pattern of feelings, meanings and other mental and physical experiences which fit together and appear or disappear as a whole. It is a Gestalt which keeps on reappearing in the person's life. If we can unlock it, we can unlock a whole big area of that person's experience.

One of the things that happens in primal work, as Adzema (1985) has recently pointed out, is that the deeper people go in recession and regression, the more likely they are to have spiritual experiences too. However, in this area there is one very common error we have to guard against. Grof (1980) points out that blissful womb states, which primal clients sometimes get into, are very similar to peak experiences (Maslow 1973) and to the cosmic unity which mystics speak of as contact with God. This has led some people – Wasdell for example – into saying that all mystical experiences are nothing but reminiscences of the ideal or idealized womb. This is an example of Wilber's (1983) pre/trans fallacy. Grof himself does not fall for this error, and has a good discussion of some different forms of trans-personal experiences. I have tried to be even more specific in discussing the various types of mystical experiences, as we saw in Chapter 2. The whole point is that we repress not only dark or painful material in the lower unconscious, but also embarrassingly good material in the higher unconscious (Assagioli 1975).

This can come out in guided fantasies, in drawing or painting, or in dreams. Dreams can be interpreted, understood or simply appreciated on many different levels (Wilber 1986). If we want to do justice to the whole person, we have to be prepared to deal with the superconscious as well as the lower unconscious. This seems to me part of the four-level listening process (Rowan 1985) which is absolutely basic to all forms of therapy and counselling.

If we believe, as Michael Broder (1976) suggests, that the primal process consists of five phases: Commitment; Abreaction (catharsis); Insight (cognitive-affective restruc-turing); Counter-action (fresh behaviour in the world); and Pro-action (making real changes); then it must be the case that the later phases are just as important as the earlier ones. In other words, working through is just as significant as breaking through. The glamorous part, and the contro-versial part, of our work is the 'primal', the cathartic breakthrough; but in reality the process of integration is necessary and equally exciting in its quieter way. For example, it is a great thing to get to the cathartic point of forgiving one's mother; it is another thing to start treating women decently in daily life, as a result of this.

Primal integration pays a lot of attention to the circumstances of people's lives, which have a great deal to do with the progress of their therapy. Sometimes these external factors have as much influence as the therapy itself. It is very important to recognize these factors and the part they play. Therapists sometimes write as if therapy sessions were the whole of life, or at least most of it, and of course this is never so. The everyday life of the client can be immensely influential in helping or hindering the kind of work which a client needs to do in therapy. And it is everyday life which lasts when therapy is over.

PSYCHOSYNTHESIS

We mentioned that one of the techniques used both in Gestalt work and in primal integration is fantasy. For example, in much of the dream work, the therapist asks the other person to relate a dream in the first person, present tense. Say the person says that she is at the top of a chute, and finds a piece of cardboard to slide down on; the therapist might ask the person to play the role of the piece of cardboard – a piece of fantasy where the person is given an opportunity to find out about some (perhaps rejected) part of her own personality.

Now it is possible to take fantasy much further than this. John Stevens (1971) has a whole book which shows how fantasy can be used in Gestalt work. This is exceptional, however, and most Gestalt work only uses fantasy incidentally. There is another discipline, however, which centres itself much more on fantasy, and that is psychosynthesis.

Roberto Assagioli (1975) was an Italian doctor, and one of the first to introduce psychoanalysis into Italy. Around 1910 he began to put forward his own version, somewhat closer to Jung than to Freud, emphasizing that dynamic psychology should not only be concerned with depth (the unconscious) but also with height (the superconscious). And he found that fantasy was very useful in making concrete the difference between therapeutic interventions which went downwards into unconscious material (caves and forests), and those which went upwards into superconscious material (mountain tops and chapels). And instead of waiting for fantasy images to arise spontaneously, one could set up guided fantasies to explore these regions in a systematic way. Assagioli's 'egg diagram' helps to make this clearer (Figure 1).

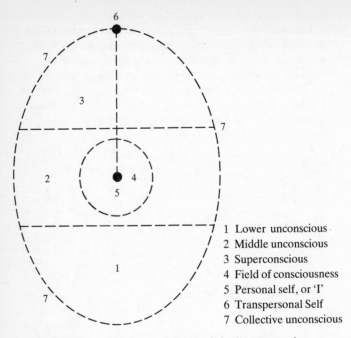

1 Lower unconscious
2 Middle unconscious
3 Superconscious
4 Field of consciousness
5 Personal self, or 'I'
6 Transpersonal Self
7 Collective unconscious

Figure 1 The Assagioli egg diagram of the human psyche

Using this diagram, and taking it quite literally that one is starting from the central point, it is easy to construct fantasies which will explore various parts of one's world. Desoille has constructed several, and Leuner (1984) has added some more (incidentally, many of Leuner's papers were first published in English in Moreno's journal – another instance of where Moreno has helped to pioneer so many of these humanistic methods), which include:

THE MEADOW Each person's meadow is different – some are green and natural, some are formal gardens, some are even like deserts. Some are actual places, some are imaginary. But often they have something to do with memories with emotional loading from preconscious areas – the middle field of the diagram.

THE MOUNTAIN This is a climb, and usually has to do with the aspirations of the climber. Sometimes there is a dragon or other opponent near the summit. Kornadt, quoted in Singer (1974), did a research study which found that assessment of striving in such fantasies was associated with achievement motivation and aspiration level.

THE DARK FOREST Here the person is told to go downwards into a deep valley, at the bottom of which there is a dark forest, and to describe what happens when he looks into the forest. The therapist may make helpful suggestions if the scene gets too frightening.

By the use of these and other techniques, the person is encouraged to explore and own the whole of the area open to her. Contacting the transpersonal self is one of the final stages of this process.

One of the characteristic methods used in psychosynthesis is the use of a fantasy which leads to the discovery of one or more sub-selves or sub-personalities. It is often found that strange habits or quirks, sometimes quite destructive, make a lot of sense if seen as a kind of sub-system which 'takes over' at certain times and dominates the whole self. And quite often it makes sense to give this sub-system a name, and to concretize it by seeing it in fantasy as a real person, with an appearance and a history of her own. James Vargiu (1974) has written a whole workbook about this, where he says that the way to deal with these sub-personalities is in five phases: recognition, acceptance, co-ordination, integration and synthesis.

I have myself done some research on this, and it does seem as though the idea of sub-personalities makes a lot of sense. There seem to be six main sources of sub-personalities which cannot be reduced to one another:

a THE COLLECTIVE UNCONSCIOUS – if Jung (1971) is right, this is where the archetypes come from, and the Shadow certainly seems to come out in this type of exercise. *Anima* figures are also quite common.

b THE CULTURAL UNCONSCIOUS – this is the internal representation of the external structures of society. In our case, we live in a patriarchal society, and one of the sub-personalities often encountered is the Patripsych (Southgate & Randall 1978):

By this we mean all the attitudes, ideas and feelings, usually compulsive and unconscious, that develop in relation to authority and control . . . In general, men tend to internalise mastery and control. In general, women tend to internalise self-effacement and morbid dependency.

This is similar to what Steiner et al. (1975) have called the Pig Parent – an internalised form of cultural oppression. It also seems close to what Doris Lessing (1970) calls the 'self-hater'.

c THE PERSONAL UNCONSCIOUS – the super-egos and ids and complexes and internal objects and ego states and top dogs and underdogs described by Freud, Jung, Guntrip, Berne, Perls and others.

d CONFLICTS OR PROBLEMS – sometimes the two or more sides of an internal conflict or problem situation may become vivid enough to seem to require an identity each, as is often found in psychodrama or Gestalt therapy, as well as of course in psychosynthesis itself.

e ROLES – the way we appear to one group may be quite different to the way we appear in another, and each role may bring out a different sub-personality. This may also apply to social frames, as described in Goffman (1974).

f FANTASY IMAGES – we may identify with a hero or heroine, or with an admired group, and take on some of their characteristics; perhaps sometimes two or more heroes or heroines may merge. And these fantasy figures may come from the past or imagined future, as well as from the present.

The view of psychosynthesis on this is that the sub-personalities must become aware of one another before any integration can take place, so a phase of co-ordination is necessary where this happens. During this phase, there are inner changes within the sub-personalities – they cease to be so dominant and exclusive, and start to take the others into account. The 'bad' ones are seen to have much positive energy, and the 'weak' ones are seen to be much stronger than they think. And these changes and discoveries make it easier for them to work together. Some more material on sub-personalities may be found in Chapter 13.

At a certain stage, the Transpersonal Self tends to be discovered, and this makes the final synthesis a great deal easier. There are various symbols for the Transpersonal Self – often associated with some kind of experience of ecstasy or insight. Back to *satori* again!

As a method of therapy, psychosynthesis has much in common with Gestalt therapy, though Perls and Assagioli were very different types of people, and some of the theoretical pronouncements sound very different. Some of the similarities are spelt out by Singer (1974).

PSYCHODRAMA

Also mentioned by Singer is psychodrama, which was developed by Moreno (1964, 1966, 1969). He studied psychiatry at the University of Vienna at the same time Sigmund Freud was there. In the early 1920s he built a Theatre of Spontaneity in Vienna, and worked on group therapy. He invented psychodrama, and called it the theatre of truth. He was interested in politics, and created the *Living Newspaper* – a theatre group which portrayed current events in satirical terms. In 1925 he came to the United States. In the years between 1920 and 1940 Moreno invented almost all the techniques which are used today in encounter groups and in Gestalt therapy. He believed in play, laughter, spontaneity and action, and laid a great deal of stress on non-verbal communication.

Moreno was a big, outgoing, red-headed man, with a charismatic personality and an oversized ego. Everything about him was larger than life size. He found it impossible to cooperate with anyone else, and got very upset when people took his ideas without acknowledgement. One of his friends, in a drunken moment, is reported to have said – 'You and Freud are both full of shit: with him it's constipation; with you it's diarrhoea.' And this does express something quite pertinent about the difference between his approach and Freud's.

In psychodrama you take a life situation which is loaded with feeling for you – a row with the boss, being ill-treated as a child, a parting from a spouse, anything at all – and act it out, using people from the group as characters in your play. The group leader is called a director, and facilitates the action by suggesting ways of making it more direct and more intense. The director will usually set up the scene in a concrete way – 'so the door is over here, the window is here, and there is a table . . . ' – to make the scene as evocative as possible.

After the scene has been going for a while the director may suggest role reversal; that is, the person who has initiated the piece of work (the protagonist) changes places with the person who was being talked to. This is sometimes quite revelatory in itself.

Something else that may happen is that a member of the group may feel that the protagonist is not saying what she really means. The group member may then go up behind the protagonist and talk on her behalf. The protagonist, if agreeing, repeats it; or has the option of saying – 'No, that's not right.'

There are over 200 different techniques which may be used in psychodrama, and it is difficult to invent a new technique which Moreno did not think of first. Moreno's 'multiple double' technique, for example, where different inner parts of the person all interact with one another, is a direct precursor of Gestalt cushion work on the one hand, and work with sub-personalities on the other.

The aim of the whole thing is spontaneity and creativity. And humanistic psychology has been in the forefront of attempts to consider creativity as a normal attribute of ordinary people. As far back as Schachtel, the great German psychologist who was a precursor of humanistic psychology, it seemed important to point out how everyone had access to creativity, if only they would allow themselves to know it and to do it.

Important blocks to creativity are fear of failure, reluctance to play, over-certainty, frustration avoidance, excessive need for balance, sensory dullness, impoverished fantasy and emotional lives, reluctance to exert influence and so on. If we can outwit these blocks – and Liam Hudson among others showed how this could be done – we can release the creativity which was there all the time. All of these things seem to emerge spontaneously in a good psychodrama group, and this is perhaps why psychodrama is so relevant to creativity.

Moreno's method (as also that of Carl Rogers) is to go indirectly by affecting the innermost self of the person, as contrasted with the approach of people like Koberg & Bagnall, who go more directly by directing the person into profitable patterns of external behaviour. Stein (1974) has a good discussion of all this.

My own belief is that there are several different things all going under the name of creativity, and that much of the disagreement in this field stems from this fact.

First of all there is the kind of creativity which comes from the child self, and which is all about letting go of the adult constraints, and allowing ourselves to be truly playful. This is a delightful form of creativity, free from inhibitions about what is known to be possible.

Second, there is magical creativity, based on the needs of a particular group, and using the rituals peculiar to that group. This kind of creativity hits the nerve of the group in some way, and can produce the craze or fashion that sweeps the group for a time.

Third, there is role-playing creativity, which is like a commodity served up for the benefit of some paymaster. This is where problem-solving types of creativity are most popular. It can result in a sort of technology of creativity.

Fourth, there is autonomous creativity, which springs from the individual's own personal awareness. This can sometimes be rebellious, but it is essentially independent. The person can respond with fresh, brand-new responses to events, and can also create events.

Fifth, there is surrendered creativity, which comes from a source outside the self. We speak here of inspiration or of being a channel. The person tunes in, rather than acting directly. There is an emphasis on the problem being worthy of being solved.

Sixth, though I am not quite sure about this, there may

be another form of creativity, such that we actually become creativity itself. At this stage we may not be interested in solving problems, because we can't see any problems.

If this schema could be accepted, it might save quite a number of arguments and disagreements. Moreno's main interest was in autonomous creativity, and I think it is this that he most often refers to.

The people who have been through such a process, just because they are now more creative and more sure of who they are, are in a better position to decide whether what they now want in social and political terms is conflict or cooperation. It is not a question of having a preconceived commitment to conflict or social harmony; it is a question of getting to a place where we have a real choice. It is not a question of deciding to be in opposition before we start, but of finding out what we really want, and in the process finding out what opposition there is to that both inside and outside ourselves. It is only thus that our spontaneous choices can be genuinely based on reality. Moreno continually talked of the importance of spontaneity as the key to mental health and full human functioning.

In a psychodrama group, the individual piece of work carries on until some resolution, often of a cathartic kind, is carried out. Then the other participants are asked about their reactions to what has been happening: often someone whose feelings have been stirred up will then do her own piece of work. A feeling builds up between the participants which Moreno called 'tele' – a bond of mutual sympathy and understanding. A psychodrama group is a very warm place to be.

Psychodrama has been used a great deal in a large number of settings, such as schools, mental hospitals, prisons, management training courses and so forth, and is suitable for everything from deep therapy to a game-playing exercise, depending on the needs of the people involved. For example, someone contemplating changing jobs may be asked to speak to her future self, the person who has been in each of the possible jobs for two years.

Traditionally, psychodrama lays a great deal of stress on the 'warm-up' – that is, the process which gets the group started and moving (Blatner 1973). Moreno himself seems to have needed a period with the group in which to get himself 'psyched-up' to run the group. In reality, there seems to be no more need to do warming-up, any more than with any of the other types of group considered in this book.

Recently psychoanalysis has been getting interested in psychodrama, as Powell (1986) has shown, particularly in France and Argentina.

It seems that the potential of psychodrama is much greater than has yet been achieved. The research studies, few as they are, are very encouraging, and one would like to see a much more ambitious application of some of the deeper techniques. The book by Greenberg (1974) shows some of the many things which can be done, and there is a good recent summary in the Badaines chapter in Rowan & Dryden (1987).

One problem with psychodrama is that in the hands of people like Blatner, it does tend to get over-elaborate – there are so many prescriptions about what kind of rooms to have, and the furniture, and trained auxiliaries, and so on. But I have seen very good work carried out without any of that complication, and really much prefer that.

Work has been going on in this area with video recordings. Obviously it is very revealing to see oneself on video, and one can even do things like talk directly to one's own video image, and play back the results afterwards, for some real self-revelation.

This and other questions are well discussed in the special issue of *Self & Society* (e.g. Karp 1980) which covers many aspects of the matter.

NON-HUMANISTIC THERAPY

I want to say something about forms of therapy which are non-humanistic, in the sense of not measuring up to the kind of outlook we have been in contact with so far. Some of these are obvious, and hardly need pointing out – drug treatment, electric shock treatment, psychoanalysis, behaviour therapy, behaviour modification – but there is one approach which is genuinely confusing, because it sounds so nice. This is groupwork, or group therapy, as described by Tom Douglas (1983), an unfortunately popular writer. In this approach everyone sits round on chairs.

Now one of the things which has been established (Paul Goodman (1962) has in fact an excellent essay on it) is that furniture can have profound effects on human interaction. The way that the furniture is arranged in a room can say – 'Keep away from me', or 'Welcome', it can say 'We are equals', or 'You are inferior', it can say 'Pretend you are a brain on a beanstalk', or 'You are here as a whole person'. Now a circle of chairs carries a profound message. It says three main things – firstly that everyone is on the same level, secondly that only intellectual interaction is permitted, and thirdly that one mustn't move from one's position. Feelings may be all right so long as they are individual and private feelings, but statements made to another person are expected to be on a head level.

So in a 'therapy group' which is arranged in this way (as in the films *Family Life*, or *One Flew Over the Cuckoo's Nest*, for example), two main lies are being told, before the group ever starts. One is that the therapist is on the same level as anyone else, and the other is that the body is not important. The first of these lies is not so bad, as long as the therapist is not taken in by it, because it helps to reduce the 'transference' element (mistaking the therapist for Mummy or Daddy) to a minimum; but the second is disastrous, because it can prevent any real therapy taking place. People who work in this way are denying themselves the dynamic therapy which is available, and which has been detailed in this and the previous two chapters. We do know how to deal with stuck feelings; we do know how to use the body and its energy; we do know how to cut through the phoney self-dramatizations; we do know how to do therapy without getting caught in the trap of 'helping'. And it is not OK to ignore all this.

It is sad to have to say this, because the people I have met who are involved in this kind of approach seem very nice people, and idealistic with it. They are often laying themselves on the line in a very real and honest way. But if I were involved in one of those groups I would want to get the full benefit from whatever skills were available to get me into a better space, and go through whatever was necessary to get there in the least time possible.

SELF-HELP AND THE SYSTEM

There is one danger with humanistic psychotherapy, and that is that it becomes absorbed into the medical system and treated as some kind of auxiliary medical aid. As we have noted already, it is not a medical matter. But there is a temptation, because mental hospitals are run by the National Health Service, to try to get legitimation through those channels. There is a double-bind operating here – if you want to be given working and research facilities, a career structure and all the other normal things, you must do it through medical channels; but if you get it through medical channels, you will be put into the wrong box, have to work under medical supervision, have all your work misunderstood, have to fight to keep your identity, and maybe have your work twisted out of recognition.

But the whole problem of accreditation has been much improved in recent years through the formation of the AHPP (Association of Humanistic Psychology Practitioners). No longer is it true that someone who wants to practise an unorthodox speciality must get a qualification in something quite different, to give her the right to do what she wanted to do in the first place. Through the AHPP, accreditation can be given to someone who has had a very unorthodox background, so long as that person can demonstrate that she has the requisite training and experience to do what she does, and that she is having supervision and continuing to work on herself. She must also be willing to sign a statement on ethics and good practice which means that she can be held to account in case of any breaches of the guidelines. Some further details are given in Chapter 12.

There are now more courses and more books (for example the excellent Brammer & Shostrom (1982) which is very nearly complete) in the kinds of therapy we have been describing, and the position is more encouraging than it was ten years ago. Qualifications can now be taken directly. See again Chapter 12.

One way of avoiding the whole question of accreditation is to encourage the setting up of self-help centres, where people can practise co-counselling and group therapy of various kinds on each other. There seem to be fewer of these about than there were, which seems a pity. For some other people, Women's Liberation Groups are an answer. These groups do not exist in many areas, however, and it is quite a task to get one started. Also these groups tend to do very well at first, and then get stuck, partly for lack of the techniques and methods which could take them further. But the excellent book by Ernst & Goodison (1981) shows just exactly how a self-help group can use all the methods outlined in the present volume with great advantage, and now that this book is available, self-help methods are much more possible. It really makes a good companion volume to this present one.

Another approach to self-help is the technique of *Focusing*, as outlined by Gendlin (1981) in his book of that name. This is a method by which the person, either in company with another person or persons, or on her own, gets in touch with her own felt experience in a therapeutic way. This is not only very good in itself, but it also enables the person who has done it to work much more effectively in any of the other forms of personal growth, counselling or psychotherapy.

CHAPTER SEVEN

———————— ❦ ————————

EDUCATION

HUMANISTIC EDUCATION takes the principles we have been meeting all the way through, and applies them fully in the educational field. This means moving away from the superior/inferior relationship between pupil and teacher, and towards a process in which everyone is learning something. There is a basic trust in the student, as someone who has curiosity about the world, a desire to relate successfully to others, a set of values which are partly fixed and partly changing, a whole lot of feelings which sometimes help and sometimes get in the way, and a real physical body – someone who is a real person with a history, and a number of projects, and who is here now.

ROGERS

Carl Rogers (1969) has said a lot about education, and has been responsible for starting a number of research projects, to find out what works and what does not. His own position is that he finds teaching of little value, and prefers to adopt the role of a facilitator of learning. And it then turns out that the three most important things for a facilitator to do, if she is really going to permit learning to take place, are the same three as are needed for a person-centred counsellor or a person-centred encounter group leader. Back to genuineness, non-possessive warmth and empathy!

And it turns out that these things work. Rogers replied to an attack on his methods by two establishment psychologists

(Brown & Tedeschi 1972) by quoting research which they had apparently overlooked. In these studies these three qualities of the teacher had actually been measured in the classroom, and the comparative levels of different teachers established (Rogers 1972):

> It has been shown that they are significantly and positively related to a greater gain in reading achievement in third graders (Aspy 1965). They are positively related to grade point average (Pierce 1966); to cognitive growth (Aspy 1969; Aspy & Hadlock 1967); they are related to a diffusion of liking and trust in the classroom which in turn is related to better utilization of abilities by the student and greater confidence in himself (Schmuck 1966).

In other words, if the teacher adopts the person-centred approach, she finds that not only does the class atmosphere improve and become warmer and more nourishing, but also the children actually do better in terms of marks. The National Center for Humanizing Education mounted a very impressive research study (Aspy 1972) which found that 'Students learn more and behave better when they receive high levels of understanding, caring and genuineness, than when given low levels of them.' Two decades of this sort of research was summarized in a book (Aspy & Roebuck 1977) whose title speaks volumes.

Since then, a great deal of further research work has been done, much of which has been summarized in Rogers (1983). Not only have the findings been supported in different sub-cultures in the USA, where the work was first done, but also in Germany, which is of course a very different culture. It is of course a common form of resistance to any behavioural-science findings to say 'It wouldn't work here', and nine times out of ten this turns out to be false. This mass of solid research work must make us pause and consider the details of this approach to education.

When one walks into such a classroom, it looks different and it sounds different from a conventional one. Children are working in small groups rather than sitting in lines, and there is a lively hum or buzz which is unlike either the silence of a 'good' class (in custodial terms) or the rowdyness of a 'bad' class. And the basic health of the situation shows itself when the children are outside the classroom, as David Sturgess (1972) has noticed.

In Rogers's (1983) book, he gives the space of four chapters to eight people who have tried out his approach, and from these one can see the kind of problems which arise when one makes the attempt. One of the teachers was working with twelve-year-olds, one with sixteen-year-olds, one with a range of fourteen- to seventeen-year-olds, four with undergraduates and one with teachers. One of the nice things about humanistic teachers is that they are open to talk about their personal experiences, without a lot of cover-up and defence. What happens when you let children set their own goals, and work on them in their own way? What happens when you allow children to make their own contract as to what they will do today? Barbara Shiel (in Rogers 1983) says:

> I must exercise great control when I see a child doing nothing (productive) for most of a day; providing the opportunity to develop self-discipline is an even greater trial at times. I've come to realise that one must be secure in his own self-concept to undertake such a programme. In order to relinquish the accepted role of the teacher in a teacher-directed programme, one must understand and accept oneself first.

Just like the encounter leader or the counsellor, the person-centred teacher must be prepared to work on herself – develop her own self-understanding, deal with her own internal 'shoulds'. But if she does this, the whole job can change. As Barbara Shiel says again:

> I have been constantly challenged, 'but how did you teach the facts and new concepts?' The individuals inquiring apparently assume that unless the teacher is dictating, directing or explaining, there can be no learning. My answer is that I did not *teach*; the children taught themselves or each other.

And the children did teach themselves; the actual results

from the class were impressive. Yet they were not exceptional children: there were 36 children in the class, with an IQ range of 82 to 135 – many of them labelled as socially maladjusted, underachievers or emotionally disturbed. There were discipline problems, lack of interest and difficulties with parents.

And it does not appear that Shiel was a charismatic, amazing personality, who would be a success no matter what she did. She comes across as a person who was interested in what she was doing, and was determined to try something properly, and adapt it intelligently – most teachers have all the qualities necessary to do this. One does not have to be a saint, but one does have to be prepared to look at oneself, and drop some of one's own defences against one's own experience.

A special issue of *Self & Society* came out (vol.12, no.4 Jul/Aug 1984) about self-directed learning, and this gave a good deal of information on how it actually works out in practice in Britain.

Rogers's views and methods are very important, and have been very influential in humanistic education, but as we have seen, his approach is not the only one.

CONFLUENT EDUCATION

One of the other main streams is called confluent education – the flowing together of intellect, emotions and the body into a single educational experience. The first book in this area was the one by Brown (1971), based on work done under the impetus of a Ford Foundation grant. Here, as in the other areas we have looked at in this book, the way in which people have moved away from Rogers has been in the direction of more intervention. The teacher has a bigger role to play, and also is more conscious of bodily movements and interactions than is Rogers. This is obviously very easy to achieve in a drama class – the body is involved already, and there is little resistance to getting the whole thing moving, either on the part of the students or of the teacher. In an English class, it may be possible to work quite naturally in that direction – after all, drama and English are quite close. But how about science? William Romey (1972) has written a very interesting book about how he, as a science teacher, went over to humanistic education. One of the key discoveries he made was that he was playing a really nasty game with his students; he was asking them questions to which there was only one answer. The result of playing this game was that he was seeing his students in terms of who answers right and who answers wrong, who answers quickly and who answers slowly, who is actively engaged and who is withdrawn and evasive, who disturbs others and prevents them from answering correctly.

Categories soon emerge from this process – 'bright' and 'dull', 'helpful' and 'disruptive', 'earnest', and 'lazy'. The 'bright' are those who like playing the game and have a talent for it; the 'dull' are those who, for one reason or another, are turned off the game of question-and-answer, and have decided it is not for them. The 'helpful' are those who may or may not be much good at the game, but want to be cooperative – they admire or love the teacher, and want to help her. The 'disruptive' are those who actively reject the situation and the game being played. The 'earnest' are those who are not very good at the game, but try extra hard to make up for their difficulties. And the 'lazy' are those who can play the game but often feel insufficiently involved to do so.

All these categories arise from the system of social relations which are set up the moment the teacher stands up in front of a class and begins to play the game. And Romey decided that these were not very constructive roles for students to play – they narrowed and oppressed the students, whichever way they went in an individual case. And so he made a resolution, which sounds weird but exciting to anyone who went through the orthodox system: 'I will never again ask a learner a question to which I already know the answer, unless he has asked me to play an inquiry game with him.' My experience of science teaching was not like this, and it is quite a shock for someone like me to conceive of a science teacher taking up this way of working.

The very useful book by Elizabeth Hunter (1972)

mentions the rule of two-thirds: that in the average classroom someone is talking two-thirds of the time; two-thirds of that time the teacher is doing the talking; and two-thirds of the average teacher's talk is lecture, direction-giving and criticism. In many classrooms, as the NCHE project discovered (Rogers 1983), it is 80 per cent teacher talk. All the research ever done, however, says that more productive learning takes place if pupils talk more; if teachers' talk is accepting and encouraging; and if teachers ask questions that go beyond recall and retrieval. So maybe Romey is not so weird after all.

But he goes further again. Hunter says that there are five kinds of questions that teachers ask in the classroom: recall; comprehension; invention; evaluation; and routine management. Romey says he is trying to give up all of these:

> Most of my teaching up until a couple of years ago consisted of trying to think up better, more stimulating questions to ask people. But I don't want learners to be confined by my questions any more. I want to learn what their questions and concerns are. We must trust each other not to pry with questions but to be ready to receive each other's offerings. It's hard for me to do, but it feels very good when people start to talk to me at a deeper level than ever before.

If the teacher can allow herself to be a whole person in the classroom, the children are more likely to allow themselves to be whole people too. Of course we really are whole people – our bodies, feelings, minds and souls are all there present in the classroom – we just need to give up pretending that we are not.

But of course there is something scary about it. Suddenly to think of oneself as an embodied self in a room with other embodied selves, all trying to make sense of a situation in which no one has a complete picture of what is going on – that sounds difficult and dangerous; much more difficult and dangerous than taking up well-formed roles, which is tidy even if no real learning takes place. It is just a question of what our priorities are. For the humanistic teacher, the priority is reality – just dealing with what is really here now, instead of what is supposed to be here now.

In terms of the Maslow levels which we have now looked at, most schools and colleges stop people developing beyond the fourth level – the level of getting esteem from others. This is because of the great emphasis on roles. In a hierarchical organization there is an extreme emphasis on role separation; sometimes, indeed, people are called by the name of the role instead of by their own name, to show that the organization needs that particular role, but does not need that particular person. Now there is a certain deep opposition between playing a role and being oneself. We have been seeing all the way through this book that the aim of humanistic psychology is to explore all the ways in which human beings can be more themselves – more authentic and less phony, more in charge of their own lives and less at the mercy of pressures from outside and from inside. Dorothy Emmet (1966) paraphrases Sartre when she says:

> To accept a role is to evade the responsibility of seeing that one is free not so to act, and of freely deciding what one wants to be. It is to evade freedom by sheltering behind one's social function.

And this Sartre calls bad faith, or self-deception. Certainly it seems to be true that, for the self-actualizing person, a role can only be something false. It is a game to be played, and one has given up playing games. The whole aim of the kinds of growth, counselling and therapy work which we have been considering here is to enable people to give up playing games. This is quite explicit in the title of Eric Berne's most famous book (1964), and in the encounter literature we find titles like *The Game of No Game* (Thomas 1970). Or one can continue to play games, but this time one does not need to play games, one can just go into them and out of them consciously, like a game of chess or a game of tennis. This is the approach of Romey. The game here is quite explicit and not mystified into a hidden norm.

Again, in Brown's (1971) book he gives two chapters over to two teachers who have actually tried these methods, and

111

they speak of their difficulties and struggles in doing justice to what they believe in.

Later Brown (1975) edited a volume of chapters by various people involved in the confluent education project, which gives far more of the feel of the day-to-day struggle. There are lots of good examples here of exactly how teachers actually cope with teaching in the new way.

One of the best books on confluent education is the one by Castillo (1978), which contains 211 exercises which have been used in the classroom, some of them general and some of them specific to language, science, reading or mathematics. There is a brief but very useful annotated bibliography on humanistic education.

EXPERIENTIAL LEARNING

We come on here to the whole question of experiential learning, which is close to the heart of the humanistic approach. Most humanistic educators do a lot of work in the experiential mode, rather than in the didactic mode. There was a special issue of *Self & Society* devoted to this subject (vol.10, no.4 Jul/Aug 1982), which gives a good deal of information as to what it is and how it works.

One of the best books in this area is by Terry Borton (1970), which not only gives an honest story of what he did himself, but also links up this whole approach to cognitive psychology. From this he derives a basic message that education is about the 'What', the 'So What', and the 'Now What':

> If, for example, a student is overly suspicious, then he must first discover What he is doing, perhaps by becoming immersed in a role-playing exercise so that he can see the pattern of his behaviour emerge there. He will then need to begin asking, 'So What?' What difference does his behaviour make? What meaning does it have for him, and what are its consequences? Finally he will need to ask, 'Now What?' Now that he sees that he is suspicious, what does he want to do? How can his new understanding

be translated into new patterns of behaviour? Does he want to experiment with a new attitude, assess its consequences, and reapply what he has learned?

Borton goes through example after example, showing how this simple structure can be applied to specific situations. He makes one important addition to the model: a curriculum based on it, he says, works best if the 'So What' part is carried out in two complementary ways:

> The first is the *analytic* mode with which most of us are familiar – hard-driving, pointed, sharp, logical, tough and rigorous. But it is difficult for people to change if they are put under much pressure, so we also employ a *contemplative* mode, a more relaxed approach which avoids picking at one's self and allows alternatives to suggest themselves through free association and metaphor.

This is the whole thing about the humanistic approach to education – it puts things together, rather than leaving things out. It also implies much more collaboration in the classroom. Johnson & Johnson (1975) speak of cooperative learning: in this approach children are encouraged to develop skills in collaborative relationships while working on academic learning tasks and other activities. Such collaborative skills include communicating in group settings, individual and group goal-setting and problem-solving skills, etc.

One thing which comes out very easily in this approach is that the personal experience of the student really matters. Somebody once said that there were four R's in even the most basic education, and that the fourth R was Respect. The experiential approach makes it easy to respect the student, because the teacher/facilitator really has to listen to the experience which comes out of the exercise, game, simulation or whatever if any real benefit is going to be obtained from it. In this way we come close to the idea of enhancing the self-concept in the classroom (Canfield & Wells 1976) – a revolutionary idea for those of us who had their self-concept severely damaged in their own classrooms.

Some of the people working in transpersonal psychology

have made important contributions to experiential education, particularly in books such as Hendricks & Wills (1975), Hendricks & Fadiman (1976) and Hendricks & Roberts (1977). The Religious Experience Research Project at Nottingham University has done a good deal of work in this area.

Another important contribution to the field of experiential education came from Sidney Simon and his co-workers, which is called 'values clarification'. Again this is not a sort of philosophical blue-sky approach, but a question of practical strategies for teachers and students.

What it says (Simon et al. 1972) is that valuing is a seven-stage process based on prizing, choosing and acting. It goes like this

1 Prizing and cherishing

2 Publicly affirming, when appropriate

3 Choosing from alternatives

4 Choosing after consideration of consequences

5 Choosing freely

6 Acting

7 Acting with a pattern, consistency and repetition

In the teaching based on this approach, the children are encouraged to follow this schema when talking about controversial subjects. And this results in far more self-respect among the students, because they now know why they think what they think, and can justify what they think in terms which will be convincing to others. Self-respect is also built up because the approach involves taking responsibility for what one thinks and does.

The authors emphasize that all school subjects on the curriculum can be treated in this way. We not only teach about rich and poor countries in geography, we ask the children what they feel and what they think about some countries being rich and others poor. The emphasis on action always makes it clear than any academic discussion of issues has practical consequences. Kirschenbaum (1977) has taken this further and shown that the general approach is applicable to organizations other than schools, too.

THE SCHOOL OR COLLEGE

So far, we have been seeing just what humanistic education is, but at the level of the individual classroom. What happens when we look at the educational institution as a whole? We find in most cases a hostile environment. There are very few places devoted to education, in this country or anywhere else, where the entire staff are committed to humanistic education.

And so one is faced with a number of difficult choices. Does one act as a teacher in an isolated way, doing what one can where one can? Or does one try to join up with other teachers who want to work in the same way, running all the risks of a subversive group? Or does one try to get the head of the organization turned on in some way? And what about the parents? And what about the students themselves? Bill Bridges (1973) says:

> Of course, I can bring them together on a purely interpersonal level (except for the 'I Ching' girl who doesn't relate well and the black nationalist who thinks that self-exploration is white, middle-class bullshit). And I can give them some growth-oriented experiences that fill up the class periods. But I can't really give them what they need, because the institution insists that we convert needs into three-unit, semester-long classes that don't conflict with one another. Until we can restructure institutions to become educational resource places, we will mistakenly, but understandably, be trying to do the impossible – make each individual classroom what the institution ought to be.

One can only do so much on an individual classroom level. It is well worth doing, but it is not enough.

Carl Rogers has insisted that this wider context is always important. In his own work, he has been driven more and more to consider the school system and the whole administrative set-up. And his latest view is now that the right place to start is at the top of the hierarchy, with an intensive group meeting (basic encounter group) with members of the administration – whoever actually makes the decisions which affect the whole school or group of schools. This would last for about a week, and be residential.

> Drawing on past experience, I think of administrators who have worked together for twenty years, and discover that they have never known each other as persons; of negative feelings which 'loused up' planning and work for years, which can now safely be brought out into the open, understood and dissolved; of positive feelings which always seemed too risky to voice . . . the intense sense of community which develops, in place of the alienation each has felt; the willingness to risk new behaviours, new directions, new purposes; determinations to rebuild family relationships and organizational procedures. (Rogers 1969.)

After this stage had been completed and digested, the next step would be to hold similar intensive groups for teachers, again on a voluntary basis. The next step would be to run encounter groups for whole classes. At the same time, groups for parents should be organized, possibly just for a weekend.

However, Rogers (1983) makes it clear that the political climate can make it almost impossible to carry through and make permanent the gains which are made through such methods. This seems to be because the humanistic approach is much more radical than at first it seems; as this begins to come through, panic sets in amongst the more conservative elements in parents, teachers and administrators. Rogers deals in a sensitive way with some of the failures in the history of humanistic education, and much can be learned from these examples. One of the big differences between this book and the earlier edition is that we are more prepared now to admit that there are failures, and to assess in a much more rigorous way the advantages and disadvantages of the humanistic approach.

116

Other approaches used in Britain are outlined in the book edited by Gray (1985), which specifically concentrates on working at the level of the whole organization, and shows a variety of ways of doing this.

There is a sort of enthusiasm which comes from the humanistic approach which is quite electrifying for the person who gets it, but quite scary for others who only see the thing from the outside. This enthusiasm almost always results in some attempt at action.

Often the jolt which starts off such action is something very simple and seemingly minor, such as marking the work of students. This is something which goes against the grain for any humanistic teacher, but it is often seen as something inevitable. It is not inevitable. It is offensive. And Romey (1972) says this:

> There is an easy way out of the role of screening people. Individual teachers need only refuse to evaluate their students comparatively. To protest that 'we have to give grades because the school requires it' is another cop-out. If the system requires grades, we need only give all students As or let them grade themselves in order to subvert the system effectively. If groups of teachers – even small groups – band together in this effort, the system can be destroyed.

And if anyone says that it is employers who need to have some evidence of education, George Leonard (1968) has given us the answer to that one. As he points out very succinctly, the job dispensing agencies are not really interested in what the job seeker has learned in the school, but merely that, for whatever reason, she has survived it.

But it is difficult to band together as teachers. Alix Pirani (1975) gave at least some of the reasons why this is so in Britain, at least:

> There is little cohesion or coordination, in spite of the frequently expressed desire for contact between at least somewhat enlightened workers, many of whom feel that they are waging a lone battle against reactionary forces . . . Everybody ultimately seems to want to do his or her own thing, in isolation and defiance.

117

So why should we bother? Why is it important? One of the clearest statements of why it is important is provided by the work of Elizabeth Simpson (1971). The question she investigated was – what is the influence of the school on basic political attitudes?

THE WIDER SOCIETY

In Chapter 3 we talked of the psychosocial spiral of development, and said that social action could either have the effect of allowing or encouraging natural development up the spiral, or have the effect of driving people down the spiral. And we saw that any form of coercion tends to drive people down the spiral, as does any form of external evaluation. This links very naturally to the view of Maslow that there is a ladder of human needs, such that satisfaction of one need level enables movement upwards to the next (see Table 1 in Chapter 1).

What Simpson did was to develop a scale which could be given to children between fifteen and seventeen, to measure which of these needs were being satisfied, and to what degree. What Simpson took as her dependent variable was a set of five fundamental democratic values:

a Faith in human nature – the belief that human beings are basically good and trustworthy.

b Belief that people have some power over their own lives, rather than being controlled by the environment, or luck.

c Desire to think for oneself, rather than accepting the opinions of others as to what is right.

d Belief in the validity of the experiences and opinions of others – they have a right to be different. High tolerance and low dogmatism.

e Belief that the rights of other people are to be respected, just because they are human beings.

Simpson argues – convincingly to me – that these five attitudes are necessary and sufficient to define a democratic outlook. Anyone who held these five views would want a democratic system of organization wherever she operated; anyone who held the opposite set of views would prefer a strong leader to take all the decisions.

So how did the research come out? On her sample of 412 children from three different schools, Simpson found a highly significant positive relationship between need satisfaction and democratic values. In other words, the more psychologically deprived the children were, the less did they tend to hold a democratic attitude or outlook.

What this means in practical terms is that humanistic education, because it is continually trying to fulfil psychological needs in such a way as to bring children up the spiral in line with their own natural development processes, makes a genuinely democratic political system possible. This would be a system where people participated fully at each level in the state, and insisted on not being excluded from decisions which affected them.

Any form of education which adopted an authoritarian approach, laying great stress on hierarchy and formal roles, would actually make genuine political democracy in adult life either impossible or very difficult. So the educational system we adopt has enormous political implications, either way.

What seems to be happening too often these days is that teachers are giving up – or being forced willy-nilly to give up – the old authoritarian methods, structures and assumptions, but are not moving over into humanistic education either. Consequently they are simply trying to survive in a very uncomfortable situation where they feel out of control and subject to many anxieties. It may even be the case that many of them are going back to more authoritarian ways of working.

Humanistic education is uncomfortable too, but it is immensely hopeful, and that little spark can give comfort to a teacher in today's world. And it doesn't take much to start. The books already mentioned give some ideas for new ways of approaching the classroom and the curriculum.

119

Jeffrey Schrank (1972) gives 101 suggestions for things to actually do. They open up lines of communication, enable students and teachers to see each other as human beings, and demand that adults in schools stop teaching-to and start learning-with.

Real freedom involves the students' ability to choose the alternatives they want rather than accept the one they are driven to. That is the concept of freedom which should be the goal of educators, yet a teacher cannot *give* it to his students. They must win it for themselves. The best a teacher can do is to teach them the processes which will increase their ability to step aside from their own way of experiencing – to wonder at it, to question it, and to modify it.

Yes. And ultimately it is impossible to separate change in the schools from change in society. One of the lines from self to society runs through schools, colleges and other educational institutions where real learning does or does not take place. Real learning affects the way people act in their own lives. And it is always self-discovered, self-appropriated learning, learning which makes a difference to who I am. That's what education is all about.

CHAPTER EIGHT

―――――――

ORGANIZATIONAL

MOST OF what is valuable in management theory today comes from humanistic psychology. It is a field in which this school has been particularly active. In the comprehensive list of management development methods compiled by Huczynski (1983) over 40 per cent of them come out of humanistic psychology.

ORGANIZATION DEVELOPMENT

It started, as we saw in Chapter 1, with the work of Kurt Lewin. In the 1950s the group of people inspired by him at the National Training Laboratories moved over from calling their work 'training in democratic leadership' (partly, perhaps, because the word 'democracy' became a bit suspect during the McCarthy era) and began calling it 'the planning of change'. And instead of talking about 'trainers', they started talking about 'change agents'.

The early books were all about T-groups (Bradford, Gibb & Benne 1964, Golembiewski & Blumberg 1970), but during the 1960s they tended to be more about whole organizations (Bennis, Benne & Chin 1970). In the 1970s a further change took place – people talked about *Organization Development* (often shortened to OD) instead of planned change. And in the 1980s the more frequently used terms have been *human resources* and *normative systems*, as in Allen (1980).

The reasons for these changes in names and titles are important. The early practitioners became so impressed by the change that they saw in people who had been through T-groups – more open, more flexible, more creative, better at communication, altogether more nourishing – that they concentrated on doing that better and better. As we have seen, that led to the development of the encounter group. But what often happened was that the person went back to her organization and was quite unable to be what she now wanted to be, because of the restrictions placed on her by the nature of the organization itself. So either she conformed, which meant giving up everything she had learned; or she resisted, which meant a long and often painful struggle, sometimes won and sometimes lost; or she left.

So the view gradually took root that it was not enough to work at the level of the individual atom. One had to start at the top of the organization, and work on changing the whole culture of the hospital, or industrial company, or school, or whatever the organization happened to be. And in the 1960s a tremendous amount of work was done – the NTL produced an offshoot, the Institute for Applied Behavioural Science, which produced a new *Journal of Applied Behavioural Science*, in which started to appear a flood of research studies describing the new kind of work which was now being done in many different kinds of organizations.

At the beginning of this phase there was a great emphasis on the trained expert in applied behavioural science going into an organization and being able to see the problems very clearly, making a diagnosis, and then getting the management to make the necessary changes. And consequently there was a great deal of soul-searching about values. The consultant must have the highest possible ethical commitment, because she had all this power.

But as the 1960s went on, the emphasis changed more and more away from this view. Organization development (OD) came more and more into line with the other fields we have been looking at already. The consultant, instead of being seen as an expert to diagnose and prescribe, now becomes a facilitator, whose job is to encourage the organization to work through its conflicts, in the knowledge that all the answers are there already.

Now one of the things which humanistic psychology has understood very well is conflict. It has a particular view of conflict which is unlike most of the received wisdom on the subject. It sets a very high value on conflict, and regards the serious pursuit of conflict as an important road to wisdom. This is clearest in some of the industrial applications, where people like Beckhard (1969), Blake et al. (1970), and Lawrence & Lorsch (1969) have spelt out in some detail how they actually encourage conflict to be developed and fully expressed, between departments of the same firm, between management and trade unions, and between functional groups in the same organization. All these people take it for granted that groups have different and perhaps opposed interests, and are not all of one mind.

What do we do, then, faced with two parties who want apparently incompatible things? There are really only three possibilities:

> *Domination*: one side wins and the other loses. This often leads to the losing side trying to build up its forces so that it can win next time round. It perpetuates or even sets in motion a win-lose relationship of low synergy.
> *Compromise*: each side gives up a part of what it wants for the sake of peace. This is always unsatisfying to some degree, and each side may try to get its missing bit in some overt or covert way. This approach always tends to diminish integrity.
> *Integration*: both sides get what they really wanted. This may need quite a bit of work to see what it is that each side did really want. Another way of putting this is to say that we look for the needs behind the wants. This way, when it can be found, is the most satisfying.

The great pioneer in this area is Mary Parker Follett (a humanistic psychologist before humanistic psychology was ever named or noticed), who takes it for granted that the thing to aim at is the interweaving of differences, because that is what one actually has got to work with. Conflicts are then carefully brought out and worked with, rather than being overridden, smoothed over or ignored. And the outcome of this is that creative solutions may emerge, which

123

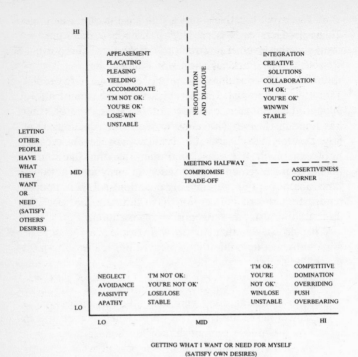

Figure 2 The Mary Parker Follett chart. After Jeffrey W. Eiseman
(1977). Added points from Berne and others

nobody had in mind at the beginning of the process. All
growth is a process of differentiation and integration, and
the differentiation is just as important as the integration.
The first rule for obtaining integration is to put your cards
on the table, face the real issue, uncover the conflict, bring
the whole thing out into the open (Metcalf & Urwick 1941).

If we do this, and attempt to bring out differences so that
they can be worked on, it is possible to meet other people
whom one knows to be opposed in interest and to confront
them as a whole person, unafraid and ready to use whatever
power one has. It is possible to be flexible and human and
at the same time to stand no shit. And it seems that this is
possible for groups as well as for individuals. It also seems

that if we want creative solutions, this is the only way to get them. (Rogers & Rybeck (1985) show how this approach works at the level of international diplomacy, another field in which Mary Parker Follett was interested.)

So the OD consultant becomes less like a doctor, and more like a therapist. Like the therapist, she cannot offer a blueprint of what the ultimate state of affairs will be. Like the therapist, what she aims at is the production of an organization which can be flexible, engage in creative problem-solving, be proactive rather than reactive and so on, at every level. This means moving away from a 'power over people' orientation towards a 'power with people' orientation (Fordyce & Weil 1971). And because the organization itself is moving in this direction, the problems about the expert having power over people seem to dissolve too. In other words, if at every level the person who knows what she is doing can feel confident enough to talk back to someone who tries to push her around or manipulate her, people will also be willing to talk back to the consultant, if she tries to push them around or manipulate them (Rowan 1976a).

HIERARCHY AND BUREAUCRACY

So much for a thumbnail sketch of the way things have moved over the past thirty years or so. But what has been said may be very confusing to anyone who actually works in an organization. 'Surely', such a person might say, 'all organizations are hierarchical, and depend for their very existence on some people giving orders, and others obeying them?' This is the voice of common sense.

But two things have happened over the years. One is that more and more research findings have piled up to show that hierarchy does harm to people, and the other is that various modifications of hierarchy have been tried, and found to work better, even in the strict terms of economic survival. This is not the place to deal with the whole tortuous business of the destructive nature of hierarchy – I have done that at length elsewhere (Rowan (1976)) – but here is a brief summary of the results.

Researchers such as Aiken & Hage, Grusky and also Lawrence & Lorsch (1969) have found these effects.

- Feelings of inadequacy.

- Inability to express oneself.

- Inability to influence anyone.

- Feelings of being shut out.

- Increase in cynicism.

- Increase in destructive feelings.

- Feeling that one has to dominate or be dominated.

- Feeling that to conform is the best thing.

- Feeling that intolerance is all right.

- Feeling that prejudice is all right.

- Feeling that new ideas must come from the top.

- Feeling that there is no way of communicating with those at the top.

These are general effects of hierarchical organization, but studies by Inkson, Porter & Lawler and others, also show that there is a big difference between the way the organization feels at the bottom and the way it feels at the top. Those at the top see their jobs as interesting, challenging, not too predictable, satisfying and engaging a lot of their personality and skills. Those at the bottom feel bored and fatalistic, hemmed in and frustrated, and that very little of them is involved in the work. A study by Kornhauser in the US car industry found that nine out of ten of the assembly line workers felt trapped in a job which they wanted to change but did not feel able to; and eight out of ten said they were boiling with frustration inside. It seems, then, that hierarchy diminishes people, makes them less than they usually are, and much less than they could be. In terms of the psychosocial spiral of development which we met in Chapter 3, hierarchical organization drives people down the spiral, rather than helping them up it.

In case anyone thinks that these findings are now out of date or reveal the prejudices of the early 1970s, the latest and much-acclaimed work of Kanter (1985) is saying the same thing, only with much greater sophistication and authority.

ALTERNATIVES

If for all these reasons we want to have an organization which does not have an oppressive hierarchy, and does not reduce people to roles, how do we actually go about it?

Again, as with the school example we saw earlier (for after all, a school is an organization too), we can either work from the top or from the bottom. Most of the literature deals with working from the top, but there is some of the other, too.

An OD consultant is often called in by a company or hospital or other organization when something is going wrong. And it is a rough rule of thumb to say that the more that is going wrong, the more ready will the organization be to make real changes that are more than superficial. If, however, there is too much going wrong, the resulting panic will make any real work on the part of the consultant almost impossible. (This is very similar to the individual case!)

The first thing an OD consultant will do is to listen, not only to the person who has called her in, but also to other people involved in the problem which appears to present itself. One never takes one person's version as the final truth of the matter. On the basis of this preliminary listening phase, the consultant will draw up a proposal as to what programme of stages seems to be necessary to tackle the problem, and what kind of costs will be involved. There may also be some discussion of the values which the consultant holds, so as to make sure that there is no misunderstanding about that.

The programme itself will very often start with a research phase. This is sometimes called a diagnostic phase, but this is not really accurate, because what is done with the data obtained (often unstructured interview plus questionnaires) is to feed it back to the people who have been questioned. This is often done at what Beckhard (1969) calls a confrontation and action planning meeting, where the consultant presents her results and they are discussed there and then, using whatever techniques may be useful to facilitate the constructive resolution of conflict.

Now I have shown elsewhere (Chapter 9 in Reason & Rowan 1981) that research itself is best seen as a cycle, and Allen (1980) shows that OD can be seen as a cycle. He has four phases of intervention within an organization, which correspond rather well with the six phases of research as I have outlined them.

Phase 1. Have you found out just what your problem really is and decided what you want to happen?

Phase 2. Have you helped others concerned with the problem understand the cultural impact of what is occurring and involved them in planning steps toward change?

Phase 3. Have you put the agreed-upon objectives into daily practice, keeping track of results as you go along and rewarding everyone for his or her progress?

Phase 4. Have you rechecked what you have done and kept your mind open to new factors that affect it?

So a whole programme may be involved here, of further meetings, further research, encounter groups, team building (Woodcock 1979), creativity training and so on, depending on what action seems to be high on the list of priorities. Specialist consultants may be called in to help reorganize accounting procedures, or shopfloor layout, lighting fixtures, etc., if these things seem appropriate to all those concerned.

The consultant in OD works like a therapist or facilitator, bringing out conflicts and helping to get them properly worked through and dealt with, at the pace which the organization finds possible. Allen (1980) makes the important point that the programme must be owned by the people affected by it; this ownership must be genuine, and it must be felt. Kanter (1985) makes the point that it is not enough for creativity to be imposed from above, as if it were this year's fashion – it has to emerge from genuine participation.

There is an important distinction in all this work between 'process' and 'task content': in any meeting some of what is going on is to do with the task which the group has on the open agenda; but some of what is going on has to do with the hidden agendas which people have brought with them into the room, and which they are also trying to work through at the same time (which may have to do with power struggles, or personal relationships, or old feuds, or private aims, etc.) – these things are collectively known as the group process. Now the consultant contributes very little at the level of the task content – she does not have the detailed knowledge necessary to make much of a contribution there – but concentrates most of her attention on to the group process. This is where her skills lie. She knows how to make what is hidden open, and what was implicit explicit; and she knows how to deal with the emotions which are revealed when this happens.

What we have here, then, is a process of *generation of valid and useful information*, which enables *free and informed choice* to be made, and leads to *internal commitment to a course of action*. Argyris (1970) has done more work in this field than possibly anyone else, and these are the three points which he emphasizes.

The humanistic point of view, then, is that choice and decision are most effective when taken closest to the event – that it is harmful to full functioning if decisions which could be taken at a lower level are taken instead at a higher level. Some of the implications of this are well drawn out in the series of books which came out of the Norwegian experience (Bolweg 1976).

But how does this affect management? Does it take away from them all their work, and leave them with nothing to do? Some people argue for precisely this, as Martin (1983) has urged quite eloquently, saying that self-managing work groups are all that is necessary. Herbst (1976) has described several ways in which hierarchies can be avoided, and Emery & Thorsrud (1976) have given many examples of how this has worked out in practice. Most people, however, feel that managers are still necessary, but have to change their function. The new concerns are with aims such as these:

1 To help set up an open, problem-solving climate throughout.

2 To make sure that knowledge and competence goes with the work.

3 To find ways of locating decision-making and problem-solving responsibilities as close to the information sources as possible.

4 To help build trust among persons and groups throughout.

5 To see that competition is made more relevant to work goals, and to increase co-operative efforts.

6 To get a reward system which recognizes both the achievement of the organization's goals and the development of people.

7 To increase the sense of ownership of organizational objectives throughout the organization.

8 To increase self-control and self-direction for people within the organization.

All these things are quite specific and possible, and each of them has methods suitable for it. But they will only be satisfying to a manager to the extent that she comes to appreciate those aspects of her work which have to do with the growth of people and her own capacity to facilitate the growth of people. And as Tichy (1977) has pointed out, this means great skill in coping with the political dynamics of organizational life.

LEADERSHIP

A great deal of research, going back to the 1940s, shows that there are two main dimensions which any leader has to consider. One of the main studies which showed this was the factor-analytic study of Halpin & Winer (1952). This was confirmed by the quite different work of Bales (1958), Blake & Mouton (1964), Fiedler (1967) and others. The two dimensions are *concern for people* and *concern for production*. The former is about social-emotional relations – paying attention to people as individuals with particular needs and feelings; a good social-emotional leader will make jokes to relieve tension, remember birthdays, show care about illness or other crises, be sociable and so on. The latter is about the task – getting the job done, being efficient, not making mistakes or wasting time – a good task leader will initiate, organize and direct in a firm and clear way, so that everyone knows what to do and when and how to do it. In the terms of Randall & Southgate (1980), who describe the healthy working cycle as Nurturing → Energizing → Relaxing, the social-emotional leader is good at the nurturing and relaxing stages of the cycle, while the task leader is good at the energizing stage.

Blake & Mouton had the idea of putting these two dimensions at right angles to each other to make a grid, and numbered each dimension from 1 (present in a low degree) to 9 (present in a high degree). They then devised tests for measuring where on each dimension a leader fell, so that each position could be described by two coordinates. They did this for managers in the first instance (Blake & Mouton 1978), and later for secretaries, salesmen (Blake & Mouton 1980), marriage partners and so on.

But Reddin (1977) suggested an interesting variation of this. He said that if we look at the four quadrants offered by this grid, and say that a leader can fall into any one of the four, we get four different kinds of leader, rather than just the two mentioned so far. In the top left-hand quadrant we get the leader who is high on concern for people and low on concern for task; this Reddin calls the RELATED leader, who is seen as supportive or permissive. So far, so good. But it is here that Reddin pulls his masterstroke: he says that the RELATED leader can either be effective or ineffective. So at each position we get two types, not one. At this position on the grid the RELATED leader can either be effective, in which case she is a *developer* who nurtures her followers at all levels and sets an example to them of how to treat people; or can be ineffective, in which case she becomes a mere *missionary* of the type who wants so much to be liked that she confuses smiling with real support, and talks about nurturing rather than being able to do it.

In the lower left-hand quadrant we get the SEPARATED leader, who is not concerned too much with either the people or the task, and who is seen as laissez-faire, leaving people to get on with their work. In the effective version, this becomes the *bureaucrat* who holds the ring and sets up conditions within which people can do what they need to do without coming up against the rules of the organization; in the ineffective version, the leader becomes a *deserter* who is simply not there, either physically or mentally.

In the lower right-hand quadrant we find the DEDI-CATED leader, the person who tells and sells, and is quite dominant in concentrating on the task in hand. In the effective version (*benevolent autocrat*), she becomes the kind of autocrat who inspires by her own dedication, and who energizes through a real knowledge of and feeling for the job. In the ineffective version (*autocrat*), this kind of leader can become narrowly and punishingly self-defensive, dogmatically dealing out blame with both hands.

And in the upper right-hand quadrant we get the INTEGRATED leader, the facilitating, encouraging type of leader who is interested both in the people and in the task. The effective type is the good *executive* – a good team worker, much concerned with motivation, adapting well to new situations; the ineffective type, on the other hand, is just a *compromiser*, unpredictable, indecisive and inconsistent.

The great advantage of putting things this way is that Reddin can now go to all the older theories of leader type and show that so often what happens is that the effective leader of one type (the type the author favours) is contrasted with the ineffective leader of another type (the type the author is against). This is what McGregor (1960) did – his Theory X and Theory Y contrasted the *autocrat* with the *executive*. This is what Lewin, Lippitt & White (1939) did – they contrasted the *deserter* and the *autocrat* with the *developer*. And this, he says, is what Blake & Mouton (1964) have done – they have contrasted the ineffective forms of all the other quadrants with the effective form of the INTEGRATED quadrant, and this is not fair.

Hersey & Blanchard (1977) also adopt the four quadrant version of the model. But they bring in another consideration – maturity. They say that maturity is the ability and willingness of individuals to take responsibility for directing their own behaviour in a particular area. And they say that Reddin's DEDICATED quadrant is the one for the least mature groups, which need strong leadership. Groups which are a little more mature need the kind of treatment given by the INTEGRATED leader. More mature again, and they come into the realm of the RELATED leader. And the most mature groups need the attention of a SEPARATED leader. Like Reddin, they also say that all these leaders can be more or less effective. Hersey et al. (1979) add a discussion of different kinds of power to this analysis, showing that the more direct and coercive kinds of power are appropriate to the most immature groups, and so on up the scale of maturity.

But Blake & Mouton have not taken all this lying down. As humanistic psychologists, they have come back very strongly to argue that this is all wrong. There is one best style of leadership – that which is high both on concern for people and on concern for the task in hand – and different kinds of situation or group do not need different styles or types of leaders. What Reddin and the others have done, they say, is to confuse *adding* concern for people to concern for the task with the *integration* of these two concerns. If you take separate statements of concern for people and concern for the task, and simply add them together, what you get is some form of paternalism. Paternalism is an issue

133

which is not dealt with either by Reddin or by Hersey & Blanchard – it is the view that the management, from a great height, will *look after* the people and get them to do the task, will *take care* of the people while the task is done. But what Blake & Mouton are interested in is genuine participation by all the people involved. This brings with it the kind of involvement which Allen (1980) and the others we have been looking at have all been talking about.

Blake & Mouton (1982) have pointed out that the questioning procedures which Reddin and Hersey & Blanchard have used in their research have actually made it impossible for them to come up with the idea that one style of leadership might be the best in all situations. There is just no room for what they call 9,9 leadership, and it could not emerge. So the humanistic view is that it is not true that in certain situations autocratic leadership is best – even if it is benevolent.

THE WIDER SCENE

Much of the older work seemed to ignore trade unions, but the more recent studies (Golembiewski et al. 1982, Nicholas 1982) show that unions can be involved with great advantage. OD can actually strengthen the effectiveness of unions, if used in the right way.

But it has to be recognized that there are three quite distinct fields within a unionized organization. The first of these is the CONTROL field, which I call level C. This is usually some kind of oligarchy, where various interests are balanced, and this is where the high-level decisions about the organization are taken. It may be called a board, or given some other name, and there may be various ambiguities about exactly where it begins and ends.

The second main field is the HUMAN region, where conflicts emerge at all levels within the organization. Many low-level decisions are taken here, and many grades and types of consultation or participation may be involved in such decisions. This I call level H.

The third main field is the REGULATORY area where

conflicts and other problems or moves are formalized through union channels. In Britain this usually takes the form of collective bargaining; other countries may have law, custom or compulsory arbitration. The outcome of the processes which take place here is a set of RULES jointly produced. This I call level R.

There is now a feedback loop whereby the rules produced at level R have to be implemented at level H. Such implementation has to be done in accordance with the norms of the workers involved, and therefore many small decisions may have to be made at this level to make the rules work.

This in turn gives us another feedback loop whereby the balance of the organization is disturbed by this change in rules, and this change is reflected at level C, where balance will have to be restored in some way, or moved to another viable state.

Now the main area for consultancy is level H, which forms a barrier between level C (where the management initiates action) and level R, where it is often the union which initiates action (though usually of a reactive kind). If level H is performing well, it acts as a damper or buffer which stops the system going into positive feedback and going out of control altogether. If too much stress is laid on level H, however, level R gets starved and may not function properly when required. Level R is necessary because the conflicts sometimes run much too deep, in terms of opposing interests, for them to be handled in an integrative way – and this is where level R comes in with a whole system of handling disputes which is adapted to this.

Humanistic consultancy does of course have something to contribute at level C (e.g. top management team-building) and level R (e.g. theories of negotiation, bargaining and conflict resolution) but its home territory and most usable set of techniques are all in level H. Rather than adopt the imperialism of total systems theory, which only serves to remind us of the imperialism of extended collective bargaining or the imperialism of managerial prerogative, we humanistic consultants would do well, in my opinion, to settle for level H, but to make good connections with the other two levels, so that we do not act in ways which deny their existence or necessity.

This would mean, for example, making personal links with each member of the ruling oligarchy, and with each of the key people involved in industrial relations negotiations on the union side. It is my impression that the former happens more often than the latter. In terms of the model, we link better with level C than with level R. And if this does happen, it is not too surprising that both the union representatives and the company's industrial relations people look on us with suspicion, and are only too pleased to say 'I told you so' when our interventions run into trouble – trouble which they might have predicted.

Perhaps enough has now been said to make it clear that quite a bit is known about how to change organizations from oppressive hierarchies into places which allow for growth, personal development and genuine participation. (I have written elsewhere (Rowan 1976) about the various levels and degrees of so-called participation.) But so far we have talked only in terms of change from the top. What about change which is initiated from the bottom of a hierarchy?

TAKING POWER

It is a quite common situation for a single individual to find herself turned-on and excited by the ideas and methods of humanistic psychology, and wanting to know how to pursue her new interest in an environment to which such ideas and methods are unfamiliar. She may try to do something on her own, which is rejected or misunderstood. She is almost certain to be asked to step back into her old role, as soon as what she does begins to be noticed. What does she do now?

I suggest that the first thing for her to get clear is the notion of synergy. Synergy is the kind of power which mutually enhances both giver and receiver – it is power through people, or with people. It is sometimes called the $2 + 2 = 5$ principle – a joining of two things or two people or two groups so that the outcome is more than the sum of

136

the two parts. Maslow (1969) quotes Benedict's definition of social synergy:

> Social-institutional conditions which fuse selfishness and unselfishness, by arranging it so that when I pursue 'selfish' gratifications I automatically help others, and when I try to be altruistic, I automatically reward and gratify myself also: i.e. when the dichotomy or polar opposition between selfishness and altruism is resolved and transcended.

Benedict used this analysis to show that some of the cultures she had studied were high-synergy cultures (the Zuni, the Arapesh, one of the Eskimo groups and the Northen Blackfoot), while others were low-synergy cultures: the Chuckchee, the Ojibwa, the Dobu and the Kwakiutl.

The high-synergy cultures tended to be secure, welcoming and high in morale: while the low-synergy cultures tended to be insecure, anxious, surly and low in morale. The high-synergy cultures were low in aggression; the low-synergy cultures had a win/lose attitude to most things, where the advantage of one individual became a victory over another.

Now I suggest that the individual stands the greatest chance of success if she keeps clearly before her mind the aim of turning the place into a high-synergy organization, where the more power you give away, the more you have. This is a tough aim, and may at first seem quite impossible; but it acts as a check at each point on whether one is moving in the right direction or not. Having accepted that, then, there are seven steps which may be necessary, as Ruth Leeds (1970) first stated. Obviously they need to be adapted to the nature of the specific organization which is in question.

The first step in taking power is finding allies. The isolated individual can do little except as a rare Titan. If one can make the person at the top of the hierarchy into an ally – and this is sometimes possible – the further steps may not be necessary; it just turns into a special case of working from the top. We are not in favour of opposition for the sake of opposition; only if it proves to be necessary.

It is better to look for allies than to wait for chance to

create them. They should have something in common which can be used as an initial focus of activity – usually some form of dissatisfaction with an aspect of the power structure, or the way power is used in the organization. One of them at least should be a popular person, preferably with powerful outside contacts. And one of them should have access to the top levels of the organization. A group with these characteristics stands the best chance of taking power.

The second step is to find some form of activity, some definite project, which is likely to achieve success. This need not be directly concerned with the overarching aim of the group – it is important mainly as a sign that the group can work together to achieve something concrete. At this stage the group may acquire a name.

The third step is to settle the leadership issue. This may need some very honest and open talking, and some real working through of emotional issues. It is all too easy for a group to be named after one person who is seen as the leader, and if this happens it makes it much easier for the organization to prevent the group from achieving anything, by removing this person in some way. So if possible, avoid having a leader, and avoid using a person's name as a label, even informally.

The fourth step is to make some realistic demand upon the next higher echelon – let us call this middle management, on the understanding that it will have different names in different organizations. This demand must now be related to the main theme of higher synergy – the present structure is holding back necessary changes, and needs to be modified. New rules and procedures are needed which will permit increased effectiveness to the work of the group, by giving it greater control over decisions which affect it. It is essential at this point to maintain a group identity as nonconformist but not deviant. Leeds (1970) explains this distinction by saying that, unlike a deviant, a nonconformist does not hide his dissent from the prevailing norms.

Much depends on how middle management react to being asked to give up some of the decisions they have had in their hands up to now. They may agree, or they may use one of four ways of fighting back: *condemnation* (threatening each member of the group and using pressures of various kinds, or trying to disperse the group); *avoidance* (memos are sidetracked, meetings postponed or cancelled, secretaries stonewall, supplies may be forgotten, delays seem to multiply, etc.); *expulsion* (direct coercive power used against one or more of the group); or *co-optation* (finding the most powerful person in the group and promoting her). None of these methods will work if the group has taken the steps outlined so far.

The fifth step is to produce a lot of good work. The work at this stage may now form one of the distinguishing marks of the group, and there will be a great deal of informal pressure on members to live up to the group norms. The number of meetings will increase. There is a great danger here of going away from other groups at the same level, who may start to see the dissident group as big-headed, standoffish, superior and generally unsympathetic. But if the earlier stages have been carried out properly, then the group will find it easy to communicate with collateral groups, and explain the issues to them in a convincing way. The outside contacts also become important. This stage may be quite prolonged, and every means of maintaining high morale will be needed.

The sixth step is where top management step in. And the tactic they are most likely to try is *protest absorption*. That is, they embrace the group and treat it as a special exception, to be treated differently from anyone else. In return, they ask for certain assurances which will stabilize the position and make it acceptable to middle management. The unit's activity is limited to a particular sphere of operation, usually that for which the leader and his followers advocated their innovation.

This is quite clearly incompatible with the main overall aim of the group – it actively prevents the whole organization developing high synergy, and virtually restores the status quo. So this kind of approach must be seen through and resisted. The group insists that it wants power to control all those decisions, and those phases of decision-making, which it has by now decided upon. And the object is, at this stage, to get top management either to approve and institute such changes, or to bring in an OD consultant who would be asked to report on the situation and take it from there. The group should, of course, insist on interviewing the consultant and having the right to veto her.

The seventh step is to make friends again with middle management, and work out a new way of living with them. For this reason it is best not to go too far in turning any one of them into some kind of symbol of evil at any of the earlier stages. In a high-synergy organization conflicts are brought out and worked through, not made an excuse for denying someone's reality (Maslow 1965).

The final outcome will be an organization which is visibly different from the way it was at the start. Some of the blocks to self-direction will have been removed. The idea of taking power will be in the air, and to that extent the feeling of being a cog in a machine will have been reduced. The organization has been started on a whole new career as a basically innovative organization.

Each of us has to make her own choice as to what to do in her own organization. It is more difficult to fight from the bottom than to make changes from the top – but maybe that is what we shall have to do, and support others when they do it. Something can be done.

Humanistic psychology is about not leaving it to experts, but taking responsibility for our own lives and our own actions. It is about human change and growth, about the realization of human potential, and about being an origin rather than a pawn. This means that you, the reader, are being at every point challenged to change and grow, to realize your potential, to become more of an origin and less of a pawn. What are you doing in your own organization?

CHAPTER NINE

TRANSPERSONAL

IT MUST have been obvious all the way through this book so far that humanistic psychology is very interested in the experience of ecstasy. Maslow with his 'peak experiences', Perls with his *satori*, Moreno with his 'spontaneity' – the list could be extended to the point of satiation. If humanistic psychology is concerned with human potential, it must include all that we have it in us to be – and therefore must include ecstasy, creativity, unitive consciousness and so on. This means that it must touch on transpersonal psychology. One of the most characteristic things which the transpersonal approach says is that just as there can be repression of what is low and nasty about us, so also there can be repression of what is spiritual and beautiful about ourselves. As Maslow (1973) puts it:

> We fear our highest possibilities (as well as our lowest ones). We are generally afraid to become that which we can glimpse in our most perfect moments, under the most perfect conditions, under conditions of greatest courage. We enjoy and even thrill to the god-like possibilities we see in ourselves in such peak moments. And yet we simultaneously shiver with weakness, awe and fear before these same possibilities.

THE TRANSPERSONAL SELF

Why should we be afraid of our higher selves? Why should we be afraid of our most ecstatic insights? What could be so bad about them? Frank Haronian (1974) offers one explanation:

> One possible reason why we do this is because the more one is conscious of one's positive impulses, of one's urges towards the sublime, the more shame one feels for one's failure to give expression to these impulses. There ensues a painful burning of the conscience, a sense of guilt at not being what one could be, of not doing what one could do. This is not superego guilt, but rather the cry of the Self for its actualization.

This mention of the Self may remind us of the Eastern approaches we noticed before. There has always been a great deal of interest in Eastern philosophy and practice, and in fact, as we saw in Chapter 2, this is one of the streams which make up humanistic psychology as it is today. Alan Watts in particular did a great deal to make a bridge between the two. We have seen that Maslow wanted science to be more Taoistic, Barry Stevens learned T'ai Chi, Will Schutz practised Kundalini Yoga and used its thinking in his encounter groups, and so on. And a lot of the talk about the 'here and now' is explicitly Eastern in its inspiration.

So this interest in what we may call the higher self (though in some ways it seems better to call it the greater self or the inner self or the deeper self) has always been a part of humanistic psychology, and in the movements associated with it.

The word 'transpersonal' was apparently used by Dane Rudhyar in the field of psychological astrology in the 1920s, and by Gardner Murphy in the field of parapsychology in 1949 (Murphy 1950). It was used by Erich Neumann in 1954 and by Ira Progoff in 1955, but it really only got popular after Stanislav Grof used it in 1967 and it then became the title of a journal in 1968. There is a good discussion of all this in Boorstein (1980).

142

But today it is becoming more important than before. Partly this is because of the increased interest in the work of Jung (1959). He is being looked at a great deal more now that all his work has been translated and made easily available. The psychosynthesis people, in particular, have done a great deal to show the relevance of his thinking. And of course Jung was very much interested in transpersonal psychology, and in such Eastern ideas as the Mandala, which is a very powerful symbol of what transpersonal psychology is all about.

Partly, too, it is because there are more and more new varieties of access to transpersonal states of consciousness of one kind and another, and the growth movement has been very hospitable to these. For example, T'ai Chi showed that there could be such a thing as moving meditation. Then Michael Murphy (1978) showed that golf could also be a moving meditation; from there it was only a short step to see that virtually any sport, any activity could be a form of meditation, leading to ecstatic states. It all depends on one's readiness to allow the experience to occur. See Leonard (1977), Gallwey (1974), Spino (1976).

There are also new kinds of meditation, such as the active meditation of Bhagwan Shree Rajneesh, which have become more easily available in Britain today. The intense breathing and violent bodily activity of these methods is far removed from the traditional picture of the sage with his legs crossed contemplating his own navel. And they seem in some ways better suited to the Western way of life.

LSD

Another method of access to altered states of consciousness is to use psychedelic drugs such as mescalin, psilocybin, Ecstasy (MDMA) or LSD. Some of the recent drugs are interesting, too, but I would like here to mention only LSD, because that is within my own personal experience. It is unwise in some ways to discuss LSD, because it is illegal, but so much that is valuable has been found out by means of LSD that it seems out of the question not to deal with it.

By 1971 there were 2000 published reports referring to treatment outcomes for between 30,000 and 40,000 patients undergoing psychotherapy with LSD. Most of these reports were favourable or highly favourable (Wells 1973). They dealt with three main types of use – psycholytic, psychedelic and hypnodelic.

(i) Psycholytic. Merely as an aid to other forms of therapy – a low-dose softening-up procedure.
(ii) Psychedelic. A powerful transcendental experience, aiming at significant change in personality organization. An unfreezing process, allowing access to hidden or buried possibilities within the person.
(iii) Hypnodelic. Patient is hypnotized before the session, and can therefore be guided into relevant areas by the therapist.

Also the therapists might use the drug themselves, on the principle that a guide to a territory should have been into that territory herself. In Czechoslovakia there was a rule that doctors must have observed thirty sessions and taken LSD at least five times themselves, before being allowed to administer the drug. A more recent account of some of this work is Grof (1980).

The approach of Timothy Leary (1970), on the other hand, was along the lines that LSD could get you into the same regions which had been described by the Eastern and Western mystics down the ages. But his account seems curiously eccentric and shallow.

John Lilly (1973) had a similar approach, and also charted various distinctions and differences between different states. This chart has now become part of the Arica training, which does not use drugs in any way. It seems to be a general truth that anywhere one can get with drugs, one can also get without.

Some of the early investigations were a little over-optimistic in the way they boosted the mystical effects of LSD – for example Pahnke (1972). It now seems clear that what you get with LSD is what is called in the mystical literature (Horne 1978) casual extraverted mysticism, which is one of the lower levels of mystical experience. It is very similar to the peak experience as described by Cohen & Phipps (1979) and by Hay (1982) based on the work of the Religious Experience Research Unit in Oxford (some of whose members have now set up their own project at Nottingham University). Such experiences are very common, about 30 per cent or more of the population having had them.

This approach to the psychedelics also produced one of the great ethical insights of recent years – the statement that 'You can't lay your trip on someone else', which we looked at briefly in Chapter 1. This seems to me an enormously valuable insight, and it applies in so many areas – for example in education, in industrial consultancy and so on. What is true for you is true for you, and there is no need, apart from insecurity, for you to try to lay it on me, and say that it should be true for me, too.

And it seems clear that LSD and its associated substances has had a great influence on a whole generation and its way of thinking. As John Heider (1974) says (and I agree with his story):

> In my experience and thinking, the single major event forcing this development (of interest in transpersonal psychology) has been the widespread use and abuse of psychedelic or mind-manifesting substances such as marijuana, LSD and mescalin . . . The psychedelic drugs gave incontrovertible proof that altered states of consciousness had reality and that paths toward transcendent experience existed. Huxley's (1963) *The Doors of Perception*, originally published in 1954, provided the seminal bridge between rational and ecstatic experience. By 1960, drug experimentation was widespread within the Cambridge-Berkeley intellectual underground and no longer in the province solely of New York musicians and ghetto blacks . . . we were hunting for ways to stay high forever and bring home the New Jerusalem, the Whole Earth.

The curious thing about this is that mystical experience had always in the past been associated with passivity and quietism (in the minds of most Westerners, at least) and here it was now leading to political activity and commitment. So perhaps this mysticism was not so 'traditional' after all – perhaps it was something quite new.

LEVELS OF CONSCIOUSNESS

One of the most common concepts of the Eastern and the Western writers about transpersonal experiences, whether drug or non-drug induced, is that there is a finite set of regions which one can get into, each of which has its own describable nature. The fullest and best account of this which has yet appeared, and which threw a flood of light on the whole subject, is that of Ken Wilber (1980), who distinguishes these eleven positions in a developmental sequence:

PLEROMA   Absolute adualism; objectless, spaceless, protoplasmic. Total oceanic, unconditional omnipotence, pleromatic paradise. Desireless, choiceless, timeless. One with *materia prima*. The most primitive of unities, on material/physical level.

OUROBOROS   First subject-object differentiation; acausality; prototaxic mode; hallucinatory wish-fulfilment; early sensory-motor stage. Oceanic euphoria and primordial fear. Primitive urge to survival. Physiological needs and awareness of these. Pre-temporal. Archaic, pre-personal, reptilian, reflex, alimentary. Ouroboric self *vs.* the ouroboric other – first incest and first castration.

TYPHONIC BODY EGO   Feeling self. Later sensory-motor stage. Acausality still. Axial-images. Exoceptual. Elementary emotions (pleasure, pain, fear, greed, rage); pranic level. Immediate survival still; the pleasure/unpleasure principle. Time as concrete, momentary passing present. Narcissistic. Klein's early stages of good breast and bad breast. Relating to the Great Mother. Magical

146

primary process thinking. Wish-fulfilment fantasies. Non-reflexive body image. Thumb-sucking. Separation anxiety.

MEMBERSHIP SELF Autistic language; paleo-logic and mythic thinking; membership cognition; temporal desires, extended and specific likes and dislikes. Proto-volition, roots of willpower and autonomous choice; belongingness. Time binding, time structuring, past and future. Verbal, tensed, membership self. Anality. The body becomes the focus of life and death. Realization of *anicca* or impermanence. Stubbornness and wish for autonomy. Language becoming extremely important. Gratification can be postponed.

MENTAL EGO Syntaxical-membership; secondary process; verbal-dialogue thinking; concrete and formal operational thinking. Concept-affects; dialogue emotions, especially guilt, desire, pride, love, hatred. Willpower, self-control, temporal goals and desires, esteem needs. Time seen as linear, extended, past-present-future. Aware-ness of ego splits and ego states, sub-personalities. Phallic stage. Oedipus complex. To conquer death by becoming father of oneself. Ego and consciousness experience their own reality by distinguishing themselves from the body. Parent-Adult-Child ego states. Incest and castration now at a mental level. Conscience and ego ideal. Preservation and enhancement of the self-image.

CENTAUR Transverbal vision-image; high fantasy; syn-thesis of primary and secondary process; trans-consensual cognition. Prehension, spontaneity, supersensory emotion, opening of heart. Intentionality; creative wish; meaning; integration; self-actualization; autonomy. Grounded in the present moment; aware of linear time as exfoliating from the present. Total bodymind being. Conscious emerg-ence of the real self; 'I create my world'. Symbols used deliberately for growth. Trans-control, trans-inhibition freedom. Highest point in the existential realm. Blissful states experienced. Cosmic love felt. Ability to transcend the ego and accept its death.

LOWER SUBTLE *Ajna* chakra – third eye. Astral-psychic; out of body experiences; auras, ESP, clairvoyance, dowsing, healing, etc. *Siddhis*. Transpersonally sensitive. Going beyond 'meaning in my life'; giving up intentionality and self-actualization; letting go of self-autonomy. Kundalini yoga. The *nirmanakaya*. The lower soul or psychic level. Intuition, openness, clarity. The transpersonal awareness of others; dropping of ego boundaries.

HIGHER SUBTLE High religious inspiration and literal inspiration. *Koans*. *Bijas* and affirmations. Symbolic visions. Blue, gold and white light. Audible illuminations and brightness upon brightness. Higher presences, guides, guardian angels, *ishtadevas*, higher self, overself. Rapture, bliss. Compassion. Experience of high archetypes. The *dhyani*-Buddha. Insight into, and eventual absorption as, Archetypal Essence. The realm of the *sambhogakaya*.

LOWER CAUSAL Deity-archetypes condense and dissolve into final-God, the Source of all archetypes. Perfect radiance and release. *Ananda. Karuna. Savikalpa samadhi*. The ground or essence of all previous stages.

HIGHER CAUSAL Formless consciousness, boundless radiance. Final-God self dissolves into its own Ground of formlessness. Samadhi of voidness. Both man and *dharma* forgotten. Coalescence of human and divine; the Depth, the Abyss, the Ground of God and soul; I and the Father are One; *nirvikalpa samadhi*; *nirguna Brahman*. The Ground of God and the Ground of the soul are one and the same. My *me* is God.

ULTIMATE Unity-Emptiness. Nothing and All Things. Seamless, not featureless. Transcends but includes *all* manifestation. Identity of the entire World Process and the Void. Perfect and radical transcendence into and as ultimate Consciousness as Such. Absolute Brahman-Atman. *Sahaja yoga*; *bhavi samadhi*, realm of *Svabhavikakaya*.

This list is so condensed as to be almost meaningless, but there is no space here to expand it. The interested person will have to go to the original. But perhaps there is sufficient to show that this is a process of psychospiritual development which we are all involved in, whether we want it or not and whether we know it or not.

Other useful maps are to be found in von Eckartsberg (1981) and in my own essay in this area (Rowan 1983a). The point I make there is that even the best maps seem to have bits missing and areas insufficiently well explored. But Wilber has achieved a magnificent task in reducing a huge mass of seemingly disparate material into some sort of order. In particular, I think he has done a marvellous job of showing exactly how humanistic psychology fits in to the whole picture. In his terms, humanistic psychology is almost all about the Centaur stage – how to take people there, how to explain what it is like, how to handle the phenomena which arise at that stage. If this is true, as I believe it is, then the function of humanistic psychology is immensely clarified and easier to carry out. It is also immensely important.

It is important because civilization, as Wilber (1981) has spelt out in detail, has now reached a stage of development which is all to do with the Mental Ego. The next stage has to do with a new spiritual step forward. But unless the Centaur stage is reached first, the Subtle stages can be quite disastrous. Because it is at the Centaur stage that we integrate all the previous stages. We go back and pick up all the pieces we discarded, as it were, at the previous stages; we fill up the holes in our personalities, we heal the splits in our personalities, and ultimately we transcend our personalities. We come out as a fully functioning person, in the terms we have learned from Rogers (1961).

In other words, it is safer and better to do our personal growth work before our spirituality, rather than leave it till later or try to avoid it altogether. It turns out that personal growth work is not an optional extra – it is an essential step on the spiritual path. In the past, people often embarked upon the spiritual path without having done this work, and promptly fell prey to demons, devils, elementals and so forth – most of which were projections of their own shadow, their own nastiness. By going the way of counselling, therapy, group work or whatever, we dispose of all these misunderstandings and confusions before we start; and hence, when we meet a demon, we know exactly how to handle it and how to speak to it, without giving it a status it does not deserve.

Similarly, in therapy we deal very thoroughly with all the big questions about oughts and shoulds and have-tos, throwing out all those compulsive guilts which plague us, and taking on instead a live conscience which lives by direct contact rather than rules. This is an immense help in dealing with the spiritual path at the subtle stage, where there are many many rules, none of which has to be taken at face value. Unless we are sophisticated about rules in the way which doing this deep work on ourselves enables us to be, we are going to be caught up in years of misery sorting all that out afresh.

So for the first time we can have a clean spirituality, not cluttered up with womb stuff, birth stuff, oral stuff, anal stuff, oedipal stuff, shadow stuff, anima stuff, parent-adult-child stuff, character armour and all the rest of it. For the first time we can relate to Deity without wondering and worrying whether what we are relating to is just a projection of our own parents. So this argument of Wilber about levels of consciousness is very important for the understanding not only of the transpersonal, but also of humanistic psychology and its function in the whole process of development.

One practical thing about this process may be of interest. Some work by Elmer & Alyce Green (1971) suggests that on the way from the Mental Ego level to the Centaur level there is a particular feature which is quite often experienced – a narrow tube, tunnel or path. This is referred to independently by several Eastern traditions, and has been discovered by therapists such as Ira Progoff in the West. It seems that often in fantasy work, when the person is approaching the level of the real self (the Centaur), she will visualize a tunnel or well, and seem to be traversing it, until at the end a light appears, a golden sun or other object with which the person ultimately identifies. The Greens quote this clinical example:

The power of meditation to bring transpersonal awareness is beautifully illustrated by the case of a 30-year-old
physicist with whom we discussed occult metaphysics.
During meditation he became aware of being in a long
grey tunnel at the end of which was a bright light. With
great joy he realized that this light was his life's goal and
began running toward it. As he neared the light,
however, its brilliance began to hurt him and he saw that
the light came from an intensely illuminated figure of
himself which was upside down, balanced head-to-head
on top of another figure of himself . . .

The symbol of the illuminated man balanced upside
down on the head of his normal self is particularly
meaningful because it is generally maintained by teachers
that the upper levels of man's nature have a correspon-
dence in lower levels, highest to lowest, etc., and that
man's personal and transpersonal natures meet at the
fourth level, the point of balance. Merging with the
illumined being consists of folding him down so that his
feet come to the ground and the resultant figure is a completely integrated man. This is, in essence, Aurobindo's
idea of the necessity in modern times of bringing down
the transforming power of the overmind and supermind
so that the man and his environment both benefit.

This is certainly something to watch out for when helping
people to come to terms with the Centaur level.

PERSONAL AND SOCIAL IMPLICATIONS

Some of our hangups come from repressing those things
about ourselves which we do not like (and this we can deal
with very well in our personal growth work), but some
come from repressing those things about ourselves which we
do like. As we saw in the earlier part of this chapter, there
is also such a thing as the repression of the sublime. But we
do not need to suppress these aspects of ourselves any more
than the others. They can all be explored, understood,
transformed and made parts of our being (Tart 1969).

But what if we do? There is a persistent fear, which we mentioned in Chapter 2, that concentrating on one's spiritual path may make one passive in social matters. This may be true of some of the Eastern doctrines in their original homes, but it does not seem to be true of the versions we have been looking at which are integrated with humanistic psychology.

Many people have been through a lot of phases and come back to the community – there is now a great deal more work being done outside the growth centres, by people who learned what they know inside those centres (and see Chapter 11).

My own way of looking at it is that there is a pulsation or cyclic movement in my life, so that at times I go inwards, and at other times I go outwards. This rhythm may have different periods in different people's lives, but I believe life is quite often like this. There is no need to fear that if one goes into a trance one will never come out of it, any more than there is a need to fear that if one once starts crying, one will never stop.

As we go up the spiral, more possibilities open up, and these are possibilities both for more intense personal experience and more intense social involvement and commitment. There are possibilities for more effortless personal experience and more effortless social involvement and commitment. How can it be intense and effortless at the same time? It is.

PAGANISM

Many people in the human potential movement have moved out in recent years into the sphere of the guru. Some of the best therapists I know have joined up with Rajneesh or Sai Baba or Da Free John. Many others more informally adhere to Buddhism in some shape or other. There is a natural tendency, once one gets interested in the trans-personal, to specialize in it more and more, and to take up some kind of religious devotion. But I believe that there is an important political question to raise here. What is the type of religious devotion that is more helpful to the earth at the present time?

It seems to me that paganism has some claim to be considered, because of its close relation to the earth and its care for it. This connection has been well drawn out by Sjöö & Mor (1980). The group called Pagans Against Nukes has issued a very good brief summary of the pagan faith, which among other things says the following:

> We consider as fundamentally Pagan all folk who hold the Earth sacred, who try to live in such a way that no living creature need suffer that they might live, regarding the plants and creatures as kinfolk, whose needs are to be treated with respect; who seek to prevent the exploitation and poisoning of our Mother Earth; who seek to re-establish a culture that will live lightly on the Earth, taking only enough for its needs, and living in peace and harmony towards the Earth, fellow creatures and other human beings.

One of the big advantages of paganism as compared to the monotheistic religions is that it is pluralistic. There are many names for the Goddess and many ways of approaching her. There are many names for her son and consort the Horned God. As the PAN statement again makes plain:

> Paganism is not a dogmatic faith. We have no holy books, prophets or saviours. There is no One True Way with Paganism – rather a great diversity of approach to the faith, and a great variety of creative ways in which it finds expression, naturally arising from the infinite diversity of life.

This is perhaps the reason why paganism is becoming more popular today, as Margot Adler (1979) has described it with a wealth of detail. Excellent authors like Starhawk (1979) and Barbara Walker (1983) have opened up a broad path on which we can now walk in our examination of these questions.

Furthermore, it is paganism which has become the most political expression of the women's movement. Not only the Greenham Common women, but also many of the strongest protest groups in the United States, use the pagan symbols of the spider's web, the snake, the ritual circle, the bird, the maze and so on. And so we get Starhawk (1982) telling us:

> If we are to survive the question becomes: how do we overthrow, not those presently in power, but the principle of power-over? How do we shape a society based on the principle of power-from-within?

This political concern is found in many places today where women's spirituality is being developed, as we find in Spretnak (1982) and in McAllister (1982). I have argued strongly elsewhere (Rowan 1987) that men's spirituality also needs this kind of connection with politics if men are to come to terms with patriarchal consciousness – the biggest social problem of our time.

These are relatively new thoughts for me, and much has still to be done in working out how best to present them in print. The word 'paganism' has rather unserious connotations for many people, and it is hard for such people to take anything like this at all in the right spirit. But it seems so important that we just have to take the risk of being misunderstood.

CHAPTER TEN

FEMALE/MALE/GAY

IN THE late 1930s, Maslow began to study the relationship between sexuality and what he called 'dominance feeling' or 'self-esteem' or 'ego level' in women. He found that the more dominant the woman, in these terms, the greater her enjoyment of sex and her orgasmic potency. It was not that these women were more 'highly sexed', but that they were, above all, more completely themselves, more free to be themselves. They could give themselves more freely, because they had more of themselves to give.

Today we would tie this in to Maslow's self-esteem level, which we met in Chapter 1. Once a woman gets to this level, she ceases to underestimate herself in relation to men, and is able to gauge her own abilities accurately and realistically. As Maslow (in Friedan 1965) says:

> Such women prefer to be treated 'Like a person, not like a woman' . . . Rules per se generally mean nothing to these women. It is only when they approve of the rules and can see and approve of the purpose behind them that they will obey them . . . They are strong, purposeful and do live by rules, but these rules are autonomous and personally arrived at.

Now we have seen over and over again that it is difficult for anyone to get to this level. Our culture does not make it easy, and all of us need special help if we are to do it at all. It is as if our society puts a slope in the ground, so that psychosocial development always takes place against resistance – always an uphill struggle.   What has been

155

found, however, over and over again in many independent pieces of research, is that the gradients are not equal for men and for women. If the gradient is 1 in 20 for men, it is more like 1 in 2 for women. The number of men who get to the self-esteem level is small – the number of women seems to be even smaller. Most of us get stuck at the level of role-playing.

SEXUALITY

Even sexuality become a matter of role-playing. There have been two sexual revolutions in our time. The first was about getting rid of restricting and hypocritical Victorian morality. This reached its peak in 1962, with the invention of the Pill. The Pill was going to liberate sex once and for all from its old shackles. Now we could all be sexually free. With the fear of pregnancy gone, the road would be clear for us all to do exactly what we had always wanted to.

But pretty soon it became obvious to some women that what had happened was in fact that the way had really been made clear for women to do what men had always done – enjoy sex without responsibility. But was this what they had actually been wanting to do? It seemed highly dubious to them. Let Ellen Willis (1981) tell it:

> The libertarians did not concern themselves with the quality of sexual relationships or the larger social and emotional causes of sexual frustration. They were less influenced by feminism than their counterparts in the twenties; in theory they advocated the sexual liberation of women, but in practice their outlook was male-centred and often downright misogynist. They took for granted that prostitution and pornography were liberating. They carried on about the hypocrisy of the sexual game – by which they meant men's impatience with having to court women and pay lip service to their demands for love, respect and commitment. No one suggested that men's isolation of sex from feeling might actually be part of the problem, rather than the solution.

So the second sexual revolution was about women discovering that the first one was not in their interest, and trying to find out what sexuality might mean in their own terms.

This process of discovery has been long and difficult. It was made even more difficult by the fact that the family did not go away in the 1960s, as some of the liberators had hoped. It remained as unfinished business to be settled. As Willis (1981) has pointed out so sharply:

> There is a neat irony in the fact that leftists are now romanticising the family and blaming capitalism for its collapse, while ten years ago they were trashing the family and blaming capitalism for its persistence.

It is only the feminists, she says, who have consistently analysed the family and shown how sexuality is distorted and confused for both men and women in a patriarchal society. Her remark – 'Women in a patriarchy have every reason to distrust male sexuality and fear their own' – is a poignant cry about an impossible situation.

And the more recent writing on male sexuality (Reynaud 1983, Metcalf & Humphries 1985, James 1985) show all too clearly that the situation does not become any less impossible with the passage of time. The kind of authenticity which the humanistic approach makes possible still seems a minority affair. Most people rest content with roles.

SEX ROLES

But there is something particularly insidious about sex roles. They seem to be tied in with our identity in a way that most of our roles are not. We are sometimes told that the differences are biological, but humanistic psychologists do not believe this. We believe that women are just as capable of moving up the developmental spiral as men, and that if they are not doing it, this must be due to some internal or external barrier.

What has happened in recent years is that women themselves have become more and more aware of the arbitrary and hurtful nature of these barriers, and in increasing numbers have tried to dismantle them. In doing so, they have found it necessary to separate to some degree from men, because when men are present the old patterns reassert themselves all too easily. Or to put it another way, men are actually the reason why many of the barriers are there – it is actually in the interests of men's comfort and peace that women are pushed into service roles. No wonder it is hard to dismantle the barriers in the presence of those who put them there, or who at any rate maintain them.

At first, men reacted with antagonism or guilt (or a mixture of the two) to being accused of these things, but gradually they began to see that the culture, while narrowing women in one way, narrowed men in another. In 1970, a 'women's caucus' was formed within the AHP, and issued the folowing statement:

> Men are discouraged from developing certain traits such as tenderness and sensitivity just as surely as women are discouraged from being assertive and 'too bright'. Young boys are encouraged to be incompetent at cooking and child care just as surely as young girls are urged to be in-competent at mathematics and science . . . If sensitivity, emotionality and warmth are desirable human character-istics, then they are desirable for men as well as women. If independence, assertiveness and serious intellectual commitment are desirable human characteristics then they are desirable for women as well as men.

Both sexes have lost touch with their inner selves, replacing them with roles. To achieve a society of whole people, it is essential that these lost selves be found and realized. Potentially we are all whole human beings, but both men and women have been diminished and distorted.

The difference between this kind of distortion and the ones we normally come across in personal growth work is that it is a kind of distortion which is socially created, socially maintained and socially approved. And so it is what the Freudians call 'ego-syntonic' – that is, if in the process of working on ourselves we come across it, we ignore it, because both the therapist and the client take it for granted. As Judd Marmor (1974) has said:

One of the clinical facts that has forced itself strongly upon my awareness has been the repeated observation of people who have undergone prolonged and painstaking analysis and yet have been left with clear-cut residual patterns of narcissism, exploitativeness, social aggression, rigidity, compulsiveness and other similar character-ological attitudes.

In other words, if the culture tells us that such and such behaviour is normal, we will not try to work on it as a problem, even if it is causing suffering to others.

This is what we called earlier the result of living in an alienated society. It seems that we must take it as a basic premise that unless a person has worked consciously and often painfully at exploring and discovering her real self, she will automatically be alienated and shut off from her innermost core of being. In other words, to be alienated is to have developed normally. To be non-alienated means a conscious interference with normal development, in our male-dominated society, as Robert Seidenberg (1973) urges:

> Although it is a vast oversimplification to attribute mental illness to one cause, we are becoming aware of social forces that filter down to the family and mother-child unit. The effects of a male-dominant society on 'mothering' cannot be overlooked as potentially and actually disinte-grative . . . In the unconscious of men as found in psychoanalysis, there is a deep-seated fear and loathing of women. All the songs of love do not displace this underlying contempt for those 'unfortunates' with gaping wounds where a penis ought to be. It is the loathing of differences that encourages and maintains the male homosexual culture from which females are regularly excluded . . . Women are different, but most of their purported differences are cultivated in the minds of men in order to justify oppressing them.

The difference between an enlightened Freudian like this and a humanistic psychologist is that we don't see any of this as inevitable. It is because the 'fear and loathing' is permitted and encouraged by a million social forms that it becomes powerful. If it were denied by the culture it would become an individual quirk with few consequences.

One small instance, which feminists have drawn attention to, is the use of personal pronouns in books. A person of indefinite or general sexual reference, when referred to again, is called 'he' and the words 'him' and 'his' are also used. This produces a cumulative impression that the active subjects of sentences are male. In other words, most of the active and interesting things which are talked about in books are done by the male of the species. And this reinforces any cultural prejudices which are floating around which says that men are interesting and women are boring; that the things which men do are noteworthy, while the things which women do are not worthy of record. In this book, I am doing the opposite, not because I think it will have much effect, but just to show that it does look odd – it goes against our expectations, which are perhaps not even conscious until they are contradicted. There are good discussions of this whole area in Miller & Swift (1979) and in Spender (1980).

This is a minor one. There are also major ones, and medium heavy ones, and everything intermediate between these. And their cumulative effects are extraordinarily powerful – they actually affect our own consciousness of who we are. As Angela Hamblin (1972) says in a superb essay:

> When we accept our role and lose touch with the vital core of ourselves we are sick . . . It is a sickness that doesn't show, it doesn't noticeably affect our bodies, it doesn't impair our capacity to function. It doesn't prevent us from acting out our role. We are just dead inside . . . And most of the time it seems like normality. It is the striving for health, the groping towards self-realization that seems unnatural, unreal somehow . . . This is because in our sick role-playing society this inner core of self is never accorded recognition or legitimized. It is never acknowledged that such a thing exists, so how can it be lost?

Of all the roles which we can try to escape from, our sex roles are the hardest. Women have found that consciousness-raising groups help a lot in some ways, but are also very painful. To permit oneself the knowledge that one is oppressed, to open up one's awareness of the way that one's life has been fucked-up, is a recipe for pain. In such a group one may also find much laughter and new feelings of power, but in the end there is so much to fight against that it makes one mixed-up and angry and resentful. Su Negrin (1972) has written about this very well.

It is almost as if in order to be a woman, one had to give up being 'a woman'. As if being a woman in relation to women was different from and incompatible with being a woman in relation to men. One simple way to resolve these contradictions is to become gay, or at least to open up to the possibilities of relating to other women on a body level, as well as on a mental and emotional level.

And something also happened with men. Men started meeting separately, and consciously experiencing their own feelings about relating to each other (Farrell 1974). They discovered how competitive they were, how devoted to power they were – often seeing couple relationships in terms of power rather than in terms of sex. (Key question – 'Which gives you more pleasure, making love to a woman or getting her knickers off?') And again, after a while, this led to a real feeling of despair – there just seemed too much of it, there was no end to the ways of dominating women and putting them down. So maybe a simple answer was not to relate to women – at least one couldn't be accused of oppressing them then. And the gay men drove the point home:

> You claim to want to struggle against your own sexism and yet you refuse to make central and primary and before everything else, the task of breaking with gender-roles. You want to stop being men, but without stopping being men. You want to postpone it until you've stopped being men . . . There are a thousand ways to deceive yourself. But in the end the only way forward is to *really* open yourself up to the mirror image of yourself and

experience through another, *yourself as a man* (you are a male, remember) – and build something from the ruins of your male ego that will result. (Anonymous contribution to *Brothers Against Sexism*, 1974)

This was a strong challenge, and really got under the skin of those who were most sincere about trying to do something about their false socialized male selves. But it was very rare to be able to find a situation where anything could be done about this. I ran a workshop with a woman once, where we tried to get into these areas, and in it one of the men was confronted by the women over a period of about two hours. This led, with the help of Gestalt therapy, into his being able to have a kind of amazing vision of what it would be like to be a non-sexist person – and actually behaving like a real person. But it needed all that period of breaking down before he was ready to make that leap. Most of the time women are unable or unwilling to get together and spend that amount of time on one man, and it just doesn't seem to work very well to get men to confront each other.

SOME WAYS AHEAD

If this bit of potted history is anywhere near right, it seems that what has been happening is that some women have become aware that society is run in a patriarchal way, for the benefit of men. They have discovered that their alienation can be pinpointed very accurately as due to the separation of roles in a male-dominated society. Angela Hamblin (1972):

The political class of men oppress and exploit the political class of women. *Within* the political class of men a few dominate and oppress the rest. It is for the benefit of these few that the patriarchal role-system is maintained, although *all* men derive direct or indirect political benefit from it. At no time is this system of benefit to women. This is why it is women who will bring it down . . . We have to dismantle the hierarchical power structure built up and maintained through social role-playing. And we

162

have to start with ourselves. We have to put ourselves together again. We must become real. *When we are real, then we are a real threat.*

But we have also seen that men find it incredibly difficult to change, partly no doubt because we do derive direct or indirect benefit from the existing state of affairs, but also because the social conditioning works at an unconscious level as well as at a conscious level. I have written about this at much greater length elsewhere (Rowan 1987).

Now this seems very much like the situation between blacks and whites, in the relationship we call racism. Racism is the pattern where whites feel it is 'all right' to oppress blacks in various ways, because it is socially sanctioned. It is a mixture of prejudice and discrimination. And in recent years, of course, blacks have begun to resist this pattern, and to undo the ways in which their own selves have been made to feel inferior. Now the corresponding pattern between men and women is called sexism, and it seems to me that the analogy is very close, as Hacker (1951) has suggested.

If this is at all true, perhaps some of the same approaches which have been used in tackling racism might be useful here too. Jones & Harris (1971) tried using small groups to produce real change. They used six to eight weekly sessions of an hour and a half, followed by a six-hour session, with groups of ten to fifteen people, some white and some black. One leader is white, and one black. Their project showed that certain phases seem to be constant, and regularly arise to be worked through as the sessions progress:

1 Introductory phase. The main theme is of white people claiming to be free from prejudice.
2 Information phase. Black members come back with details of how they have suffered.
3 Competitive phase. The whites come back with stories of how they, too, have experienced discrimination or persecution, because of being Jewish, Catholic, long-haired, revolutionary, etc.
4 Competitive response. The blacks then emphasize how much worse their problem is, and it becomes

clearer that it is *white* society which is responsible in their eyes.

5 Dissociation. The whites then try to dissociate themselves from white society generally, and also accuse the blacks of exaggerating. One way or another, they avoid accepting the black statements as applying to them.

6 Impasse. It becomes clear that the blacks and the whites are on two different wavelengths. There is a feeling of being stuck. Evasions of different kinds are tried. It seems that nothing is going to change or happen.

7 Moment of truth. Eventually one of the blacks will express unequivocal anger, strongly and honestly. The group now knows him or her well, and canot fail to be impressed.

8 Follow through. The other blacks in the group sooner or later support the member who has spoken out. The emotional reality of what it is to be a black and not a white comes through clearly.

9 Realization. The whites gradually and painfully see the contrast between sympathetic understanding, warm-hearted liberalism, and the real awareness of the black experience. They see that they have been living in a different world, and systematically deceiving themselves about it.

10 Digestion. The whites start to go over their past experiences with blacks, in the light of the new consciousness they have now of what it means to be black. The blacks feel relief and surprised delight that the whites are really listening and struggling to understand.

11 Consensual validation. Both whites and blacks are able to work on their, and each other's, individual problems in an atmosphere which at last is relatively clear.

The main purpose of making this comparison is to show that deep-rooted ways of thinking and feeling need a great deal of effort to work through. Even in these groups, there were some people who never got the message, and semed unreachable. It seems to me that there is no reason to believe that sexism is any easier to deal with than racism. And therefore something corresponding to these stages may need to be worked through between men and women too. There may even be more to it than that; I have suggested elsewhere (Rowan 1987) that the prejudices of men are so deeply ingrained that work at the unconscious and at the spiritual levels may be quite necessary, in addition to this kind of work at the conscious level of daily conduct.

One thing about it needs pointing up, perhaps, and that is that the blacks in these groups had an experience of expressing deep anger, and seeing it work. Casriel (1971) distinguishes four types of expression of anger, and says that it is only the fourth which is really effective in changing people. The first type is intellectual anger, quietly thought and expressed; the second is riddance anger, screaming but mixed with anxiety, coming from the throat; the third is more in the chest, a murderous rage:

> Individuals have to feel that third level before they can get to the fourth level. They have to feel secure enough for that third type of anger in order to feel the fourth level, which I call 'identity anger'. People feel it in their belly, and it comes out as a feeling that 'I'm angry because I've been hurt; it wasn't fair what happened to me, Goddammit, and I'm angry; I'm angry and nobody is going to do that to me again; no more. I'm not going to let anybody do that to me. *No more; no more!*' You feel it in your total body, and you feel aware of a total you, a total whole identity.

This means that these groups not only reduced prejudice in the whites, but also gave an important therapeutic experience to the blacks. Similarly, if this work were done with men and women, it would not only be of benefit to the men (by confronting them and helping them to change) but would also be of benefit to the women, by enabling them to get into their identity anger, in the presence of the actual object of that anger, and with the support of the whole group structure.

It is important to be clear that we are not asking for people to take off one set of social clothes and put on another set. It is not a question of learning how to be 'Mr Nice Guy' so that one can get on better with feminists. For both men and women, it is a question of learning how to take off the clothes of social conditioning and walk naked. Or to put it more accurately, it is a question of getting in touch with the real self, and reintegrating the personality around it. This is the same process we have been looking at all the way through this book, only now it seems to have a more scary feel to it, as Angela Hamblin (1972) suggests:

> It will be a difficult journey back. It means peeling off layer after layer of social role learning. It is frightening. As more and more is discarded there is the fear that when the final layer is removed it will reveal nothing. This is existential terror, and it is this that makes us scurry back to the safety of roles, to the safety of what is known, and to deny our selves. It takes courage to go on – the 'courage to be'.

This is all true, and yet, as we saw in the last chapter, there is no need to worry. In that scary void beyond catastrophe lives the real self – who we really are. The way to wholeness and union is through the gateless gate.

But there is another area which we need to look at. So far, we have been assuming that the whole world is heterosexual. But it is quite clear, from the little bit of history which we looked at, that the various movements within sexual politics have now become very much aware that an important alternative is to be gay or lesbian.

And once we start to look at this, we find that just as men in quite real and important ways oppress women, so the straight world in quite real and important ways oppresses the gay world.

Now humanistic psychology does not have a particularly good record in relation to gay people, and some therapists who otherwise have a right to be included in this book have been excluded from it mainly because of their strong prejudices against gays.

Most people in humanistic psychology seem to be quite open to homosexual expression, and quite accepting of gay people, but somehow they don't talk about, don't write about, don't research about anything to do with the gay experience. They just leave it alone, quietly and politely. I'd like this to change. But gay people are going to have to do the real work of confronting and raising the issues, just as women and blacks had to do the real work before straight men and whites would take them seriously.

In February 1975 I helped to organize the first 'four-way workshop' to be held in Britain (Rowan 1975a). This had two gay and two straight leaders, and enrolled both gay and straight men and women. We all learned a great deal from this, but it was very hard to arrange, and a planned follow-up workshop never happened.

There are two good papers on the difficulties involved here in the book on radical psychology edited by Phil Brown (1973), and Su Negrin's (1972) book helped me a lot in getting some understanding. She says:

> To me, lesbiansim is not so much a sex issue as it is a life-style issue and a political commitment. The life-style aspect involves putting my energy into relationships with women, finding my pleasure in the company of women, developing my sexuality among women, struggling with my oppression in solidarity with women, satisfying my daily needs in community with women. My habits always oriented me to relate in these ways only with men, as straight women do . . . Being a lesbian helped me to become a whole person. As a straight feminist I got in touch with anger; but I experienced myself as a rhetoric reciting, vengeful, conflict-ridden ghost. As a lesbian, I got in touch with love; and I experience myself as a more confident, joyful, powerful person.

It would seem quite wrong to me to say that Su Negrin was sick, or needed treatment. The ability to love somebody of the same sex seems to me a valuable quality, which should be wider spread than it is. (I feel uneasy about that 'should' but let it stand.) I don't do it myself. I have very few close relationships with men, and those that I do have are not on

167

a physical level. But I would like to think that this would not always necessarily be so. (See also Clark 1972.)

And the implications of this include a complete change in the way we might think about sex education. I have never seen a book by a humanistic educator which included suggestions about sex education to include an understanding of same-sex relationships. Yet every book I have ever seen on counselling adolescents says that worries about homosexuality are high on the list of concerns which come up in their sessions. There is a contradiction here.

There is a lot of work being done now on breaking down sex roles in children's books and so on. But whenever an anxious parent raises the question – 'But won't playing with dolls make little Johnny into a homosexual?' – the answer is always given – 'Certainly not'. Which is fair enough, in factual terms, but leaves all the prejudices intact. Maybe we could think of some alternative answers now:

- We believe that each child has the right to be gay in his or her own way, and we wouldn't try to force it.

- We try not to indoctrinate them with any particular sexual orientation.

- We try to help children to be as adaptable as possible in a fast-changing world.

- This is not a single-sex school

- Are you prejudiced against homosexuals?

Perhaps heterosexuality is like Anglicanism – something we used to teach in schools, but now you have to go to a special school if you want to get it; the ordinary schools are interdenominational. Then sex education would be sex education, not heterosex education.

It is interesting that recently there has been some attempt to put these thoughts into action, and that the backlash has been very strong, assisted by the current anxieties about AIDS. Acknowledging homosexuality becomes encouraging homosexuality, and encouraging homosexuality becomes abetting buggery, and abetting buggery becomes the spread of AIDS. It seems obvious that each of these links is very shaky and can be challenged very easily.

In general, it seems that humanistic psychology needs to be a lot more consistent in its approach. If it is in favour of the full development of human potential, this must mean the full development of sexual potential too. In the present historical situation, where there is such considerable inequality as between men and women, straights and gays, this may have to include periods of separate development and separate exploration. But it also needs to include new kinds of coming-together.

It seems to me that humanistic psychology has a lot to offer in helping to understand these phases, and work them through. It is not afraid of sex any more than it is afraid of any other of the basic motives of human beings, and it has a lot to say about human relationships. The basic principles outlined by Bach and Wyden (1969) in their book on couple relationships apply not only to heterosexual couples but also to homosexual ones, and even to larger intimate groups than the couple.

And this may mean shattering our self-image. Specifically, it may mean shattering our image of ourselves as a woman, or a man. This is what we have been saying all through this book, though. Fritz Perls (1969) puts the point with his customary bluntness:

> Many people dedicate their lives to actualize a concept of what they *should* be like, rather than to actualize *themselves* . . . This difference between *self*-actualizing and self-*image* actualizing is *very* important. Most people only live for their image. Where some people have a self, most people have a void, because they are so busy projecting themselves as this or that.

And what we have seen over and over again is that this void is *all right*; it is only by going into that void that we can have any inkling of what it might be like to be a real person, who is free to play games or not to play games, and never *has* to play games.

This process is never easy, and in an historical situation where the straight white male has to do very little to win, and the others have to work like hell to avoid losing, it is harder still. The problems and burdens of men are real enough, as Pleck and Sawyer's book (1974) makes clear, but they are the burdens of privilege; the game is not even. There is a long way to go.

CHAPTER ELEVEN

SOCIAL ACTION AND COMMUNITY DEVELOPMENT

IT SEEMS clear from all that we have seen so far that humanistic psychology has a real investment in the social and ethical implications of its work. It is not surprising, therefore, that virtually every one of the central figures in humanistic psychology has come out and said challenging things about society, as well as about the individual. All the time the emphasis is on change, real change, and not on adjustment to the existing order. Maslow (1973), for example, says this:

> If we were to accept as a major educational goal the awakening and fulfilment of the B-values, which is simply another aspect of self-actualization, we would have a great flowering of a new kind of civilization. People would be stronger, healthier and would take their own lives into their hands to a greater extent. With increased personal responsibility for one's personal life, and with a rational set of values to guide one's choosing, people would begin actively to change the society in which they lived.

Well, that sounds all very well, but how likely is it? And how do we perform this task of education? Do we have to do it individual by individual? Do we have to set up innumerable small groups? Do we have to pass laws in Parliament?

Some people who are seriously interested in politics see the whole approach of humanistic psychology as being a diversionary palliative which can only be illusory. Barry Richards (1974) says of activities based on it:

> They are a means of drawing large numbers of intellec-
> tuals into active promotion of extreme individualism,
> hedonism, and the psychotherapeutic ideology – the ideol-
> ogy of personal adjustment as opposed to political
> commitment and organization, of self-fulfilment as op-
> posed to social change, and of serving self and not serving
> others.

Let us check this out by seeing what activities have been initiated in the social field by those who are identified with the position outlined in this book.

DRUG PROJECTS

Some very characteristic projects have been those set up around people who used drugs in largely self-destructive ways, and who began to want to stop doing this. Marilyn Kolton (1973) and her associates carried out a study of seventy-two such programmes in the States, and found that the more humanistic programmes were those for young people. And one of the first things they decided was that it was a mistake to emphasize the 'drug addict' label, or any other label; it was better to regard the people as people with problems in living:

> If you focus in on one thing, if an adolescent goes into a
> Buddhist kick, if you then assume that's permanent and
> unchanging, he doesn't have a chance to get off that kick.
> Because you're relating so much to that. If he focuses on
> drugs, and then he stays on drugs, and you stay on drugs,
> and the structure of the community stays on drugs, well
> then that keeps him from shifting to something else.

So there was little or no attempt at diagnosis, or of applying some kind of medical model to the person. Instead, there was much more of a real attempt to get on with the person, and learn something from that, in a genuine two-way interaction. There was a genuine respect for the person's praxis: the underlying assumption about the behaviour of an individual is that her strategies are from choice, and are the result of decisions made to cope with certain situations.

But there is also a respect for the environment, and its power to impose very real sanctions on the person. Lester Gelb (1972) gives this example:

Several years ago I was asked by a social agency to see a 13-year-old orphaned boy, depressed, failing in school and often truant. The reason given for his numerous transfers was that he was a 'severe behaviour problem' and 'unmanageable'. I.Q. was 79 at age 11. My attempts, through psychotherapy, to provide a 'corrective emotional experience' were to no avail. He complained continually about his difficult life situation. He improved after I was able to share with him my understanding of a truth that he had sensed or known all along – namely, that he had been the victim of poor teachers and a series of foster homes where he had been cruelly exploited. The several foster parents had suffered from poverty and had used the foster agency payments as a way to improve their own standard of living. Meanwhile the children were used to do chores and housework. Partly as a result of my joining my patient in his angry reaction, the agency reorganized its foster placement programme and provided family counselling. After my acknowledgement of the appropriateness of the boy's anger, he was ready to accept educational opportunities, including courses in photography. His I.Q. had risen to 129 by age 17. He is now a highly respected photographer at age 26.

When one begins to see people's dilemmas as consequences of their positions within an oppressive environment, the solution involves direct intervention, creation of concrete alternative communities, and helping them develop a strategy of social change which will enable them to meet their legitimate needs. Rather than adjustment to a difficult situation with resignation, the goal might be to develop a sense of personal movement and change so that a new environment can be created.

And this has been pushed further in the field of

community development, where we look beyond the individual and her immediate environment.

COMMUNITY DEVELOPMENT

We understand the word 'development' reasonably well by this time, having seen the concept applied in a rather precise way in so many fields in previous chapters. But the word 'community' needs some explanation. It sounds so nice and so comforting, and yet it can be quite misleading. It seems that the beginning of wisdom here is to recognize that community is actually very rare and vanishing fast, and that if we want it we have in a sense to create it.

It hardly needs to be said that the effects of industrialization include the breaking down of local communities. Whether people live in tenements or the suburban semi-detached, in housing estates or in detached acres, in caravans or in bedsitters, they find neighbourly relations difficult to maintain and less than satisfying. This is part of a wider process, as Orrin Klapp (1969) has pointed out:

> Such a malady is not just a failure of particular interactions and personal efforts but a blight on the forest of meaning which a child needs to grow up into a man, a grandparent, finally an ancestor. Any of its causes are difficulties in the way of a person in a mass society finding meaning to, for, and in himself: dehumanized work, extreme impersonality, destruction of places, social mobility, lack of identifying ceremonies, pile-up of objective (meaningless) information, mediocrity of bureaucratic and white-collar self-images, explosion of expectations from impact of mass communications and increasing leisure, and fragmentation of identity from multiplicity of personality models.

So to even think of developing a community or a sense of community, we have in a way to believe in the community without being able to see it. We have, as it were, to have a faith that community is there somehow, even though it may be hard to see any signs of it. And this is very similar to the

174

truth which we have already encountered, that in therapy, or counselling, or personal growth we have to assume or take for granted that there is a real self, before we can even dream of actualizing it. Just as humanistic psychology takes the view that the person is basically OK and to be trusted, it also takes the view that the community is basically OK and to be trusted. As William Biddle (1965) says in his basic text:

> The attitudes that a worker with people has toward them contributes substantially to their development or lack of development. People respond to their perception of attitudes as these are expressed in gesture, word and deed. If the worker acts as though he believes people are unworthy, not to be trusted, or selfishly motivated, his influence is not likely to awaken generous initiative. If he acts as though he believes people have constructive ideas (often despite evidence to the contrary) and potentialities for development beyond their present limitations, he is likely to prove more encouraging.

The case studies given in his book make it clear that these are neither pious hopes nor sly tricks – they actually tell us something about the way of working which was adopted in reality. One of these studies was rural and one urban, and in both projects local people emerged as leaders with initiative, originality, ideas of their own. This leadership was not discernible before the projects began and some knowledgeable onlookers had predicted that it would not be found. Furthermore, when certain emergent leaders proved inadequate or had to step aside, other leaders developed out of and were refined by the process.

Out of this work, Biddle arrived at a definition of community: 'community is whatever sense of the local common good citizens can be helped to achieve'. This is clearly a view which assumes that local conflicts are ultimately reconcilable. To put it another way, it makes the assumption, which we also found in considering organizations, that high synergy can always be aimed at.

Now it is precisely this assumption which most often upsets

those who are more politically committed. As the anonymous authors (1973) in Rat, Myth and Magic succinctly say:

> The essence of all 'participation' schemes is the reinforcement of structures of class-collaboration . . . The pay-off for the capitalist class in all this is the re-creation of a more docile work force . . . and the abolition of 'difficult' communities – to avoid the recurrence of localized 'no-go' areas or total rent strikes (as in Ulster or Liverpool).

My own view is that this analysis is too one-sided. It takes opposition as the only thing that matters, as if the only decision which had to be made was which side of the barricades to be on. This is wooden-soldier politics, where the main virtue is not to listen to the enemy. And it produces a certain syndrome within the left party itself, where the members are also not able to listen to the enemy within. And so within the left party member there grows up a secret fifth column of which she is quite unaware. In spite of her conscious wish to be democratic or equalitarian, and in any case adult, she unconsciously treats the party, and in particular its 'fathers' as a feared but loved parent. She becomes dependent and unable to fight intelligently for changes in policy. She becomes a 'child' in relation to its parents, or a 'hack' in party terms. So we do not get away from class-collaboration by merely wishing to.

I don't believe in a revolution which is only about structural changes in social institutions and says nothing about how we live our lives and run our own organizations. I see the real social change which I am interested in as basically about better social relationships, and as being achieved through better social relationships, which in themselves force structural change. As Jerry Rubin (1973) has said:

> My definition of 'political' has now expanded to include the food we eat, the excitation in our bodies, how we raise our children. People out of touch with their bodies cannot make a revolution. The political battles of the 1960s included too many crazy meetings, bureaucratic hassles, ideological wars because people were not aware

of their own need for personal growth. In the 1970s we are going inward and discovering that we are the creators of our experience. Soon the spiritual and political revolutions will be joined: the inner and the outer.

It is in community development that we can most clearly see the tensions appearing which we have ultimately to deal with, in all their aspects.

One particular approach has become codified well enough to be described in some detail, and applied in some seventy different communities. This is the so-called 'Charrette' programe developed by Barry Schuttler (1975) and his associates. It has five stages: preparation; conference design; fact-finding task forces; intensive problem-solving conference; and implementation.

The preparation stage consists in some person or group in a community or would-be community taking the initiative to call in an experienced 'conference manager'. This person is a humanistic facilitator with some kind of organization development or similar background, and experience in handling community development projects. This manager helps the sponsors to set a realistic budget in terms of time and money, and if necessary to get further support to make the work possible.

The conference design stage consists mainly in setting up a steering committee to work out what the community needs and resources are. It is important to get a fairly neutral and respected person to convene this committee, and someone similar to be the first chairperson, elected by the committee once it is operative. This steering committee is open through the whole process, and permits all groups to be heard; if it gets too big, an executive subcommittee may be set up. At this stage everyone is wary and watchful to see if there have been any predecisions or political alignments set up. Specific interests begin to emerge, and the issues which are going to be important start to come to the surface. Fantasy and fact intertwine, but the issues are sorted and tested within the group and the objectives of the forthcoming conference begin to take shape.

During this stage, too, the budgeting starts. This

consideration of costs sharpens the debate, and as it becomes clear that practical questions are being considered, other groups in the community, who had remained outside, now begin to want to participate. The committee enlarges, and the leadership tends to shift to those who are happy working in an open situation like this. At the same time it becomes clear that certain groups or individuals have to be invited to join, if certain issues are to be dealt with in any adequate way. The committee will also probably decide to pay a local co-ordinator to handle the increasing amount of administrative work.

The fact-finding stage begins when it seems clear what the main issues are, and those issues are properly represented on the steering committee. A task group is set up to consider each of the issues.

At this point several things begin to happen. The members of the committee are forced to declare themselves by identifying which issue is most important to them. The steering committee management checks its assumptions about the priority of the issues and notes which issues have strong or weak support. And the members of the task groups now can see who their allies are. (Schuttler et al. 1975)

The groups collect data which bear on their particular concerns, usually with the help of local officials or other bodies with access to the relevant facts and figures. Such groups usually run for three or four months, and may involve action research, desk research and just plain talking to a lot of people. Another task of the groups is to select technical consultants who may be useful. During this stage, the steering committee sets up a subcommittee to handle publicity, so that everyone in the community can know what is going on and feel fully informed. At a certain point a deadline for the conference is stated and held to.

The intensive problem-solving conference runs for between five days and two weeks (partly depending on the size of community) and may be held for something like sixteen hours a day. It can, however, also be run in evenings and weekends. Normally it is best, however, to have a full working day, and then an evening forum with public participation. The agenda is very flexible, but the process is controlled by a tight system of deadlines, to ensure that whatever emerges is properly worked out and feasible.

The participants are free to caucus, bargain, scheme and realign their interests, but they are taken through a series of steps that includes goal definition, problem clarification, solution analysis, programme planning, feasibility analysis and then a final push for consensus, commitment and an implementation strategy. (Schuttler et al. 1975)

Where possible, it is an advantage to have a graphical presentation, with charts and diagrams, at the evening meeting to make clear what the outcomes of the day's work are. Architectural students are often very good at doing this task. They can also be asked to make physical models at the end of the conference, where that is appropriate.

Much of the work is done in small groups, and it is for each of these groups to decide if and when it needs or wants to combine or consult with other groups with different interests, different issues. Halfway through the conference, there is a presentation to the local officials, at an open meeting where radio and TV are also present. This pulls the deliberations together effectively, and trial solutions are put forward here.

The officials' forum is a turning point in the process. Much of the rhetoric and early confusion disappears, and a core of determined community leaders begins to take charge . . . An air of excitement begins to grow . . . What seemed to be an amateur effort doomed to defeat now begins to look like a professional planning conference with a scope of solutions and new concepts never expected and seldom, if ever, seen in a community setting. (Schuttler et al. 1975)

This leads up to the final presentation, also public and attended by the relevant officials and the media. Politicians are invited to endorse key aspects of the plan which have won community support. This opens the way to implementation by the local authority during the coming months.

The implementation stage is particularly difficult. Officials may leave office or back out of their public commitment, committees may change their composition, funds may

179

disappear and community enthusiasm sometimes wanes. What counts now are the community leaders and the network of allies they formed during the earlier stages. They have to make sure that the final report is printed and published, that a time-schedule is drawn up including all the meetings of the relevant committees, and that appropriate pressure is put on to make sure that decisions are not forgotten. If this is done thoroughly, much more can be achieved than if everyone just sits back and congratulates themselves.

These are the five stages, then, of this particular plan. It is only one way of going about the matter, and has only been quoted at length because it is reasonably detailed and specific – much more so in the original than in the brief summary given here.

More recently, Byron Kennard (1982) has given a very good account of community development, emphasizing the need for community activists to look hard at their motivations for engaging in social causes. Besides the fact that most of us expect a lot in return for the efforts we put in to social movements, we often become overcommitted to them and put the rest of our lives out of balance. We are sometimes motivated by deep wells of anger and bitterness and the struggle becomes more important than the outcome – even than success.

He also emphasizes how community organization is a process of bringing out creativity. Humanistic psychology has always been certain that there is more creativity in people than they normally allow to emerge. This is connected with the repression of the sublime which we have alluded to earlier.

And humanistic psychology has been in the forefront of attempts to consider creativity as a normal attribute of ordinary people. Again there is a big difference from the approaches of other psychologies. For the psychoanalyst Kris, for example, creativity was 'regression in the service of the Ego', and this view has been widely accepted by Freudians and others. It means, in crude terms, that the creative person got his new ideas by, as it were, plunging into the Id and coming back with the goodies.

It was Schachtel (1969) who pointed out the error in this. He showed that far from losing oneself in the boiling cauldron of the Unconscious, one finds oneself in the object, idea or problem which is the focus of the creative endeavour. And he went on to say

> What distinguishes the creative process from regression to primary-process thought is that the freedom of the approach is due not to a drive discharge function but to the openness in the encounter with the object of the creative labour.

This is an important difference, because it enables the humanistic psychologist to assume that people only need a slight twist, in the form of a situation which gives them permission to be creative, and that they will then have such capacities available and on tap. The experiments of Liam Hudson (1970) in this country are very striking here – he only had to ask schoolboys to pretend that they were a bohemian artist or a successful computer engineer, and the quantity and diversity of their responses on a creativity test went up sharply.

Due to the efforts of people with a humanistic bias over the years, it is now possible to teach people very directly how to be creative, and manuals are now available which are easy to follow and very stimulating, for example Koberg and Bagnall's (1974) *Universal Traveller*. There are other more erudite volumes, such as Stein (1974), which tell you all about the research and extant knowledge about creativity without actually being in any way creative themselves.

And there is an interesting relationship between creativity and peak experiences. A peak experience can be the turning point in letting someone believe that she is indeed creative; but also an experience of creativity can itself be a peak experience. Indeed, every breakthrough in problem-solving or art work feels like a mini-*satori*. The 'Aha!' experience is not far from ecstasy, be it mild or intense. And as Carl Rogers (1970) says:

> The mainspring of creativity appears to be the same tendency which we discover so deeply as the curative

181

force in psychotherapy – man's tendency to actualise himself, to become his potentialities. . . . This tendency may become deeply buried under layer after layer of encrusted psychological defences; it may be hidden behind elaborate facades which deny its existence; it is my belief however, based on my experience, that it exists in every individual and awaits only the proper conditions to be released and expressed.

What we are saying, then, is that community development can be a way of getting people to get in touch with their own functioning, and awaken their perhaps long-dormant belief in themselves.

And so the important thing is not the actual achievements, which may be large and impressive or rather small and seemingly minor, but the process by which people become more competent to live with and gain some control over local aspects of a frustrating and changing world. This is a process planned by the participants to serve goals which they more and more choose. And in and through this process people grow and develop their capacities and their confidence and their self-esteem. So it is about personality growth through group responsibility for the local common good.

The people who have been through such a process, just because they are now more creative and more sure of who they are, are in a better position to decide whether what they now want is conflict or cooperation. And this is the answer to the political arguments we looked at earlier in this chapter. It is not a question of having a preconceived commitment to conflict or social harmony; it is a question of getting to a place where the people involved have a real choice. It is not a question of deciding to be in opposition before we start, but of finding out what we really want, and in the process finding out what opposition there is to that both inside and outside ourselves. It is only in this way that our choices can be genuine ones based on reality and taking into account all that which genuinely needs to be taken into account.

There are now huge numbers of community development

projects going on in this and other countries, and some of them are run with the kind of perspective we have been outlining in this chapter – but many are not. Because of the extreme dislike of the British for theory, many people working in this field do not even know that it is humanistic psychology which is at the back of the ideas and methods they are using, even when they are using them.

This may now be changing, and there are some signs that workers are becoming more conscious of what they are doing. There has been a training scheme for community development workers which combined the approaches of Saul Alinsky and Gestalt therapy, and this made a number of interesting discoveries. Ultimately it seems that some combination of political awareness and the awareness of personal growth must be more effective than either of these alone. As Jerry Rubin (1973) says:

> To love your body, to accept yourself, to know your own personal rhythm, to go inward, gives you better control of your own life, and makes you better able to change the oppressive economic and political structure. Awareness of self is the first step to awareness of cultural oppression.
>
> In fact, true self-awareness leads to the realization that full self-growth is impossible in a corrupt, repressed and polluted society. Therapy by itself can become very narrow and result in an overwhelming absorption with one's self. The final therapy is a social revolution.

What humanistic psychology is asking for, all the way through, in field after field, is for all of us to exchange the pain of alienation for the pain of awareness. And this is a hard thing to ask. It is hard because it is possible to switch off the pain of alienation by becoming numb. It is not possible to switch off the pain of awareness, once we have awoken to the realization that we are responsible but unfree. There is nothing for it but to go all the way. As Julian Beck (1972) once said:

> When we feel, we will feel the emergency;
> When we feel the emergency, we will act;
> When we act, we will change the world.

PART THREE

THE FUTURE OF
HUMANISTIC
PSYCHOLOGY

CHAPTER TWELVE

——————— ➤●❦ ———————

THE SPREAD OF
HUMANISTIC PSYCHOLOGY

AS WE have seen, the Association for Humanistic Psychology was formed in 1962. All through the 1960s the thing was growing in the United States, but outside there was little overt sign of the ideas or methods catching on. Probably most of what activity there was tended to be in the established fields of counselling (the Rogerian influence) and in organizational psychology (the influence of Maslow, largely channelled through the National Training Laboratories and other management professionals).

It was not until 1969 that the AHP started in Britain, through some people happening to come together at a conference of the British Association for Social Psychiatry. It was out of that meeting that Ruth Lassoff and John Wren-Lewis and Leslie Elliott started the British organization off. And in 1969 the first British growth centre was started up by Paul and Patricia Lowe, and called itself 'Quaesitor', which means seeker.

The AHP in Britain began by running a number of open experiental events, attended by some fifty to sixty people each time, and quickly built up a mailing list of about 500 names and addresses. It began to issue a Newsletter early in 1970, and set up a task group to decide how best to organize. The group consisted of Mel Berger, Eve Godfrey, Roger Harrison, Caron Kent, Ruth Lassoff, Paul & Patricia Lowe, Hans Lobstein and Bill Schlackman. Anne Elphick, Nina Quinn and John Adams were also involved at the start of 1970.

By May 1970 the AHP had forty-one members in Britain,

and the committee included Ann Faraday, Val Peacock, Peter Spink and Colin Sheppard, in addition to those mentioned before. Already there was pressure to start a British journal, and make specific contacts with industry, education, social work and academia.

In 1970 a big boost came through the visit to London of several leaders from the Esalen Institute, who put on two big events at the Inn on the Park, and also two for students, in Paddington. Michael Murphy, Stuart and Suki Miller, Alan Watts, Jackie Doyle, Will Schutz, George Leonard, Betty Fuller and others were here, and aroused a great deal of interest in the whole area. By August 1970 the membership list had gone up to seventy-six.

In 1971 it was decided to make a definite attempt to become better known in the field of academic psychology, and to get more members from that area. So the AHP set up two evening events on the campus of Exeter University, at the same time as the annual conference of the British Psychological Society. The first event was a talk by John Heron on the different ways of attending to behaviour, followed by an experiential event led by Paul Lowe and Jackie Doyle; and the second was a talk by Jacob Stattman on the concretization of affect in groups, followed by an experiential event led by Carmi Harari and Stanley Graham. These two events were extremely successful, about a third of the entire conference attending one or other of the events, and most of these attending both. To explain and supplement the experience, a booklet was handed out, containing a general introduction by Charlotte Buhler, information about the AHP, a book list and a sprinkling of quotations. This was also available later in the main conference office.

This event gave a lot of confidence that the British AHP knew how to do things, and knew where it was going. And it reflected some things which were going on elsewhere. In August 1970 the first international conference of the AHP had been held in Amsterdam, and participants came from the USA, the Netherlands, Britain, Denmark, Sweden, Norway, Belgium, France, Germany, Switzerland and

South Africa. Also in 1970 the first groups were started in Israel under the AHP banner.

In Japan in 1970 there were something like 400 people leading groups ranging from T-groups to encounter and psychodrama. This again started in the organizational field but became more oriented towards personal growth. Some became quite political, wanting 'to popularize the movement for the masses to liberate individuals from all that keeps them from being themselves'. There was an Institute of Group Dynamics at the University of Fukuoka and a professional association of T-group trainers with a membership of 150. A great deal of work was being done by the Japan Institute for Christian Education, with forty trainers doing a wide variety of workshops, many of which have no connection with the church as such. Some indication of the level of interest at that time was shown by the fact that the complete works of Carl Rogers had been translated into Japanese (eighteen volumes).

At the same time in the Philippines there was a great deal of activity and a Philippine Institute of Applied Behavioural Science, with a growing network of trainers doing groups for industry, the church, the university and a variety of community development projects. There was also a good deal of interest in the Department of Psychology at the University of the Philippines in developing a research programme on humanistic psychology.

All this was reported in the second number of the Bulletin which the British AHP started to bring out in 1971. Also reported in the same bulletin was the very successful conference held by the Group Relations Training Association (GRTA) that September. This was organized in a much more flexible way than the average conference, and included a much wider variety of activities – talks, demonstrations of leadership style, board games, encounter tapes, intergroup exercises, large group experiences, a marathon, a couples group, creativity training, achievement motivation training, Gestalt awareness exercises, 'The Marriage Grid', management simulation, and so on. It was arranged like a fair, with plenty of choices and repeats of some sessions, and it was very cheap. Before it happened some of the session leaders were worried about the disjointedness of the thing, and worried about how their work would be separated off. But:

> What happened in practice was that feelings generated in one session were often carried over into other later sessions. In effect, what was created was not a tightly-bound series of self-contained learning groups, but a much more flexible and open learning community. (*AHP Bulletin* 1971)

The GRTA is not committed to humanistic psychology, but this particular conference probably went further in the direction of that orientation than anything they have done before or since, both in form and in content.

In April 1972 the first Scandinavian Conference on Humanistic Psychology took place at the University of Stockholm, with about 140 people.

And in the same month the British AHP participated in the annual conference of the British Psychological Society, this time on an official basis, with a half-day symposium on humanistic psychology. This started off calmly enough with papers by John Heron and Peter Smith – but the third paper was by Sidney Jourard, who had come over from Stockholm specially for this session. It was called *Psychology for control, and for liberation of humans*:

> The agencies that believe it worthwhile financing research into human behaviour typically believe that their interests will be furthered if man's behaviour becomes less unpredictable. They want men to be transparent to them (while they remain opaque to the others), and they want to learn how to make men's actions more amenable to control . . . My hypothesis is, that unless the behavioural scientist explores the broader social, political and economic implications of his work, then he is a functionary indeed; worse, if he does not realize it, then he is being mystified by those who employ him.

This was hard-hitting political stuff, and it fitted in very precisely with the concerns of many people at the conference, who had in fact organized an informal meeting on ethics the previous day. They had been saying much the same thing – only here it was being said more fully and more eloquently, and by a distinguished professor, and in the name of humanistic psychology, to a packed audience in a large lecture theatre. (Two years later Sidney Jourard died in an accident, which was a sad loss to us and to the world.)

The rest of that conference was dominated by these events, which formed a major topic for the open meetings which followed. And out of this conference it was decided that the time had come to start a British journal. The time was ripe.

The international conference was held in Tokyo in 1972, and aroused a great deal more interest in Japan, though it was rather far to travel for anyone from this country.

In September 1972 the AHP (by this time I had been the Chairperson since the departure of John Wren-Lewis and Ann Faraday to America) together with the GRTA and Leslie Elliot's 'Ananda' organization, put on its most adventurous event yet, a four-day workshop under the title 'Creative change in Higher Education'. This again was arranged in 'fair' style, with many choices, but this time the afternoons were devoted to small group sessions where people could find ways of taking back what they had learned in the mornings to their own home environments.

About 150 people attended this event, and it showed how much interest could be aroused in the whole humanistic approach to education. Those giving presentations included:

Roger Harrison
Gurth Higgin
Angela Steer (later Summerfield)
Brian Thorne
G.W.H. Leytham
Jacob Stattman
Bill Tibbett & Laurie Cureton
Emily Coleman
David Warren Piper
Eve Godfrey

Peter Spink
Anthony Blake
Nick Georgiades
John Heron
Alan Dale
John Shotter

This was an encouraging event, which should have led to a spurt in activity; but around the end of the year (1972) Leslie Elliott left to live in America and Bill Schlackman withdrew from active participation. Both of these two men had contributed substantial resources of premises and secretarial facilities. We realized how much we had depended on these generous subsidies. From then on, everything we wanted we had to pay for, in time or money or both.

Not to be too parochial, however, it was also in 1972 that the AHP had a very successful meeting in Moscow on psycho-energetics and parapsychology, with 70–80 people, half from the USSR and the rest from France, Belgium, Austria, Switzerland, West Germany and the United States. Stanley Krippner and Carmi Harari, as well as several others, brought back information about important experimentation going on, essentially relating to tapping fields of psychic energy, which corresponded to the work of a number of US scientists closely associated with the AHP.

In 1973 the second AHP Scandinavian conference was held at Roskilde University; 250 people attended, and about 100 had to be turned away because of lack of facilities.

And in March 1973 the first issue appeared of *Self & Society*. This was the culmination of a year's thought and struggle, often difficult and trying. It was an independent venture by Vivian Milroy, but had a close relationship with the AHP, printing two pages of AHP notes every month. As soon as it could be formally arranged, it was made part of the AHP subscription package, thus ensuring a basic circulation. This made a great difference to the whole identity of the AHP in Britain; for the first time it had a living demonstration that humanistic psychology was active in a wide variety of fields. Contributions started to come in from many countries, and clearly it was of more than narrow interest.

At the same time the University Circus was operating. This was a small group of people within the AHP who were willing, for expenses only, to go to any organization which could provide twenty people at least and suitable premises, and put on a five-hour presentation of the theory and practice of humanistic psychology. This proved to be a successful enterprise, and the Circus went to over twenty different universities and colleges.

In July a big seminar was held in India, and a number of visits made, which aroused such interest in Indian universities that a conference was mooted for the following year. The main centres were Dehradun and Aligarh, and many important connections were made between humanistic psychology and Indian philosophy.

In September the International Conference was held in Paris, and several British members went to it. It was poorly organized, and a great deal of dissatisfaction was expressed that it seemed to be an American event held in France, rather than a European event. This was really the turning point in setting off the idea of a genuinely European conference.

In October in Britain the AHP attempted to get together all the organizations working in the field of humanistic psychology, so that they could actually meet and see each other. This turned out to be very exciting, and there was a lot of enthusiasm to take things forward and see whether some form of cooperation might not be possible. Two more meetings were held in November and December, but it became clear that if anything concrete was to come out of this, a great deal of time and energy would be needed. It seemed that a professional organization, separate from the AHP, was one possibility, but nobody wanted to found it. It was not until 1980 that this idea was brought to fruition with the formation of the AHP Practitioners group (AHPP).

The winter of 1973–4 was very active for the AHP in Britain, with six monthly workshops, including an important one on therapeutic communities, which was attended by seventeen different organizations, most of them outside the National Health Service. It was quite apparent that humanistic psychology and therapeutic communities fitted together, and that much could be gained by making those working in such places much more aware of how much they were using our approach, and how they could gain by doing it in a more self-conscious way.

In April 1974 we again put on a symposium at the BPS annual conference, with papers by John Staude, Peter Spink and myself, followed by an experiential event. About 300 people came to the papers, and 100 to the event. Also films of Fritz Perls were put on by Ken Holme of the Churchill Centre. By this time we were also able to distribute the AHP booklist, which we had got together the previous autumn, and which had been printed with the great help of George Brosan of the North-East London Polytechnic. This gave an annotated rundown of the books in the area of humanistic psychology which were felt to be central, and it was updated twice over the next four years.

International conferences were again held in Scandinavia and in India, at Andhra University. Later in the year, there was an important AHP symposium put on at the Inter-American Congress of Psychology at Bogota, in Colombia. As a result of it, an AHP chapter was set up in Venezuela. In the following year, the sixth international conference was held, this time in Cuernavaca, Mexico. About 500 people came, and it was felt to be a big success.

1977 was a very important year in a number of ways for Europe. In Britain the Association for Self-Help and Community Groups was founded by Hans Lobstein; the Antioch University MA in Humanistic Psychology was set up by John Andrew Miller; the first Primal Integration course was set up by William Swartley; and the first European Conference was held in London, organized by the AHP in Britain.

This conference, entitled 'Self Renewal', was very successful. About 200 people turned up, and seemed determined to make it a high-energy event. Five major presenters failed to turn up, and nobody seemed to mind too much. The schedule of lectures and workshops was in a continual state of flux. But some very important ideas were put forward. One presentation on 'A basic qualification in psychotherapy' sparked several efforts in the next year or so to start up training institutes with the humanistic approaches. And another on 'Research in the human sciences' started in motion the formation of the New Paradigm Research Group and its publication later of the book *Human Inquiry* (Reason & Rowan 1981).

In 1978 Michele Festa was inspired to put on the first Italian Congress of Humanistic Psychology in Rome, and to start publishing a magazine, *Psicoterapia Umanistica*. Carl Rogers went to Spain and put on a big international workshop and then came to England and did a week workshop for the Facilitator Development Institute. A second European Conference was held, this time in Geneva, thanks to the marvellous entrepreneurship of Sabine Kurjo and her centre, Vision Humaniste. As a result of the success of this enterprise – again about 200 partici-pants came – the European Association for Humanistic Psychology (EAHP) was formed, with Arnold Keyserling as its first President, and Sabine Kurjo as Secretary-General. In September a French AHP was formed, with Jacqueline Barbin as the most active moving spirit.

Nor was this all. In Britain two very important educational enterprises were started. One was the Institute for the Development of Human Potential, initiated by David Blagden Marks together with John Heron, Tom Feldberg, David Boadella, Frank Lake and others. This ran a two-year diploma course, which was later extended to run at a number of different centres all over Britain. The other was the Institute of Psychotherapy and Social Studies, which put on a three-year diploma course in psychotherapy, covering both the psychodynamic and humanistic approaches, to-gether with a good deal of attention to the social context within which all psychotherapy takes place. This was initiated by Giora Doron, and in the first year the staff included Joan Meigh, Helen Davis, Alan Cartwright, Luise Eichenbaum, Susie Orbach and myself. Unfortunately this was too heady a mixture, and there were splits and problems, leading to Helen setting up her own somewhat similar course under the title of the Association for Psychotherapeutic Process (later changed to the Minster Centre). The IPSS still continues with a high-level course involving people such as Ronald Laing, Morton Schatzman, Tom Feldberg, Petruska Clarkson, Dina Glouberman, John Southgate and myself.

In America Jean Houston was elected President, and initiated a three-year programme of social involvement. This led in the following year to an event which is best described in Jean's own words:

In April there was an extraordinary conference in Easton, Maryland. The US Departments of Commerce, Energy and the Interior pooled resources and under the sponsorship of the National Institute of Public Affairs brought together over 120 leading government officials and change agents from virtually every department to consider with AHP leaders how the possible human could lead to the possible society. For three days of intense exchange, speeches, small group seminars, and, yes, physical and mental exercises, we explored together the implications of humanistic values and practice on social change. Linear-analytic thinkers were in abundance as were hardnosed bureaucrats whose pathos was one of hopelessness. In the opening small seminars there were ten negatives given for every suggestion, the conversation rife with current trappings of Catch-22. But as we all continued in the atmosphere that we tried to create of real caring, of shared and deep inquiry, of acknowledgement and empowerment as well as fun and fanciful disinhibiting exercises, many among them came to feel differently about themselves and their roles. They discarded despair and began to explore in depth and detail the practical policy alternatives that could help engender the possible society. Networks were formed there, transformational lunch bunches agreed to meet and share regularly to enable each other's vision and to help bring these perspectives into government policies. We in the AHP were asked by a number of key officials to continue to assist and consult with their departments. And several weeks ago *The Washington Post* featured a long editorial applauding the conference and its efforts to improve government by first extending the vision and mind-sets of bureaucrats.

This was an activity which some of us would like to see reproduced in many other countries and much more frequently. But to the best of my knowledge it has never been repeated.

However, on the 28 August 1979 another aspect of the new attention to social action came to fruition, when at the Annual Meeting of the AHP at Princeton University entitled 'Evolutionary Ethics: Humanistic Psychology and Social Change' a resolution on nuclear power was passed. This was something quite new: the AHP had always set its face against political involvement. The resolution was so important that it seems worth while to give it here in full:

NUCLEAR POWER AND SOCIAL TRANSFORMATION

We the Executive Board of the Association for Humanistic Psychology wish to affirm our positive vision of the human potential and our conviction that a truly free, just and peaceful way of life can be achieved in our times. We believe, in fact, that our society may well be at the beginning of a new era of human progress.

But our reliance on nuclear power and nuclear weapons – the two are inseparable – endangers and could destroy this positive prospect. The immediate possibility of nuclear accidents and the difficulty of containing radioactive wastes for thousands of years threatens our children and their children with a legacy of birth defects, cancer, and an environment that will not support life. The excessive security requirements of safeguarding nuclear materials and vulnerable nuclear facilities threaten our political liberties. The institutional requirements for the concentration of wealth and power in huge, publicly unaccountable bureaucratic organizations, and the need for secrecy and public deception threaten to undermine democratic government. The safety requirements of infallible operation for thousands and tens of thousands of years put intolerable demands on fallible human beings and social systems. The expansion of nuclear technology increases conflict, stress and anxiety throughout the world.

We believe that all these dangers can be avoided. A more humane, less extravagant way of living is easily possible through greater emphasis on conservation, appropriate technology, and renewable sources of energy. We believe, in fact, that the turn away from nuclear power can mark an historic turn toward a more human-growth-oriented society.

Nuclear expansion depends upon a distorted image of the human being as a consumer whose well-being and sense of identity demand an ever-increasing use of energy and other resources. An evolution to higher levels of personal and social development requires the unfolding of a more holistic and positive vision of human nature. Beyond the failing nuclear dream is a new dream, a dream of deeper human relationships and more humane institutions, of lifelong learning and growth, of greater personal responsibility, more supportive human community, of lifestyles that are more efficient in the use of scarce resources, gentler on the earth, more ethical, more fulfilling.

We therefore resolve to take initiatives in support of research, education and social action dedicated to the emergence of a non-nuclear, human-growth-oriented society. We will seek helpful ways of dealing with the social and psychological transitions that must inevitably accompany a collective change of mind about nuclear power. And we will strive to articulate and realize new adventures of person and planet.

We of the Association for Humanistic Psychology publicly call for global nuclear disarmament, a moratorium on the construction of nuclear power plants, a phased decommissioning of existing plants, and a comprehensive program to conserve energy and implement the alternative, renewable energy technologies which already exist.

This was approved unanimously and confirmed in 1980. AHP in Britain adopted it in 1980. Some members did not like us taking this stand, and one or two actually resigned over it, but it marked a turning point in the history of attitudes within humanistic psychology. No longer could anyone maintain that it was neutral or value-free.

In Europe we had, for the most part, not gone that far; we were still occupied with spreading the word more generally. The European conference in 1979 was entitled 'Reaching Out', and a strong attempt was made to do exactly that. And it was very successful – again in Geneva organized by Sabine Kurjo, and this time under the aegis of the EAHP. There were 650 participants, and 100 presenters from 14 different countries – the biggest gathering in Europe we had had up to that time. *Self & Society* was inspired by this event into renaming itself the *European Journal of Humanistic Psychology*.

In the following year, the Association of Humanistic Psychology Practitioners (AHPP) was founded, with John Heron as its first Chairperson. This was another ground-breaking effort, because this had never been done in America, and still has not been done there or in any other country. What it does is to set up and maintain standards in all the fields where humanistic psychology is applied. There is a strict accreditation procedure whereby people first of all assess themselves, and then are assessed by their peers. Individuals are accredited in a specific area of practice for three years only, after which they come before a Review Board for re-assessment.

Members of this group have to satisfy strict criteria of training and experience, and since education is seen as a lifelong process, they are required to continue their own professional and personal development while they are members. They must subscribe to a code of ethical conduct and professional practice which means that any dissatisfied client has recourse to a complaints procedure which has ultimate powers of expulsion.

This group in its first year developed a method of self- and peer-assessment which has spread to many other groups and other countries. It consists of a formal sequence of operations, where a person conducts a live counselling session (or other activity) in front of a group of peers for 20 minutes or so, and then gets feedback from the group. This is extremely valuable for purposes of professional development.

In 1981 came a new magazine – *Human Potential Resources* – from the enterprise of Maureen Yeomans. This is a quarterly which contains many advertisements for humanistic practitioners and centres, and also interesting articles about humanistic approaches. It has survived various changes and continues to be a valuable source of information.

Later in the year came the fifth EAHP Congress, this time in Rome. This was an excellent conference, with Laing and Laborit as the two main protagonists. Five hundred people came to this one, mainly from Italy. The sixth Congress was in Paris, and even more people came to that one, breaking all records with about 800 participants.

It was interesting what was happening at this time. Two quite different movements were both progressing at the same time – one towards an increasing interest in the social aspects of humanistic psychology, and the other towards an increasing interest in spirituality. In 1982 there was a joint conference with the Wrekin Trust – rather New Age type of people at the spiritual end of the spectrum – and a special issue of *Self & Society* around psychology and spirituality.

The two things come together in Joanna Macy (1983), who in 1982 and 1983 began to do far more work on what she calls 'pain for the world'. This is a particular kind of pain, which is not psychological in the sense of being due to early trauma or existential *angst*, but is both social and spiritual. She runs workshops where people can face and own up to their despair at the state of the world – nuclear threats, ecological devastation, political oppression and all the rest – and come out the other side feeling refreshed and empowered. She is very much in favour of networking.

And networking was the theme of the AHP Annual Meeting in Toronto in 1983. Out of it came a number of networks and an extraordinary initiative by Wendy Roberts. She had had advance notice that a film called *The Day After* was to be shown on TV in some months' time – a film about what happens after a nuclear attack. She had the idea of setting up at least 100 Community Forums where people who had seen the film and been affected by it could talk to each other and find common cause and common meaning through it. Not only did she succeed, with a lot of help from AHP members and members of Joanna Macy's Interhelp groups, but in the end over 500 Community Forums took place, involving some 25,000 people, not only in the USA and Canada, but also in Hawaii, Britain and Germany. That same year there was a special issue of *Self & Society* on Peace, and the following year one in the *Journal of Humanistic Psychology*, which normally never has special issues on any political subject.

In 1983 came the first issue of the *Japanese Journal of Humanistic Psychology*, edited by Shoji Murayama. In September of that year thirty members of the International Association for Humanistic Psychology visited Moscow and other centres in Russia. This was to be the first of many yearly visits, usually for a fortnight, talking to Russian psychologists and other practitioners about matters of common interest.

March 1985 saw a big celebration in San Francisco of a quarter century of humanistic psychologies. All the big names were there, and over a thousand people took part over the three-day event. In the same year there was something quite new – a conference which started in Baden and then went over the border into Budapest. This was the first time that a really strong effort had been made to have a joint conference with a country like Hungary, and it was mainly due to the initiative of Laszlo Honti that it happened.

In 1984 and again in 1986 there was an attempt made to set up a real international committee which would genuinely represent humanistic psychology worldwide. But it seems that it is very difficult to do this, and maybe it is not really necessary. We shall see what the future may hold.

But of course the spread of humanistic psychology does not depend on the efforts of the AHP alone. Organization psychologists, counsellors, people in various fields of education and ordinary people who feel their consciousness to be changing are all affected. They read Carl Rogers, they learn group work and discover Moreno, they attend more to their peak experiences and find Maslow, they do management training and are exposed to the work of Argyris,

Blake & Mouton and the rest, they go to self-help groups and learn about Fritz Perls and Gestalt awareness, they go to demonstrations of body work and hear about Lowen and Reich, and so on and so forth.

It seems that still there are many people – perhaps most of those affected – who have the ideas without the experience, or the experience without the ideas. Both of these are lacking – it is as if the former had the words without the music, and the latter had the music without the words. But humanistic psychology is the kind of song which needs both words and music to carry its full message and its full effect.

So in the spread of humanistic psychology there are a number of contradictions. On the one hand it is probably more universal and less culture-bound than any previous psychology, but on the other it is always seen as very American, and arouses a lot of resentment and anti-Americanism. On the one hand it deals with what is common between people and works more often than not in group settings, but on the other it is seen as very individualistic and does actually seem to lead to people working separately rather than together. On the one hand it is very well integrated and consistent, but on the other it is seen as very fragmented, and leads in practice to people working in a fragmented way. On the one hand it is very open and receptive, opposed to laying trips on people; but on the other, it is seen as very intrusive and aggressive, and very heavily laden with values which it is busily pushing. On the one hand it is seen as too active, leading to panic and breakdowns; but on the other it is seen as too passive, leading to withdrawal from political involvement, and personal responsibility.

There have always been criticisms of humanistic psychology, and I suppose there always will be. We have touched on many of them in this chapter.

I don't profess to be able to answer or deal with these contradictions. I feel them myself. But it seems that humanistic psychology has been able to spread on a world scale in spite of them, so maybe it can go on doing so. In the next two chapters we shall be looking at some of the directions in which we might go in our search for answers.

CHAPTER THIRTEEN

———————— ✥ ————————

DIRECTIONS FOR THE SELF

IS THERE any way of drawing the threads together and seeing what is common to all the fields we have been studying?

First of all, is there any consistent message about the self – any indication of where we might go from here? Let us start off with that which seems most obvious – the personality.

THE PERSONALITY

What now seems to be true, and to be coming through from the ever-increasing amount of research now available (Verny 1982), is that experience starts early, way back in the womb, if not before. The mass of respectable academic research now being done on infants shows that babies are perceiving the world and making decisions about how to interpret it right from the word 'go' (Bower 1977). As far back as we know how to make any kind of tests, we find that babies are *making sense* of the world, not just responding to it blindly or automatically.

And in doing this, they soon find that certain kinds of ways of relating seem to work for them; they may be about getting what they want, or they may be about how not to care when they don't get it, and so on (Mahler et al. 1975). As time goes on, babies find that they have to relate differently in different circumstances; what works for one person does not work for another, and what works in one setting does not work in another. Also processes of identification are going on – 'This is me; this isn't me' – and people in the environment start to get internalized in this way, often under strong pressures. All this makes the personality, even in the first couple of years, become *differentiated* – one region, as it were, becomes specialized in one way, and others in other ways. And in all this there is a powerful element of fantasy – this specialization is not done in relation to the environment as it might appear to an impartial observer, but as it appears to a panicky person with a rich fantasy life, very willing to make up stories and paint pictures, and with very little sense of time before and time after (Segal 1985).

So by about four years old, the child has made some very important decisions about the world and her relationship with it, and split off various regions within the personality to deal with the people and situations which have been noticed.

I have put this in rather general language, but the same kind of story is in fact common to most forms of psychology which have attempted to deal with the same ground. Kurt Lewin (1936) puts it like this:

> The degree of dynamical connectedness of the different parts of the person can be nearly equal within the whole region of the person, or certain regions can separate themselves to an especially high degree from the others and develop relatively independently. This can be observed in the normal person . . .

If we take this point seriously, it makes us wonder why there is no discussion of this sort of thing in any of the texts I have been able to discover so far on the study of personality. But if this is true, it makes a great difference to the way we do our research and conceptualize our results. Which sub-personality is answering our questionnaire? Which sub-personality is taking part in our experiment? Which sub-personality is attending our group? As Gurdjieff (Ouspensky 1949) put it dramatically:

Man is divided into a multiplicity of small I's. And each

separte small I is able to call itself by the name of the Whole, to act in the name of the Whole, to agree or disagree, to give promises, to make decisions, with which another I or the Whole will have to deal. This explains why people so often make decisions and so seldom carry them out. A man decides to get up early starting from the following day. One I, or a group of I's decide this. But getting up is the business of another I who entirely disagrees with the decision and may even know absolutely nothing about it. . . . It is the tragedy of the human being that any small I has the right to sign cheques and promissory notes and the man, that is, the Whole, has to meet them. People's whole lives often consist of paying off the promissory notes of small accidental I's.

Once we begin to think in these terms, many things become clearer – we can start to see how our sub-personalities torture each other, how they play games with each other, how they play into each other's hands, and often how little they know each other. And once we know our sub-personalities and give them names, and find out what their nature is, what their motives are, they become powerless to harm us. A shadow is only strong when it is dark; once some light is shed on the scene, it changes colour and may disappear altogether.

But not only does this way of looking at things do good in freeing up our own internal world, it also does good in our relationships with others. Elizabeth O'Connor (1971) explains this very well:

If I say 'I am jealous', it describes the whole of me, and I am overwhelmed with its implications. The completeness of the statement makes me feel contemptuous of myself. It is little wonder that I fear letting another know when my identity with the feeling is such that it describes the totality of who I am . . . If I respect the plurality in myself, and no longer see my jealous self as the whole of me, then I have gained the distance I need to observe it, listen to it, and let it acquaint me with a piece of my own lost history. In this way I come into possession of more of myself and extend my own inner kingdom.

If each of us understood herself in this way, she would be able to give up saying things like 'Well, if she is that way, I want nothing to do with her', as though the 'way' of a person could be known just because one of her selves was glimpsed for a moment. We are able to listen to one sub-personality, and do justice to that, because we are not forced into the judgment that that is all there is. We can wait for the dialectical movement which is going to bring the next sub-personality out into the picture – maybe a directly opposed one. And this makes the job of listening much easier, because we have given up the impossible task of understanding a person better than she does herself. We can genuinely give ourselves up to following the energy to see where it leads today.

The theory of multiple selves seems to make a lot of sense, but it gives a lot of problems for the researcher. Kenneth Gergen (1972) has shown one approach, and James Vargiu (1974) another – I have also done some work on this myself, which was mentioned briefly in Chapter 6. It is obvious that if we have a number of sub-personalities and also a number of levels, then the possibilities for the number of combinations extend alarmingly.

Multiple selves also raise problems for the therapist. If we are busy trying to get people to take responsibility for themselves, is it not a cop-out to allow them to say – 'Well, you see, it was this sub-self that did it'? This is actually not as difficult in practice as it might seem in theory. Whatever form of therapy we go in for, we almost always come across sub-personalities in some form or other. It may be Freud's Ego, Id or Superego; or Jung's complexes or archetypes; or Berne's ego-states; or Perls's top dog or underdog; or Klein's internal objects; or Shapiro's (1976) sub-selves; the names change, but the reality is still there. It may be interesting to point out that even behaviourism, in the person of B.F. Skinner, (1974) has its version – in this case 'repertoires of behaviour'.

Humanistic psychology prefers to talk in terms of sub-personalities rather than regions or repertoires because this makes them easier to deal with in practice, and also because it seems truer to the pictorial way in which they are laid down in the first place.

Now it often happens that one of these sub-personalities becomes a general functionary, and gets given more and more jobs to do. This is usually the most highly socialized of the sub-personalities, and is often closely tied in with the male or female role. This is the one which most of the people in the child's circle will call forth by their expectations, by rewards and punishments, by referring to cultural norms. It is the sub-personality which we know we are *supposed* to be, whatever we actually are. When people praise us, and try to raise our self-esteem, it is often this sub-personality that they are boosting.

Now the tragic thing is that we can easily be taken in by this, to think that this sub-personality is our real self. It is so much us. It is what everybody knows and relates to – why wouldn't it be who we really are? But in fact it is just what Esterson (1972) calls an alterated identity – that is, it is something trumped up for someone else's benefit; it is something they wanted, and we survived because we produced it (see also Winnicott 1975).

To the extent that we firmly feel identified with this false self, it will be dangerous for us to entertain notions of self-actualization, self-realization and so on. What it will mean for us is some form of ego-boosting, some kind of inflation of this sub-personality. And we know very well that this is just going to magnify our existing faults and impose them more fully on other people. So the whole enterprise becomes ridiculous. And if, in spite of this, we go along with the therapy group or therapist or guru or whatever, and come to believe that we have achieved *satori* or some other kind of enlightenment, we are likely to have incredible difficulties in reconciling our sainthood with our humanity, and have to resort to all the methods which pseudo-saints down the ages have used. McNamara (1975) has a very good discussion of some of these points.

As Perls said, it is the difference between self-actualization and self-image actualization. The latter leads to the desperate straits of the man who said to me once – 'I think

I've got this spiritual thing pretty good now, but I still can't get on with my wife.'

The more we can work with the sub-personalities and really get to know them, the more easy it is to see that none of them is the real self. And when at last we allow ourselves to get in touch with the real self, we find that we don't have to take any special measures to deal with our sub-personalities – they take care of themselves and just become colourful facets with a lot of light, but no harm in them.

This may seem hard to believe, particularly because there is often one of our sub-personalities which seems evil, destructive, black and horrible. This may come to light during therapy, or in some other way, but it seems always to be a heavy experience to go through, when we discover it. Jung (1938) has described this as the archetype of The Shadow:

> Unfortunately there is no doubt about the fact that man is, as a whole, less good than he imagines himself or wants to be. Everyone carries a shadow, and the less it is embodied in the individual's conscious life, the blacker and denser it is. If an inferiority is conscious, one always has the chance to correct it. Furthermore, it is constantly in contact with other interests, so that it is steadily subjected to modifications. But if it is repressed and isolated from consciousness, it never gets corrected. It is, moreover, liable to burst forth in a moment of unawareness. At all events, it forms an unconscious snag, blocking the most well-meant attempts.

But this again is just another sub-personality, sometimes brought into being as a servant whose job it is to destroy the child's enemies, but who then starts to take over and get out of hand (the basis of the fascination with the Frankenstein story). But there is no need to destroy it; it contains a great deal of locked-up energy and excitement, which when released makes the person more alive and spontaneous. There is a lot of real love and real anger tied up in that congealed hate, and when it melts and starts to flow the results can be incredibly beautiful.

Although he uses different language, this is also the view of Mahrer (1978), who speaks of deeper potentials. These deeper potentials, he says, always have a good form, although they usually appear to us at first in a bad form. And again the answer is to own up to and enter into the deeper potential, so that we can reclaim the original good form it always really had.

Another person who has gone into this matter and said some helpful things is Watkins (1978) who draws on the work of Federn (also drawn on by Berne) to suggest that there are a number of ego-states, which amount to sub-personalities. We get into them by a process of ego cathexis, which he carefully distinguishes from object cathexis.

So it seems that this way of looking at the self, and the personality, and the sub-personalities, is potentially very rich, and deserves much more research to discover how best to conceptualize and describe the phenomena. Also perhaps there may be ways of handling children which are less likely to produce these very deceptive and over-inflated socialized sub-personalities, which as we saw in the chapter on sex roles can be very destructive both to men and more particularly to women.

Research in this area might also be productive because it may be that the way in which we treat people in our environment is closely connected with the way in which we treat our own sub-personalities. If one's first reaction to a sub-personality judged to be bad is to say – 'Cut it out, destroy it' – then this will perhaps be one's attitude to social, financial or political enemies. It might make sense to say that sub-personalities are to the whole person as social classes are to the whole society. There are many thoughts we could pursue along these lines, as I have suggested elsewhere (Rowan 1983b). If we can find out how to deal with the internal society, this may help us in our understanding of the larger society we live in.

The important thing is that in humanistic forms of therapy we do not try to get rid of the sub-personalities, but we do try to transform them (or allow them to transform themselves or each other). Ultimately we want all the sub-personalities to be merely seen as integrated filters to the real self.

THE REAL SELF

Using the term 'real self' in this way suggests that the sub-personalities are in some sense false. And in so far as they act independently they are false. They are not an adequate expression of who I am. They are partial versions of me, scraped up to meet a particular purpose, and resorted to in a kind of panic of choice.

But, as we suggested in Chapter 2, there are very difficult paradoxes involved in any notion of the real self. Let us see how they arise by taking it very slowly and watching our language very carefully. Do we simply mean the body? This is what Rogers (1961) calls the organism. From one point of view, it is identical with the self, and from another it is part of the environment of the self. It is this ambiguity which makes the body schema or body image such an important source of discontent for most of us, as Seymour Fisher (1973) demonstrates. Masters & Houston (1978) have shown with a wealth of detail how important the body is as a centre for our identity.

Or do we mean some kind of original self? This can be thought of from the inside as the 'I' (first person use) and from the outside as the 'me' (third person use). Heron (1972) refers to the primal self, and says that it can be looked on as a set of hypothesized potential capacities. Duval and Wicklund (1972) call it the 'causal agent self', and they make the point very strongly that this self does not need any outside agent to bring it into being – it is there all the time. But it has no namable characteristics – nothing specific can be said about it. When it relates to the internal or external world, it is the content of the relation, and itself the process of relating. It is empty and void of any content, and at the same time full of energy and life.

Or do we mean the embodied self? Will Schutz (1977) makes the important point that any really adequate approach to psychotherapy or to group experience must take the self and the body as being a unity, and he often speaks of the body/person/process where another writer might refer to the person. He makes the point, too, that the body contains the whole history (or histories) of the self in its encounters with the world. Perhaps the best discussion of this point of view is to be found in Dreyfuss & Feinstein (1977), where they say:

> Contemporary understanding of human functioning is tending to abandon the old notion that mind and body can be thought of as being separate entities and is adopting more holistic concepts, such as the soma: the total living, breathing, experiencing, indivisible *being*, whose parts cannot be meaningfully considered except in light of the whole person.

They go on to consider the body as a map of the past, as a map of our limitations, as a map of our potentials, and as a map of our universe. But it is also a gate to transcending the map. They talk about unhindering and unfolding, in the typical humanistic fashion, and this has been even more thoroughly brought out in Houston (1982).

Or do we mean the deep intention of the person? Sartre (1963) makes the point that in an important sense our projects are the most significant part of our self structure. What I want to do, what I want to be, what I want to happen – this is what defines my direction. It arises out of my values, my needs, my wants:

> The most rudimentary behaviour must be determined both in relation to the real and present factors which condition it and in relation to a certain object, still to come, which it is trying to bring into being. This is what we call *the project*. Starting with the project, we define a double simultaneous relationship. In relation to the given, the *praxis* is negativity; but what is always involved is the negation of a negation. In relation to the object aimed at, *praxis* is positivity, but this positivity opens onto the *non-existent*, to what *has not yet* been . . . Man defines himself by his project.

Again, this is not easy stuff to handle. But it is simply a part

211

of the truth which we have to come to grips with if we are going to make any sense in this area. There is no particular reason why men and women should be as simple as noughts-and-crosses. It is intentionality which makes the difference between behaviour and action (Torbert 1972). In humanistic psychology we are often reluctant to talk about behaviour, and are more interested in talking about action, for this very reason.

Or do we mean the realized self? Heron (1972) talks about this as the personality as re-created by systematic self-direction. We have seen a great deal about this in the course of these chapters. With Charles Hampden-Turner we can perhaps best see this as a spiral or helix where we have gone away from the original self into all the complexities of personality and role, and where we now come back again to the original self, only now on a higher level. Mahrer (1978) has an excellent discussion of integration and actualization as two distinct steps in the process of realization. This would also be the view of Jung, in his work on individuation (von Franz 1964).

Or do we mean the transpersonal self? When we first come across this, it always seems to appear as an outside force. We picture it as something which in some sense has something particularly to do with us, but a something unchangeable, which is not moved by the wheel of fortune. It is 'above the battle'. It has 'stopped the world'. It is like a star to guide us, or an angel to watch over us, or like a wise person on a mountain peak who can see it all. And we can be this star, be this angel, be this wise person.

All these different versions seem to have some claim to be considered as the real self. But recently the work of Ken Wilber has given us a way of sorting out this business much more satisfactorily. By referring to his map (Chapter 9) we can see that the primary self is not really relevant – it is too bare and too primitive to be much use to us, except as a conceptual starting point. At the other end, the transpersonal self goes beyond the realm of humanistic psychology and therefore cannot be what we are looking for. The body is again too primitive, going back to the very earliest forms of experience. The realized self is perhaps a bit ambiguous, but as described by the people we have quoted, it seems close to what we mean by the real self. Similarly the embodied self, because it implies a process of realization, can be very relevant to us. And the deep intention of the person also seems relevant; it is crucial to what Wilber calls the centaur stage, which is what we are mainly concerned with here.

We have avoided talking here about the soul, because up until recently there has been no treatment of the soul which seemed at all useful to the humanistic psychologist. But recently in the work of Frances Vaughan (1986) we do have a version which seems to make sense, and to be quite usable. One of her main points is that – 'How the soul is envisioned depends on the level of consciousness from which it is perceived.' In the years to come we shall see whether this approach fulfils its promise.

MULTIPLE LEVELS OF CONSCIOUSNESS

One final point we need to make here is that there is not just one condition or state to be studied under the heading of 'human consciousness'. People move into and out of a number of different states and stages in their development. And this is true not only in the trivial sense that we are sometimes awake and sometimes asleep; we are talking about a wide range of different 'spaces' that we can get into.

Now it is true that there is as yet no agreement on this variety of states, or even as to what kind of dimensions might be useful in describing them. Leary (1970) has seven levels. Lilly (1973) has nine levels. Stanley Krippner (1972) describes twenty states, but the waking state is just one of them. Maslow, Kohlberg, Loevinger and Piaget (see chart in Chapter 1) describe six or seven states, but they are all waking states. Ring (1974) describes nine different states, most of which are contained in one of Krippner's. And so on. It seems that we have a great number of things here, few of which have been studied in any detail, by psychologists or anyone else.

But the main point to see about this is that if we are

genuinely trying to explain human behaviour, or understand human actions, or interpret human conduct, it must be absurd to ignore these different conditions.

Tart (1975) has talked about state-specific science, and has suggested that a phenomenon can only be studied from a state of consciousness which is adequate to that phenomenon. Wilber (1983) has reinforced this view, and has criticized academic psychology for not paying more attention to this. We have already seen in a previous chapter how he has his own list of such states.

So what we are talking about all the time is a set of levels or states which a person can move into and out of, though not necessarily merely by wishing to. It is here that a question arises which seems worth discussing thoroughly: should we talk about levels (which seems in some ways an elitist way of talking) or should we talk simply about states, or spaces, with no implication at all that some of these are more rarefied than others?

It seems as though those who have gone furthest into the whole business of altered states of consciousness are all of the same opinion about this. Whether we look at John Lilly or Abraham Maslow, at the Greens or at David Wright; whether we look at the Eastern tradition or Western science, the same answer comes out – it is a matter of levels, and some levels are higher than others.

And there is a precise sense in which this is held; the higher levels are higher in that they include the lower levels, in a way which is not true the other way round. From a lower level, one cannot understand a higher level; but from a higher level, one can understand a lower level. This is, of course, related to the fact that one progresses from one layer to the next, so that one cannot rise above a level, in any genuine sense, without having been through it. So the person at a higher level can understand the lower level not least because she has been through it. A fuller account of this argument may be found in Wilber (1982).

Now is this elitist? It seems that it is only so if two conditions are satisfied: firstly there is an implication that only a few can reach the top levels; and secondly there is an

implication that those at the top levels are generally
superior to those at the lower levels.

As to the first of these points, humanistic psychology
says that people can naturally reach the further levels, and
that it is only if they are held back (by cultural pressures or
their own choices) that they will fail to do so. There is an
innate capacity for self-actualization, which only needs a
supportive environment to be realized. So it is not elitist in
this respect.

On the second point, humanistic psychologists are not
always fully in agreement. Rogers is quite clear that his
'fully functioning person' is just one possibility, and that
some people would rather aim at a person who is tightly
controlled and rigidly disciplined; and he certainly doesn't
come across in his films or books or tape-recordings as
someone who thinks of himself as superior. Maslow is quite
clear that his 'self-actualizing person' has faults and defects,
and is by no means free from guilt, anxiety, sadness, self-
criticism and internal conflicts. Perls I am not so sure about,
but if we take Barry Stevens as a living example of what
Gestalt therapy is all about, certainly she doesn't see herself
as superior to anyone. Here is where she is talking about
Herbert Talehaftewa, a Hopi Indian who was at this time
working on a construction job as a carpenter, while Barry
was on the same job as office manager (Stevens & Rogers
1967):

Cab, the owner and boss, was a Boston snob who looked
down on *everyone*, belittled them to the point where most
people who were subjected to it went to pieces and had to
pull themselves together again. One day I saw this man
look and speak to the Hopi in this way. Cab was a small
man, and the Hopi was quite tall and broad, but Cab still
managed to look down on the Hopi. I saw the Hopi look
at Cab so *equally* that he drew Cab down to his own
level – precisely, and not one bit lower – so that they
seemed to be two people eye-to-eye. I was so impressed
by this that I looked up to the Hopi as though he were
some sort of god. The Hopi turned to me with that same

strong *equalness* in his gaze, and I felt myself being drawn up until we were on the same plane.

Whatever we may feel about the language in which this is expressed, it seems to express an attitude pretty clearly, which is not an attitude of superiority. It is an attitude which, if anything, is critical of assumed superiority.

So it seems to me that, at least in its most central and substantial representatives, humanistic psychology is not elitist in this way either. It says that being a real person may be very rare at present, but it is just ordinary, not a cause for exaggerated respect, and not carrying with it any special privileges.

Some of the Eastern approaches seem to be much worse in this respect. If someone calls himself a Perfect Master, and carries on as though he did have a general superiority, this seems to be indefensible. But no one within humanistic psychology has yet done this.

It seems, then, that although the concept of levels is a dangerous one, and we rightly look upon it with suspicion, it does not necessarily lead to an elitist view. And we can surely accept this conclusion when we look over the various fields dealt with in this book, and see how in every field there is a general opposition to hierarchical social relationships.

CHAPTER FOURTEEN

―――――――――⋙◉⋘―――――――――

DIRECTIONS FOR SOCIETY

AND SO we come to the social scene. What does humanistic psychology have to say about that? Again it seems important to be personal here. This is not just an abstract question. One of the main discoveries I made is that there are three approaches to politics: one is to develop the best possible intellectual case, so that you can be more correct than anyone else; one is to be so militant and so activist that you never cease from some kind of action or other; the third is to see politics as about feelings and the way you live. It is the third kind of politics which seems to be closest to what humanistic psychology has to say. And when I get in touch with my feelings, what do I find?

When I look at most of what goes on in psychotherapy I get angry. When I look at the relations between men and women I get angry. When I look at the relations between straight and gay people, I get angry. When I look at what goes on in our offices and factories I get angry. When I see what happens in our schools I get angry. I have tried in this book to be positive rather than negative; to say what can be done, and what has been achieved, rather than dwell on the worst aspects of what is. But really I agree with Michael Glenn (1971) where he says:

> Therapy is change, not adjustment. This *means* change – social, personal and political. When people are fucked over, people should help them fight it, and then deal with their feelings. A 'struggle for mental health' is bullshit unless it involves changing this society which turns us into

217

machines, alienates us from one another and our work, and binds us into racist, sexist and imperialist practices.

And it is in and through the growth movement that I have come to see the world this way. It is with a taste of liberation, a touch of some new sensibility, that what I see around me turns into ugliness and horror.

I see a society which compels the vast majority of the population to get a living in stupid, inhuman and unnecessary jobs; which conducts its booming or failing business on the back of ghettos, slums and internal and external colonialism; which is infested with violence and repression while demanding obedience and compliance from the victims of violence and repression; which uses its vast resources for waste, destruction and an ever more methodical creation of conformist needs and satisfactions; which systematically puts children down under the guise of educating them; which turns women into drudges and men into image-defenders; which condemns marijuana and LSD while swimming in a bath of alcohol and cigarettes; which does not care about the environment, does not care about pollution, does not care . . .

The courts are not all right, the police are not all right, the local councils are not all right, the mental hospitals are not all right, the nuclear family is not all right, the universities are not all right, the medical profession is not all right, the way handicapped children are treated is not all right, the newspapers are not all right, IQ tests are not all right, what happens to the homeless is not all right; Star Wars is not all right; nuclear power is not all right; international diplomacy is not all right.

Even language is not all right. Somehow those who want things to stay as they are have captured the language itself (Miller & Swift 1979, Spender 1980). We find ourselves using their categories, fighting on their ground, talking in their terms, copying their style. I have tried to write this book directly, without jargon and without hiding what I meant under a hail of words – and of course I have failed. The horror and the twisting and the distortion are not just out there – they are right here, in me. I have written about the pain of awareness – well, this is it, this is what it feels like.

If, in spite of all this, it is all going to come out all right, we need to be really strong, and not let it overcome us. Luckily we don't get the awareness without the strength – they come together, in the same package. As Joanna Macy (1983) tells us, the only worthwhile hope comes up out of despair. In her workshops we learn just how this works. And they enable us to see that not only must we not give up, we mustn't get desperate about the pathways of change. The absurd situation is that the established democracy still provides the only legitimate framework for change and must therefore be defended against all attempts to restrict this framework – but at the same time, preservation of the established democracy preserves the status quo and the containment of change. There are no one-way, open-and-shut answers. All we know is that we have to struggle with love as well as opposition in our hearts. If we just have the love (as some of the New Age people suggest), the old ways continue their disgusting course, only touched with a certain glow, like phosphorescence; if we just have the struggle (as some of the political groups suggest), we soon become wooden soldiers fit for nothing but being pushed around by some leader. It is about love and struggle.

There is a very important misunderstanding here. New Age people often say that by paying attention to some evil we give it energy, we somehow feed it. But it was the people who ignored the Nazis who allowed the death camps and the pogroms to continue. It is not enough not to give energy to some social evil – we sometimes have to question it, to raise awareness about it and if necessary to fight it.

Once we see the way we treat our bodies as political, the food we eat as political, the raising of children as political, the way we look at people sexually as political, we cannot rise above or turn away from the challenges which face us day by day and hour by hour.

The ideology of Thatcherism is so hostile to everything we stand for that we cannot just stand back and see it rise and rise without any comment and without any response. We have to care for our fellow human beings who are alienated and deprived: material deprivation is common enough, but emotional and imaginative deprivation is important too. When I notice these things, I find it hard to keep calm.

That is where I have to start from. But although anger is

a good starting point, it is not much good as a guide to what to do. In trying to spell out the implications of this, I want to say that there have been two phases in the way humanistic writers have spoken about society. In the first phase humanistic writers talked mainly about humanity as a whole; while in the second phase there has been more awareness of the depth of the patriarchal split which has divided women from men. For example, one of the researchers who has been found most valuable in this book is Lawrence Kohlberg (1981), but anyone who has come across the feminist critique of his work by Carol Gilligan (1982) will know that there is much that is deeply wrong with Kohlberg's approach, and in particular the assumptions he makes about the way that men see the world and the way that women see the world.

So let us start with phase one.

PHASE ONE: THE UNIVERSAL APPROACH

One of the best writers in this area is Christian Bay, who has written a number of pieces, the best known of which is the book *The Structure of Freedom* (1968). He was a political scientist, and wrote:

> I am convinced that our profession will never help us advance from our wasteful, cruel pluralist pseudopolitics in the direction of justice and human politics until we replace *political systems* with concepts of *human need* and *human development* as the ultimate value framework for our political analysis. (Bay 1967)

He made an important distinction between politics, which is all about the power to satisfy real needs, and pseudopolitics, which is all about satisfying the vocal demands of pressure groups, no matter how narrow the interests being served. The crucial thing is not to obstruct human development:

> How can people construct a society so as to provide for maximum growth opportunities and satisfaction of their needs? (Bay 1965)

Bay argues that only a society in which people are positively encouraged to reach Maslow's self-actualization level can ever be truly free. People at this level actually have a capacity to cooperate voluntarily, and not to demand control. At this level social freedom is possible, because people can set up a structure which allows the necessary opportunities to act or refrain from acting as they desire. (See also Bay 1971.)

Another writer who has written along these lines is David Wright, a sociologist much influenced by the research of Jane Loevinger (1976) on ego development. Her well-researched and empirically grounded work ties in, in a remarkably strong and apt way, with the more speculative work of Maslow. In particular, the final stage which she calls *Integrated* fits in very well with Maslow's (1970) self-actualization level. Wright says of people at this level that they are autonomous and genuinely individual:

> Yet 'autonomy' and 'individuality' should not be mistaken for 'individualism'. There is a social context to their independence that is implied by their principles. By taking everyone's perspective into account in any particular situation, they are explicitly 'other-oriented' (though not 'other-directed') and view their selves within a larger context of mutual interdependence. Moreover, these people have a deep feeling of identification, sympathy and affection for human beings in general and they view their selves and others as part of a common humanity. (Wright 1973)

Wright makes an important distinction between indoctrinated control and voluntary co-operation as a basis for social order, and argues that the former comes essentially from the middle levels of development, and holds people back at those levels.

> Thus, to emphasise the contrast, one basis views meaning and action as derivative from the social order; the other sees the order itself as derivative from the people's meaning and action. One postulates the society's creation and control of members; the other postulates the people's creation and control of their society. (Wright 1974)

In a major effort at theory-building, Wright uses Maslow's ideas to build a synthesis between the conflict perspective of people like Marx and Dahrendorf and the equilibrium perspective of people like Parsons and Smelser. He points to the necessity for social transformation involved in taking Maslow's ideas seriously:

> In sum, we have presented support for the view that people located at stage 6 and the self-actualized need-level tend to actively respond to situations of perceived injustice. Thus, people at earlier need-levels will struggle to become self-actualizing and, once there, will tend to act on their universal moral principles. As a result, change is ubiquitous and continuous, no matter where people are located on the need-hierarchy. (Wright 1973)

Wright therefore argues that it is worth contending for a society where this happens more readily – a society where the positive nature of human needs is better recognized. Charles Hampden-Turner (1971) is excellent on the whole process of psychosocial development and its problems, and what Wright is saying here chimes in well with the position taken up by Hampden-Turner.

A third writer who has spoken of these things is Walt Anderson. He again speaks of the higher levels of human development, and of what happens when the social scientist reaches those levels:

> Scientists will no longer think of themselves as detached from nature, as disembodied intellects in the sense Hannah Arendt (1958) meant when she described the rise of modern science as the point, the place to stand *outside* the world. Rather, they will understand and feel that they are a part – the conscious, deciding and *responsible* part – of the very evolutionary process they study. (Anderson 1973)

So he, too, comes out in favour of a society where more people are encouraged and allowed to reach the higher levels of development – Maslow's self-actualization, Loevinger's integrated state, Kohlberg's level of conscience and principle – and he sees this as definitely possible:

I believe that the drive toward self-actualization is, as Maslow insisted, species-wide and not peculiar to any race, culture or sex. The predominance of white males among the historical figures considered to be examples of self-actualized people is not so much a flaw in Maslow's research as evidence of the inadequacy of a society which offers such a narrow spectrum of its members the opportunity to reach their fullest development as 'human beings'. I would argue, therefore, that the middle-class bias is relatively superficial, and that humanistic psychology is in fact a comprehensive set of ideas relevant to the needs of *all* people. (Anderson 1973)

It is this sense of important possibilities being ignored which runs through all the arguments we have been looking at here. Society as organized at present has little notion of human development in the Maslow sense, and holds people back to the levels at which they can play fixed and predictable roles most efficiently.

When we look at politics this way we naturally turn our attention to the things which obstruct human development. And I believe that the most important single limiting factor is the idea that any society has about what the possibilities of human development actually are. A stunted or narrow conception of the human potential, especially when deeply built into cultural norms and reinforced by a society's art and science and philosophy, is as narrow a form of tyranny as any political institution. (Anderson 1973)

Another implication of all this is that the person-centred society would be decentralized. We have seen that in organizations it has been found best to place the decisions as near as possible to the place where the knowledge to make those decisions first becomes available. The same applies in society generally. It is bad for a larger and higher organization to arrogate to itself functions which can be performed efficiently by smaller and lower bodies. There is work to be done at every level, and the responsibility for what can be done at lower levels must not be allowed to gravitate to the top. The general principle of autonomization applies all the way through.

In a more recent book, Anderson (1983a) carries on the theme of decentralization, and many of the contributors to this book have much to say on how we have to go beyond liberalism.

This means that each citizen can and should have the experience of genuine participation, which means having a direct say in the political decisions which affect her. There is a spirited discussion of this whole area in Hampden-Turner (1983). The desire for this kind of participation comes both from greater opportunities, and also from the feeling of being competent. As Brewster Smith (1974) says:

> the motivational core of competence is a cluster of attitudes toward the self as potent, efficacious, and worthy of being taken seriously by self and others. Such a cluster of attitudes sets a kind of self-fulfilling prophecy in operation. In the favourable case, the individual has the confidence to seize upon opportunities as they present themselves. He tries. He therefore acquires the knowledge and skills that make success more probable – which in turn lend warrant to his sense of efficacy.

Such a society would be likely to be high in synergy, since there would be no need to see everyone else as competitive for limited goods. The power of imagination would be released to solve problems creatively.

Thus this scenario has a gradual movement towards a different state of society, along the lines outlined by Charles Reich (1972) in his popular book. Instead of Consciousness I (go-getting individualism) or Consciousness II (conformity, the organization man and the domination of technique) we have Consciousness III (person-centred). A similar view has been put in different terms by Capra (1983) and by Ferguson (1982). Or as Maslow (1973) puts it: 'The movement toward psychological health is also the movement towards spiritual peace and social harmony.' If only it were as simple as that.

EVOLUTION OR REVOLUTION?

So what is this saying about evolution and revolution? Just that it seems wiser to have at the back of our minds the notion of revolution, rather than the image of evolution. Just as couples can stand more honesty than they think they can, so groups and communities and whole nations can stand more change than they think they can.

But perhaps words like evolution and revolution are just debating points – alternative maps which really reveal the same territory. I don't feel very comfortable with either of them – the one suggests some kind of biological determinism, and the other suggests red-eyed mobs. Perhaps we should take a leaf out of the book of the organization specialists, and talk about 'social development' as what we are really interested in.

So where does that put us politically? We are not Fascist, because we value thought, and theory, and science; and we do not value great leaders or hierarchical structures of authority. We are not Conservative, because we want change, and radical change at that; we have some severe questions about the nuclear family and traditional female/male relationships; we do not value nationalist symbols such as the flag. We are not Liberals, because although we are somewhat individualist, we do not believe that people work in terms of conscious rational calculation very much of the time; we do not believe that the capitalist system is basically innocent. We are not Labourites, because we do not believe in smooth unbroken progress; we do not believe that all necessary changes can be made from the top; we do not believe that economic tinkering produces any real change. We are not Marxists, because we do not believe in public ownership and national planning (but rather in generalized self-management); we do not believe in class war and revolution (but rather in collaboration through conflict); we do not believe in massive class movements based only on material interests (but rather in the quality of individual personalities developed through living/learning experiences). We are not Anarchist, because we believe in construction

225

rather than destruction; we believe there is a place for experts and teachers, so long as they do not become identified with their roles; we are willing to work with the system, as well as being ready to bring it down.

To people who are used to the conventional political spectrum, humanistic psychology is hard to place. Probably we are closer to the politics of experience (as described by Juliet Mitchell (1971) than to the politics of platforms and programmes; probably we are closer to the developmental Left (as described by Hampden-Turner) than to the dogmatic Left; we have something in common with the libertarian Left, and something in common with the Christian Democrats (Fogarty 1957); we have a great deal in common with the Green movement (and will come back to this in the next section, where we also look at eco-feminism); and we have a lot of sympathy with Marcuse (1969) when he says:

> Socialist solidarity is autonomy: self-determination begins at home – and that is with every I, and the We whom the I chooses. And this end must indeed appear in the means to attain it . . . If the socialist relationships of production are to be a new way of life, a new Form of life, then their existential quality must show forth, anticipated and demonstrated, in the fight for their realization. Exploitation in all its forms must have disappeared from this fight: from the work relationships among the fighters as well as from their individual relationships. Understanding, tenderness toward each other, the instinctual consciousness of that which is evil, false, the heritage of oppression, would then testify to the authenticity of the rebellion. In short, the economic, political and cultural features of a classless society must have become the basic needs of those who fight for it.

Personally, I don't like the word 'Socialism', because historically it has become associated with a great number of horrific events, far from anything which I could see as humanistic in any sense. It has been associated with great disappointment and great betrayal, and I don't trust it any more. But I think I know what Marcuse is talking about, and I don't think we are that far distant from one another. (Also Rowbotham et al. (1979), the same applies.) I think the kind of society which is implied by the vision of humanistic psychology could be described as a classless society.

As humanistic psychology gets into sociology and into politics it grows and changes. The book edited by Glass and Staude (1972) shows how sociologists are finding in the humanistic approach a new inspiration and some new directions. In the months and years to come more and more effort needs to be put into this area, as humanistic psychologists see more and more clearly the social implications of their work and start to cooperate with professionals and lay people in other disciplines.

And as this happens, I think both psychology and sociology will become less and less academic specialisms open only to the few, and more and more open dialogues with those who are actually affected and actually involved with specific social changes. There will be fewer experiments and surveys, and more action research, intervention research, participant observation, self-study (Gouldner says that this new sociology would prefer the seeming naïveté of soul-searching to the genuine vulgarity of soul-selling), co-operative research (which we consider at length in the next chapter), and generally more deep involvement.

> One wonders if these biases (cultural, national, class and gender) can be understood only through self-study and through study of societies, or if such self-understanding of society must be accompanied by attempts at changing both self and society on multiple levels. Humanistic sociology would do well to opt for the latter. (Stein 1972)

In this way comes the knowledge we need for intelligent and creative social change.

PHASE TWO: QUESTIONING PATRIARCHY

All this sounds perfectly plausible, but there is something still missing from it. And what is missing is any real

227

appreciation of the feminist critique. Feminism has raised the issue that in our present society women are put down and all that is female is downgraded. In a future humanistic society, they say, that could easily continue. Just because so many men in the field of humanistic psychology have developed their feminine characteristics to some extent, and have to that degree stopped downgrading the female inside themselves at least, that does not mean that they will stop oppressing women. It often means that they do it better, more efficiently. In a typical centre for training people in the caring professions, 80 per cent of the participants will be women, but 80 per cent of the leaders will probably be men.

So if we are to do better than this, if we are to enable some kind of non-oppressive society to dawn, we have to understand something about patriarchal consciousness and how it works to the detriment of both women and men – not to mention children, animals and nature.

The diagram below, taken from Gray (1982), shows the

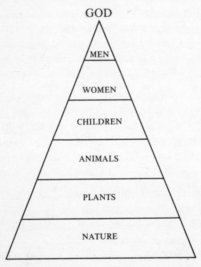

Figure 3 The world map of patriarchy. Taken from Elizabeth Dodson Gray, *Patriarchy as a Conceptual Trap*, Roundtable Press 1982

basic structure of patriarchy. It exposes, with pitiless clarity, the simple nature of the oppressive structure. All other oppressive relations are based upon this model. This comes first. And once we see the world exposed in this way, it enables us to connect the political with the personal, it even applies to the conscious and the unconscious mind, it includes the material and the spiritual.

> Patriarchy is a society which worships the masculine identity, granting power and privilege to those who reflect and respect the socially-determined masculine sex role. (Warnock 1982)

But patriarchy is an historical structure, which came into being and can go out of being, and has internal dynamics which are changing it. It is nothing to do with biological determinism, as some critics suggest. It is about socially/historically defined gender, not about biological sex.

It was feminism which allowed us to see that all the struggles against oppression are one struggle, the same struggle, the struggle with patriarchy. And this includes the struggles for children's rights, animal rights and the concern for ecology against the exploitation of nature. It is very important that the black struggle and the lesbian and gay struggle are one with the women's struggle. A member of the National Black Feminist Organization said:

> We are often asked the ugly question, 'Where are your loyalties? To the Black movement or the feminist movement?' Well, it would be nice if we were oppressed as women Monday through Thursday, then oppressed as Blacks the rest of the week. We could combat one or the other on those days – but we have to fight both every day of the week. (Quoted in Dunayevskaya 1982)

I have argued at length elsewhere (Rowan 1987) that questioning patriarchal consciousness is just as important for men as it is for women, blacks, lesbians or gay people. Men lose a great deal under patriarchy, and would gain a great deal from a non-patriarchal society. It is in the interest of men to work for change in this area (Farrell 1974). But it is harder for men to change than it is for women, because at a conscious level they often seem to gain from patriarchal power (Reynaud 1983), at an unconscious level they are at the mercy of their conditioning (Metcalf & Humphries 1985), and at a spiritual level they have no notion of the Goddess (Starhawk 1982). So men often have to work at all three of these levels in order to change their internal responses to women and to power in the world. And unless they are willing to do some of this work, they are going to stand in the way of the oppressed groups who need change much more urgently.

Women have already seen a lot of this, and particularly, it seems, those women who have made links with ecological issues, peace issues and the issues around the development of a new spirituality. Hazel Henderson (1982) has made an acute economic analysis showing that we have to keep all the connections in mind if we are to think reasonably about society. It is not enough to talk about decentralization – some very dubious politicians can talk about decentralization too, in their own way – we have to keep in touch with all the relevant factors, and listen to the voices from below.

And this means listening to nature. Henderson (1982) says about this, after discussing the basic economic realities:

> The planet, Gaia, and the universe are now teaching us humans directly, nudging us along in the direction we must change, reconnecting us with the most fundamental living force, the urge to become all we can be, to evolve and to love it. We have this optimal program encoded in the proteins of our DNA. We *know* how to be healthy, how to co-operate as well as compete. These are older, deeper programs than our cultural programming. We are learning to tune back into them and to Nature, our surest teacher.

This speaks of a kind of eco-feminism which goes beyond the male eco-philosophy which preceded it. It speaks of what Wright (1982) calls moonpower. See also many of the contributions in Spretnak (1982).

POWER AND CHANGE

All this, of course, makes us ask the question – 'What do we do about it?' How are we to take power to change the patriarchal system? And how are we to use it? Zaltman (1973) has given us seven types of power; Hersey et al. (1979) give us seven bases of power; combining the two gives us these nine forms of power:

1 *Physical force; coercive power*   This is a form of power which can produce compliance. It is seldom any use for any length of time, unless accompanied by one of the other forms of power.

2 *Connection power*   Based on connections with influential or important people. Induces compliance from others because they try to gain favour or avoid disfavour of the powerful connection.

3 *Rewards and punishments; reward power*   Another form of coercion, where the stick and the carrot are used to ensure compliance. Not very effective unless accompanied by fear on the part of those on the receiving end.

4 *Manipulative*   Behaviour is influenced rather than ideas. Rewards and punishments may be used as in behaviour modification. All sorts of Machiavellian tactics, including cue control. Many examples in the book by Varela (1971).

5 *Normative-legitimate; legitimate power*   Norms, rules and values are referred to in using and maintaining power. The strength of this will of course be strongly related to the strength of the relevant norms, etc.

6 *Expert power*   Based on possession of expertise, skill and knowledge. The expertise to facilitate the work behaviour of others. This leads to compliance with the leader's wishes.

7 *Charisma; referent power*   A non-coercive form of

power which relies on identification as the psychological mechanism for ensuring the correct behaviour. People will go along as long as they feel drawn to the leader.

8 *Rational-persuasive; information power*   Use of relevant information to persuade and influence, such data being related to the subject in hand rather than the person to be influenced.

9 *Synergy*   Growth-oriented power, obtained through facilitation of the needs and interests of others, as in organization development, individual therapy or experiential learning, or community development. This is the one which is often called power-with, as opposed to power-over, and it is compatible with what Starhawk (1982) talks about as power-from-within. Can be creative.

These categories can of course overlap, or be mixed. But they make quite a useful list of what is available. The question now is – which of these can be used in dealing with the problem of patriarchy? And as soon as we ask the question it must be evident that many of these forms of power actually reinforce patriarchy, or take it for granted. If we want to question patriarchy, we must question some of the ways of attacking it. Types 1, 2, 3 and 4 seem very difficult to use without setting up the very social relations which we want them to overthrow. Types 5, 6, 7 and 8 are also rather dubious, though much will depend on the actual content of the norms, etc. If the norms or values are deficiency-motivated, they are likely to be helpful to patriarchy, while if they are abundance-motivated (see Chapter 15), they are likely to be incompatible with patriarchy.

But the type of power which is most useful for dealing with patriarchy is obviously synergy, since this is all about power *with* people, rather than power *over* people. And one of the most distinctive and characteristic features of patriarchy is that it is dedicated to, and depends upon, the notion that power is always over people.

232

However, synergy is by no means an infallible password, any more than is decentralization. For example, I find Peter Russell's (1982) discussion of synergy to be far too blue-sky and over-optimistic in the New Age manner. I think we have to keep our feet on the ground with synergy as with everything else.

With this in mind, let us look at the acute analysis of social action developed by Philip Kotler (1973) where he makes some very important distinctions. He suggests that there are five main elements:

- *Cause*   A social objective or undertaking that change agents believe will provide some answer to a social problem.

- *Change Agency*   An organization whose primary mission is to advance a social cause.

- *Change Targets*   Individuals, groups or institutions designated as targets of change efforts.

- *Channels*   Ways in which influence and response can be transmitted between change agents and change targets.

- *Change strategy*   A basic mode of influence adopted by the change agent to affect the change target.

Now what is the cause here? It is tempting to see it as the overthrow of patriarchy, but it seems more modest and more appropriate to see it as the questioning of patriarchy, so that at least it is not taken for granted and hidden or mystified. Another point worth clarifying is that when we question patriarchy, it is not because we want to put matriarchy in its place – it is the whole system of domination of one set of people by another set that we are questioning, and not the substitution of one set of dominators by another.

Kotler suggests that there are three basic types of cause; *helping causes*, which seek to help the victims of a social problem; *protest causes*, which seek to discipline the institutions contributing to it; and *revolutionary causes*, which seek to eliminate the institutions contributing to it. The cause of questioning patriarchy seems to contain elements of all three: there do need to be answers for individual victims; the contributing institutions do need to be disciplined; and ultimately we do want to eliminate patriarchy. This being so, it seems that more than one change agency might have to be involved. This is a problem which extends from the family to the whole industrial system.

And there is one extra difficulty which does not apply to most other social problems: in questioning patriarchy we are questioning something which is built into the nuclear family, and therefore built into the growing psyche of each child in our culture. Juliet Mitchell (1974) has spelt out the extraordinary way in which patriarchy has entered into our language and our thinking at deep unconscious levels. John Southgate (Southgate & Randall 1978) has suggested that it makes sense to talk in terms of a Patripsych – an internal structure which exists inside all of us and which is easily hooked by authority figures, producing exaggerated reactions of one kind and another. If anything like this is true, it means that we have not only to contend with the patriarchal structures in our society, of which social class is one of the most important; but also the Patripsych inside us. This thought has also been taken up by a group of radical psychiatrists in the United States, of whom the best known is Claude Steiner. One of them, Hogie Wyckoff, (1975) has written:

> In women's groups, women can become familiar with what insidiously keeps them down – not only the obvious, overt male supremacy . . . but also oppression which has been internalized, which turns women against themselves, causing them to be their own worst enemies rather than their own loving best friend. This internalized oppression I have called the Pig Parent. It is the incorporation of all the values which keep women subordinate . . .

This is not unlike the self-denigration of minority groups, which has often been investigated. But Wyckoff and her group have been working on ways of breaking down these patterns in individual people.

So we must be concerned with the dancers as well as the dance. A system as all-embracing as patriarchy has to be dealt with on many levels at the same time – no one approach is likely to be adequate on its own. This again suggests rather strongly that more than one change agency will be required to deal with the problem.

It is enough to think of a few of the contenders in various parts of this field to see at once that not only are the various efforts very uncoordinated (for some excellent comments on this problem see Rowbotham et al. 1979), but that also there are patriarchal elements still surviving within many of them. Probably the most consistent one, in avoiding all kinds of relapse into patriarchy, is the women's movement.

And within the women's movement we find the kind of eco-feminism which is very close to the vision of humanistic psychology, deeply concerned with the integration of all the forces in nature and society. As Kornegger (1975) says so well:

> Together we are working to expand our empathy and understanding of other living things and to identify with those entities outside of ourselves, rather than objectifying and manipulating them. At this point, a respect for all life is a prerequisite for our very survival.
>
> Radical feminist theory also criticises male hierarchical thought patterns – in which rationality dominates sensuality, mind dominates intuition, and persistent splits and polarities (active/passive, child/adult, sane/insane, work/play, spontaneity/organization) alienate us from the mind-body experience as a *Whole* and from the *Continuum* of human experience. Women are attempting to get rid of these splits, to live in harmony with the universe as whole, integrated humans dedicated to the collective healing of our individual wounds and schisms.

This is very much the voice with which we have been familiar all through this examination.

Coming back to our question, then, what kind of change agency would be suitable for carrying on the struggle to question patriarchy? It seems that it must probably be an organization dominated by women, or at least the kind of vision which women have particularly been responsible for developing, and that it must be organized in such a way as not to set up all over again the social relations of patriarchy. There is a very good discussion of all this, with many practical hints, in Coover et al. (1978). We saw in Chapter 8 that organizations did not have to be hierarchies, so it is by no means impossible for such an organization to exist. But the men in such an organization would have to have been through the men's movement, or something like that, in order to be able to work in such a set-up.

The men's movement is something I have tried to describe elsewhere (Rowan 1987). Warren Farrell (1974) is quite informative, and the Pleck and Sawyer (1974) book has a useful bibliography; another excellent collection of papers is Snodgrass (1977). It arose mainly as a result of the women's movement making it clear to men that their behaviour was not acceptable in certain ways. After a number of one-to-one struggles within couple relationships, men began talking and finding that they had things in common. Their eyes had been opened to things about themselves which they did not know before. And so they started meeting to try and work things out, and see how they really felt about themselves. These meetings were often very tense, because the men felt pressured into self-examination, and defensive about many things. The meetings were often unsatisfying because of this defensiveness, usually manifesting itself in a persistent tendency to go off into theoretical diatribes or compulsive activity rather than real attempts to get in touch with feelings and to critique daily actions. But imperfect as they were, and are, these meetings are seemingly the best way for men to find out at least something about how they are affected by the social relations of patriarchy, both internal and external. The Men's Antisexist Newsletter deals with these matters, and so does the magazine *Achilles Heel*.

However, if these groups are to be effective, as I have argued at greater length elsewhere (Rowan 1987), they have to work on three levels. On the first level, they have to

enable the participants to examine their current consciousness and actions. This is the basic consciousness-raising
function which can work very well in enabling men to
change their assumptions as to what is proper masculine
behaviour, and to enable them to relate much better to
other men.

On the second level, they have to enable the participants
to go into the unconscious determinants of their actions.
This is more difficult, and requires a commitment to some
form of personal growth work. Only in this way can men
really get down to their mother stuff, their father stuff and
all that material which unconsciously prejudices them
against women and all that is female. (Many ways of doing
this are outlined in the earlier part of this book.) At the
same time this process enables them to come to terms with
the feminine within themselves, and this is also a useful and
perhaps necessary step.

On the third level, they have to enable the participants to
come to terms with female power. The only way I know for
this to happen is that we find out about the Great Goddess
and the Horned God, as we saw in Chapter 9, and to
understand something about paganism. The reason why this
is so necessary is because there are very few images of
female power in our present society, and we need to go
back and pick them up if we are to believe in them. Unless
men genuinely believe that there is such a thing as female
power, and accept it as good, they will never hand over
their male power.

It is for this reason that I do not really believe that there
are any other ways for men to pick up this kind of thing.
Those who have been through the 'hippie thing' often
picked up something of it, though not at all reliably; those
who have been through encounter groups or co-counselling,
have often discovered some of the same things, though
again not reliably; those who have mixed a good deal with
feminists have often changed quite substantially as a result.
But none of these things is on a mass scale.

It seems, therefore, that the change agency for questioning
patriarchy on any large scale is going to be rare and hard to
find. Perhaps the nearest thing to it is the Green movement,

237

particularly in West Germany, though it is now growing in other countries. But as we have been seeing, work has to be done at many different levels, and it would not be right to leave everything to a political party, no matter how enlightened.

This means that we also have to consider change agencies which can challenge patriarchal attitudes and practices at the organizational level – what Kotler calls the 'protest' approach. This is obviously an easier, though never an easy, task. But it still entails having an organization which is not itself patriarchal, and aims at synergy. Coover et al. (1978) give many hints how this may be done.

Believing, then, in the importance of conflict and the possibility of integration, we can go out for what we want as individuals, as groups, as communities and even as members of social classes.

Out of this, then, what needs to be said is that the way of working through conflict and integration favoured by humanistic psychology works best with reasonably small units, which can be easily visualized and mentally grasped.

We have already seen that humanistic psychology can handle very well the conflicts between management and unions, black and white races, gender opponents, teachers and students and opposed interest groups in local communities. Why should it not be able to handle class conflicts too, so long as these are expressed in terms of genuine demands for real needs? In fact, this outlook should make class conflict more frequent and more productive, because of its emphasis on becoming aware of what is real for each person, instead of suppressing needs in favour of what is supposed to be felt.

There is only one way through: to become real, to learn to take a stand, to develop one's centre.

CHAPTER FIFTEEN

SOME POINTS ON THEORY
AND RESEARCH

THIS BOOK is about what happened and what is going on, rather than about detailed theoretical argument. The main reason for this is that such finer details are only of real interest to a minority – those who have had psychological training of one kind or another. My other books were mainly written for them, and contain quite a lot of scholarly material which can be chewed over in the usual academic way. But in reading over this book, I have become aware that there are certain theoretical points which perhaps need to be clarified, because they are referred to every now and again without any real explanation being given, and this may be frustrating to the reader. So I'd like to try to mop up at least a few of these points here.

BASIC ORIENTATION

Humanistic psychology says that it is all right to look inside yourself. And it sets no limits on that. It is all right to look as deep and as long as you want to, on your own or in company, and whether you call it meditation, counselling, psychotherapy, confluent education or whatever.

Now there is a basic difference here between humanistic psychology and two other main dominant schools of psychology – behaviourism and psychoanalysis. Both of these other schools, in their various ways, say that it is not something to be encouraged. Let us look at psychoanalysis first.

Psychoanalysis says that if we look inside ourselves deep enough and long enough, and in the right way, what we will find, deep down underneath it all, is the Id. The Id is seen as the basic foundation for all motivation in the individual person. It is an extraordinarily dramatic concept. It seems to be impossible to describe it without excitement. It is a 'seething mass', 'primitive, repository of primitive and unacceptable impulses', 'completely selfish and unconcerned with reality or moral considerations', or 'unorganized chaotic mentality', according to various commentators. Freud's own words are 'a cauldron of seething excitement'.

The Id works on the basis of the pleasure principle – that is, it seeks immediate gratification, regardless of circumstances, ignoring other people's rights or needs in an almost crazy way. For Freud, the unconscious system works according to the laws of the Id. There is no time in the Id – past, present, and future mix without distinction. The laws of logic and reason do not exist for the Id, so that contrary wishes can exist side by side quite happily. One thing can stand for or symbolize other, incompatible things, and so on. If the Id were a person, she would be mad. There is a very sophisticated discussion of all this in Blanco (1975). This is what makes so striking the words of Groddeck, which Freud accepted – 'We are lived by our unconscious.'

There is a powerful picture here, of a primitive energy source frightening in its intensity, and actually guiding our actions. No wonder it is thought to be unwise to go anywhere near it without a highly trained and skilled therapist by our side, to see that we come to no harm! And it is not surprising that one of the main efforts of the therapist is to help the Ego to get some kind of control over the force of the libido which comes from the Id. Nor is it surprising that psychoanalysis takes very seriously the importance of social rules and norms, and believes that society is right to set limits on what we naturally want to do. The answer to the problems of the Id is good socialization, where we learn how to adapt in terms of the reality principle, and become acceptable and tamed.

Now behaviourism sees itself as being strongly opposed to

psychoanalysis. In the eyes of the behaviourist, psycho-analysis is woolly and unscientific, hard to understand and impossible to check. How surprising it is to find, then, the same message coming out also from this source. We must distinguish between two different kinds of behaviourism, because they have different foundations.

The first kind of behaviourism is based on the classical conditioning theory of Pavlov. A good example of it is given by the British behaviourist Eysenck (1965) where he says:

> [The young child] has to learn to be clean and not to defecate and urinate whenever and wherever he pleases; he has to suppress the overt expression of his sexual and aggressive urges; he must not beat other children when they do things he does not like; he must learn not to take things which do not belong to him. In every society there is a long list of prohibitions of acts which are declared to be bad, naughty and immoral, and which, although they are attractive to him and are self-rewarding, he must nevertheless desist from carrying out.

So activities like this have to be prohibited and suppressed from outside, by suitably designed punishment.

Often this is put in terms of biological drives. It is the drives which are basic, and push for immediate release. And it is only the strong conscience built up through conditioning, through good socialization or taming, which can cope with these strong forces, which have the whole power of evolution behind them. If we started looking deep inside ourselves, then, what we should find, if we went down far enough, would be these unregenerate drives with all their power and strength. So again, what we need if we want to do this at all for any reason is an expert behaviour therapist, who knows about these things and will take all the responsibility for what might happen to us. If anything goes wrong, she will know what to do.

The second form of behaviourism is based upon the operant conditioning theory of Skinner. It does not have any notion of drives, and is in many ways much less theoretically committed than the Pavlovian form. But in the classic book by Skinner (1974), he fortunately makes clear his view of how his own position differs from that of Freud. And it turns out that it does not differ at all – he merely want to rename the Id to suit his own terminology:

> In Freud's great triumvirate, the ego, superego and id represent three sets of contingencies which are almost inevitable when a person lives in a group. The id is the Judeo-Christian 'Old Adam' – a man's 'unregenerate nature', derived from his innate susceptibilities to reinforcement, most of them almost necessarily in conflict with the interests of others.

So now it is the genetic endowment, a set of susceptibilities to reinforcement, which is what we find deep down underneath everything else. And it will not surprise us to find that this most fundamental layer of the personality is defined on another page as 'selfish behaviour', which needs to be limited and trained from outside so that it will become more acceptable to others.

And if we want to look inside ourselves to go into these matters, again what we need is – this time – a behaviour modifier. Only the behaviour modifier, unlike the other two experts we have met already – the psychoanalyst and the behaviour therapist – is even more cagey about the whole thing, and refuses to look inside herself at all, or to encourage anyone else to. All the work is done on the surface, without recourse to anything like depth. This seems in a way even more frightening than the other two – like it is something you had better not do even with an expert.

It can be seen that both the psychoanalyst and the behaviourist (in both varieties) have a pessimistic view of what is going on inside human beings. This seems to be helped, if anything, by the emphasis which both of them have on the biological and Darwinian basis of man's animal nature. As Maslow (1970) points out:

> One expression of this world view has been to identify this animal within us with wolves, tigers, pigs, vultures or snakes, rather than with better, or at least milder, animals like the deer or elephant or dog or chimpanzee. This we may call the bad-animal interpretation of our

inner nature, and point out that if we *must* reason from animals to men, it would be better if we chose those who were closest to us, i.e. the anthropoid apes. Since these are, on the whole, pleasant and likeable animals sharing with us many characteristics that we call virtuous, the bad-animal outlook is not supported by comparative psychology.

So it is clear how humanistic psychology would reject psychoanalysis and behaviourism. But how would it reject the third form of psychology which has come up in the past ten years and which now dominates academia – cognitive psychology? Cognitive psychology is perhaps one of the greatest con tricks ever perpetrated.

Back in the 1950s, cognitive psychology was one of the most promising and delightful parts of the whole psychological field. In the hands of people like Goldstein and Scheerer, it offered a very sophisticated critique of behaviourism, and said that to ignore emotions, imagination, consciousness and intentions for the future was absurd. I loved these people, and quoted them constantly. And of course, when I heard that cognitive psychology was getting popular in the universities, this was very cheering.

But it turned out that what was becoming popular was not the very cultivated European cognitive psychology which I had liked so much – it was a psychology which reduced people to the level of a computer. It was all about computer analogies of how the brain might work. One of its main branches was the study of artificial intelligence – how to make machines behave like human beings (Boden 1979). It was only willing to study those things about the person which could be set up in hardware and software.

Of course it is now terribly ingenious in doing this, and in its own way as sophisticated as any of the psychologies which had preceded it; but it is basically nonsense. I remember once doing a presentation about humanistic psychology at Warwick University, and in front of an audience I asked the professor there – 'What is your model of the person?' He replied – 'The computer'. I said – 'Surely you can't really mean that?' – but he assured me that he did. This is just obscene. A computer is a thing. To use a thing as a model of the person is to reduce the person to the level of a thing. It reduces something alive to something dead. And this is not OK.

This leads us into what is perhaps the main difference between humanistic psychology and these other forms which we have been looking at. For humanistic psychology, people are people all the way through – there is no point at which they turn into animals, or inanimate objects. Deep down underneath it all, where it really counts, there is the self. And the self is all right. There is nothing there to be afraid of.

This is something which is held consistently by all those who are seen as central to humanistic psychology. Rogers (1961) says:

> When we are able to free the individual from defensiveness, so that he is open to the wide range of environmental and social demands, his reactions may be trusted to be positive, forward-moving, constructive.

His definition of adjustment is complete openness to experience, whether it comes from outside or from inside. And he says – 'There is no beast in man. There is only man in man . . . '

Perls says that rather than try to change, stop, or avoid something that you don't like in yourself, it is much more effective to experience it fully and become more deeply aware of it. You can't improve on your own functioning, you can only interfere with it, distort and disguise it. When you really get in touch with your own experiencing, you will find that change takes place by itself, without your effort or planning.

Maslow says that he sees people as living organisms with an inherent need to grow or change. This is their intrinsic motivation – it does not derive from other needs. And it leads to self-actualization – a never-ending process of going into the self and going beyond the self. It includes ecstasy, creativity and transpersonal experience, and not just everyday coping.

Mahrer (1978) says that if we delve beneath the surface of

a person, what we come down to are the deeper potentials. These are often hated and feared when they first come into awareness, but when they are worked with and entered into fully, they turn out to be positive and full of energy and helpful meaning.

May (1967) says that the core, the centredness of a person is the bedrock on which we base all our attempts at therapy. We have to assume that it is all right, because neurosis is the attempt to deny it, to hide it, to get away from it. It is this that makes true love and real encounter possible.

All the detailed techniques and applications in this book are based on these assumptions. And they seem to form what is often called in social science a self-fulfilling prophecy: that is, if you act as if they were true, they seem to check out as true. But they are not just a self-fulfilling prophecy – they make a lot of logical sense too, as we shall see in the next section.

DEFICIENCY MOTIVATION AND ABUNDANCE MOTIVATION

Most psychology, most of the time, deals with deficiency motivation. Something happens, and we have to cope with it. We have to adjust to it in some way, and we may do this well or badly, appropriately or inappropriately – often it will be possible to state quite objectively whether our reaction met the situation or was inadequate to it in some way.

There is a word to describe this, taken from cybernetics, which is often used in the literature and which is quite useful to remember: homeostasis. Homeostasis simply means self-adjustment in accordance with a standard. A thermostat, as found on the ordinary domestic iron, works on a homeostatic principle; so does the pupil of the eye. It is a principle of tension reduction, and it works by relieving some kind of want or discomfort.

Now there is no doubt that dealing with this form of action is very convenient for psychologists. It enables them to be very precise in their measurements, and to set up experiments which enable strict control to be kept and exact predictions to be made and checked.

Historically, the introduction of the notion of homeostasis in the 1950s was a very progressive move. It enabled psychology to throw off all the puzzles about 'the instinct of self-preservation', because homeostasis replaces it completely. It enabled psychology to give mechanistic meanings to such things as 'expectancy', 'purpose' and 'information', and in doing so to revolutionize our whole notion of the word 'mechanistic'. It enabled us to drop our puzzlement about freewill and determinism, since it became clear that we could construct machines which could rearrange their own internal circuits in such a way that we could be sure that they would adapt to their environment, but not sure at all of how they would do it. If afterwards we wanted to know how they had done it, we would have to take them apart to find out. If a machine could be as free as this, it was obvious that animals and still more human beings could do this and more. It is hard now to recall the excitement we felt on reading Ashby's fine book, (1952) which made all this so clear.

But now that all the hubbub has died down, it is easy enough to see that homeostasis leaves out some very important things about human beings. In particular, it leaves out virtually all the things which humanistic psychology is interested in.

In terms of motivation, what it leaves out is abundance motivation. This is the kind of motivation where we are not trying to relieve some discomfort, but actively seeking fresh stimulation and new experiences. It is sometimes called tension-seeking or tension-maintaining behaviour; Woodworth (1958) calls it outgoing motivation.

This has now been studied a great deal, and the classic by Fiske and Maddi (1961) prints a number of papers which show that even by the very strictest of scientific standards, deficiency motivation and homeostasis is not enough to account for a great deal of animal behaviour, and still less of human action.

Krech, Crutchfield & Livson (1969) explain very well the

difference between deficiency and abundance motivation, and make it clear that psychology needs both concepts if it is to do justice to what we actually find. Coleman (1969) also deals with this in a helpful way.

Weiner (1985) in a very full and lengthy examination of the whole question of motivation from a modern psychological standpoint quotes Maslow as talking about Being-values as opposed to Deficiency-values (homeostatic drives); the B-values are more to do with needs which are not deficiency-driven, such as curiosity, appreciation, love, peak experiences and so on.

Supposing that we were to apply this thinking to Maslow's model, in a way which Maslow himself never apparently considered? Maslow says that we will expect to find abundance motivation (or growth motivation, or B-motivation, as he calls it) at the self-actualization level of development; as I read him, he tends to identify the two things, or run them together. (Weiner (1985) also takes this view.) Here and there he seems to suggest that we can find some abundance motivation at the self-esteem level and at the love and belongingness level, but he never says this, to the best of my knowledge, about the safety or the physiological levels.

Now it seems certainly and obviously true that we do find abundance motivation at the level of self-actualization. But I want to say two things about this. One, that we can also find deficiency motivation at this level; and two, that we can also find abundance motivation at the two lowest levels. In other words, I want to make a dividing line right down the middle of the Maslow chart.

Very young babies show exploratory tendencies, playful activity, curiosity and self-discovery, etc.; they do not have to wait to become self-actualizing adults before they can get away from deficiency motivation. And we all know we can eat or drink from purely aesthetic motives, or as a meditation, not only from hunger or thirst. So I think we can say that at every level of activity we can find deficiency motivation and abundance motivation side by side. Maslow himself says very clearly that there can be deficiency-motivated love, a kind of love-hunger; but there can also be abundance-motivated love, which is non-possessive and not need-oriented at all. But how about self-actualization sometimes being deficiency-motivated? To people who have studied Maslow this may seem something like heresy.

Funnily enough, it was Maslow himself who discovered this. One of the key things about the self-actualization level has always been, for Maslow, the fact that it was at this level that the peak experience most often appeared. But with the coming of LSD and the Esalen Institute, it appeared that perfectly authentic peak experiences were to be had simply and directly, almost for the asking. And Maslow (1970a) turned back, appalled, from the new world he had helped to create:

> If the *sole* good in life becomes the peak experience, and if all means to this end become good, and if more peak experiences are better than fewer, then one can *force* the issue, push actively, strive and hunt and fight for them. So they have often moved over into magic, into the secret and esoteric, into the exotic, the occult, the dramatic and effortful, the dangerous, the cultish.

In other words, people could now start to say 'I'm a bit off and down at the moment, so I think I need a peak experience this weekend'. And this is precisely the language of deficiency motivation.

> Instead of being 'surprised by joy', 'turning on' is scheduled, promised, advertised, sold, hustled into being, and can get to be regarded as a commodity. More exotic, artificial, striving techniques may escalate further until they become necessary, and until jadedness and impotence ensue. (Maslow 1970a)

It seems, then, that this confirms our view that one can have deficiency motivation even at the level of self-actualization.

The actual details shown in Table 2 are speculative, and have not been checked out by empirical research. They are there merely as possibly suggestive hypotheses, and not as authoritative pronouncements.

The advantage of putting it in this way, it seems to me, is that it shows more concretely how abundance motivation

TABLE 2   Abundance motivation and the Maslow levels

Letting peak experiences come; enjoying flashes of insight; finding non-punitive humour in many places; finding ecstasy in music; being genuinely creative; being inspired and inspiring; exploring spiritual realms.	6	Searching for peak experiences out of boredom; needing a 'turn-on' desperately; using the occult to control others; being driven by one's demons; comparing and evaluating peak experiences; using spiritual talk for sexual exploitation.
Strong connection between respect for one's own identity and respect for other's identity; sureness of identity leading to flexibility in action; awareness of some of the paradoxes of identity; authenticity.	5	Strong conscience with many guilt feelings; high personal standards which are rigid and must not be infringed; identity very important but a bit precarious; need for consistency, without ability to achieve it.
Liking to be appreciated; warming to response from others; ability to receive respect as something appropriate to the situation; ability to set up 'virtuous spirals' of interaction.	4	Need for recognition from others; need for applause; need for commendation from important authorities; need for authorities to be important; need for system, law and order, hierarchy, stability.
Love which overflows and reaches out to others; feeling of being part of a wider unity of people; love which gives space to the other person in which to grow; love which does not count the cost.	3	Need for approval; fear of the group; likely to conform; wants to be 'good'; need to please others; need to know what the others think; strong desire to belong to a definite group.
Control by integration of impulses and desires; control of situations by going with the flow; understanding of some of the paradoxes of control; mastery through enthusiasm; risk-taking.	2	Need to do things the 'correct' way; need to be perfect; need to know the rules; desire for control 'over' things and people; manipulative and dominant; narrow concept of own advantage.

ABUNDANCE MOTIVATED	DEFICIENCY MOTIVATED

Seeking long-term protection; anticipating danger in imaginative ways; seeking vicarious danger so as to be ready for unfamiliar situations; playing games about dangerous situations.	1	Escaping danger; avoiding pain or harm; seeking protection in real threat situation; cutting down on stimulation; suppressing hurt; · attempts to stop environment changing. Short-term.
Eating for aesthetic pleasure; drinking for new sensations; excreting with full awareness; enjoying heat, cold or rain; luxuriating in a bath; laughing at the lightning.	0	Eating from real hunger; drinking from real thirst; excreting when necessary; having sex out of pressing bodily need; compensating for or escaping from heat or cold; sleeping when tired.

fits in to the whole picture. And it does seem to be an advantage to have a two-dimensional picture, rather than a one-dimensional one. But much more work needs to be done on this.

B-VALUES AND D-VALUES

Maslow's tendency to mix up self-actualization and abundance motivation extended also into his discussion of Being. He believed that Being was a kind of realm which one entered into by means of a peak experience, and that while in it (probably quite briefly) one found oneself living in terms of the Being-values (B-values) rather than the deficiency values (D-values). Similarly one understood the world in terms of B-cognition rather than D-cognition, understood people in terms of B-love rather than D-love, and so on (Maslow 1973). This all makes perfectly good sense, but it does always sound as if we have to be at the self-actualizing level before any of this can happen.

How can we think about this in terms of the thought expressed in Table 2? It seems to me that there are two possibilities, which deserve to be mentioned. The first possibility is that we do indeed have to cross the gap (the 4–5 Gap of Table 1) before we can enter the realm of Being. The suggestion would be that the lower levels are too heavily infused with fear and stereotyped thinking to be able to move. But after the leap has been made and the gap crossed, we can then come back down the levels and act at those levels, but now according to the principles of abundance motivation. So we would, on this supposition, go up the ladder on the right-hand side, and then come down it again on the left-hand side, 'redeeming' each level in terms of the values reached at the top. This seems to make a lot of sense, and be quite understandable.

The other possibility is that at any level we may, on a good day, move over to the left, and open ourselves up to abundance motivation, and that this may, in fact, be the way in which we do grow. Perhaps each leftward movement makes it easier for there to be an upward movement. Certainly we stand more chance of learning when we are open and receptive than when we are closed up and defensive. And it may be just this kind of self-owned learning which takes us up the levels. Perhaps each glimpse of what it would be like to cross the gap makes actually crossing the gap easier. This would make it easier to understand what happens in many encounter groups and other growth experiences, where we seem to have an intense experience at the time, which is however not reflected in our conduct outside the group. This would be a case of moving over to the left while in the group, and then moving back again once the special group atmosphere is removed. But with some more of this 'pump-priming' sort of experience, enough strength and insight may be achieved to cross the gap for ourselves, so that the group is no longer necessary. This would also fit in with Maslow's simple diagram:

GROWTH ←————————PERSON————————→SAFETY

Maslow (1968) says that the process of healthy growth can be considered as a never-ending series of free choice situations, confronting each individual 'at every point throughout his life, in which ne must choose between the delights of safety and growth, dependence and independence, regression and progression, immaturity and maturity.' This emphasis on choice is of course meat and drink to the existentialist thinkers like May and Mahrer.

The two possibilities we have been considering both seem quite plausible, and only proper research can determine which of the two is true. Perhaps they both are. It would not take much change to see them as complementary rather than as competitive explanations of what we actually find in practice.

Humanistic Research

And this takes us on to the general question of research method. There are at least twenty kinds of research which are carried out in social science:

1 PURE BASIC RESEARCH   Carried out in universities and institutions of higher learning. Concerned with high-level abstractions which may or may not have any practical relevance. Attempts to push forward the boundaries of some new or established theory. Tends to be very strictly controlled.

2 BASIC OBJECTIVE RESEARCH   Research which is designed to relate theory to real life situations. The results are intended to be relevant to the situation studied, and also to some theoretical framework.

3 EVALUATION RESEARCH   Attempts to follow up some intentional course of action in an effort to determine whether what was intended to happen actually did happen (and possibly to what extent). The result almost always comes out as some kind of evaluative judgment on the course of action. Before-and-after measures are often used.

4 APPLIED RESEARCH   Covers a wide range of
possibilities, but often takes the form of a survey of
some kind. All the measures are within the four walls
of the situation being researched, and *ad hoc* items
may often be created. Can include exploratory
studies, and may use factor analysis or other computer
processing. Carried out by expert researchers. May
include observation or unobtrusive measures. The first
four methods are those dealt with in detail in most
standard textbooks on research methods.

5 QUALITATIVE RESEARCH   This approach
uses very open-ended types of questioning, which
enable the research subjects to use their own
categories of response. For a full description see
Walker (1985).

6 PARTICIPANT OBSERVATION   The
researcher plays a role similar to the roles of the
people being studied, either owning up to it or
keeping it secret. Well described in McCall &
Simmons (1969).

7 LANGUAGE AND CLASS RESEARCH
Studies language by mixing with the people actually
using that language, and entering into their world to
some degree. See for example Labov (1972).

8 PERSONALITY AND POLITICS RESEARCH
Studies the relationship between people's personality
and the political positions they take up. Long
interviews, sometimes over months, see Knutson
(1973).

9 ETHOGENIC RESEARCH   Studies carefully
the accounts people give of their actions, and says that
the explanation of such actions must be seen in terms
of such accounts, but going quite deeply into them
over extended periods of time, as Harré (1979) has
discussed.

10 PHENOMENOLOGICAL RESEARCH
Examines very carefully the ground the researcher is
standing on while conducting the research project; all
the rules the researcher is taking for granted have to be
rethought and re-examined, as Giorgi (1975) has
outlined.

11 ETHNOMETHODOLOGY Approach
pioneered by Garfinkel, which again takes apart the
taken-for-granted aspects of social life and re-examines
them very fundamentally, experimenting sometimes
with rule-breaking situations. Good summary in
Turner (1974).

12 LSD RESEARCH Approach where a drug is
administered and the therapeutic results are carefully
monitored, the researcher also having experience of
the same drug. See Grof (1980).

13 DIALECTICAL RESEARCH Good example in
Esterson (1972) of someone who takes up an explicitly
dialectical philosophical position when doing research
within a family.

14 ACTION RESEARCH The researchers who do
the work are people who will be affected by the
results – often they live in the same place as those
being studied. The process of doing the research is
itself part of the action to be taken. Expert
researchers may be used as advisers. See Sanford
(1981).

15 INTERVENTION RESEARCH A researcher
acts in the situation as a complete person, aiming at
the provision of valid and useful information, leading
to free and informed choice, and internal commitment
to a course of action. Research comes out in the form
of shared experience, which may or may not be
reducible to 'knowledge' which can be handed on to
others. See Argyris (1970).

16 PERSONAL CONSTRUCT RESEARCH
Research done according to the theory and precepts of
George Kelly, as exemplified in Fransella (1972). Close
co-operation between researcher and subject.

17 EXISTENTIAL RESEARCH   The researcher
acts as her own measuring instrument, using thoughts,
emotions, bodily reactions to register what is going on
as fully and deeply as possible, as in Hampden-Turner
(1977). An attempt is then made to play this back in
such a form that it can be re-experienced by others.
This may need a high degree of literary or other skill.

18 EXPERIENTIAL RESEARCH   This is done by
two people researching each other, and themselves. It
involves a two-way, systematic but creative interaction
between persons who may take up the roles of agent
and facilitator. Each session may be recorded and
analysed afterwards, or this may only be done for
certain agreed sessions. Hypotheses may be checked
by an attempt to produce certain changes, in self or
other, as Heron (1981) has described.

19 ENDOGENOUS RESEARCH   Here the
researcher turns the subjects, or some of them, into
co-researchers who are equally concerned with the
results of the project. See Maruyama (1981).

20 PARTICIPATORY RESEARCH   Pioneered by
Hall (1975) in several different countries, this
approach entails the co-operation of the research
subjects in a very close and detailed way, such that
they become co-owners of the research project.
Sometimes called collaborative or co-operative
research.

The first four of these tend to be alienated types of
research, which put people at some disadvantage, and treat
them as objects to be described externally. They all belong

to the field of Old Paradigm Research. Often the people studied are deceived in some way about the purpose of the study, and the extent of this massive deception has given rise to much worry in recent years, as Kelman (1968) has noted.

Types 5 to 16 are much more ambiguous. Depending on who is doing them, and for what purpose, they may be more or less alienated or deceptive. People involved in them may not be very clear themselves as to what paradigm of research they are following. However, these methods have in the past tended to be much more genuine, in that people are not deceived, and are allowed to express themselves in their own terms and in their own way.

The last four types are in the field of New Paradigm Research, which is relatively recent, and relates much better to humanistic psychology. It is described rather thoroughly in Reason & Rowan (1981). All these types of research from 17 to 20 seem particularly suitable for investigating theories of personal growth and human potential. This is a fast growing field, and those interested in New Paradigm Research should also look at Mitroff & Kilmann (1978), Part 2 of Darroch & Silvers (1982), Lincoln & Guba (1985) and Berg & Smith (1985). A challenging new look at research in the field of counselling and psychotherapy is to be found in Mahrer (1985).

CRITIQUES OF HUMANISTIC PSYCHOLOGY

Over the years, there have been a number of critiques of humanistic psychology. Most of them are very feeble, and hardly any of them show any real understanding of the fact that the whole thing is based on experience rather than abstract logic – what in Chapter 1 we called the paradigms.

Some of the criticisms are very well answered in Shaw (1974), who shows that the general theory of self-actualization holds up very well in answer to various criticisms made up to that time. Others are dealt with in several articles of mine which have appeared in *Self & Society* at various times.

256

Someone who has looked at humanistic theory from a sociological perspective is Roy Wallis (1985), who examines the idea that the movement has gone in the direction of more spiritual concerns in recent years, and that this means a kind of failure, a substitution of false compensators for real rewards. He goes into this at some length, and in the end disagrees with it, saying that it seems rather that:

> Spirituality may be pursued as a way of providing an explanation for what has been achieved, and out of a desire to gain *additional*, rather than substitute, values and effects.

But he says that the most consistent feature of the human potential movement is its epistemological individualism. I think what he means by this is quite acceptable, and reflects the emphasis on the real self which is so characteristic of humanistic theory. It fits very well with what Wilber (1980) calls the centaur stage of psychospiritual development.

Another critique comes from Geller, who takes a rather logical positivist position, and says that the whole theory is incoherent because it tries to mix biology and psychology in a way which does not logically hold water:

> Implicit in Rogers's view, I suspect, is the erroneous if not incoherent assumption that the true self is an immaterial, unchanging thing-like substance that can be an object of exploration and discovery but not a subject or agent. (Geller 1982)

This was answered very fully by Ginsburg (1984) a couple of years later, who showed that this view was not sustainable, and was also based on a type of logic which could not even in principle work in the examination of humanistic psychology. He points out that 'Geller makes his argument against Rogers by converting phenomenological experiential statements into metaphysical propositions'.

And he goes on to reply to Geller's point that authenticity is a logically incoherent notion by saying that:

> The test of whether one knows what it means when one says 'I am being authentic' or 'I am behaving according to

the dictates of my inner self' is in the experience of doing
so and the experience of difference in testing this strategy
against previous possibilities. The difference is a difference
in somatic experience of oneself, and is therefore
empirically verifiable in the most direct sense.

So that even by Geller's own standards this has to be
accepted as valid.

Geller (1984) tried to come back, but only made his own
position more untenable, by making such a radical gulf
between knowledge through language and knowledge
without language that the two became quite impossible to
relate together, never mind develop one out of the other, as
must obviously be the case.

More recently, we have had Lethbridge (1986) trying to
attack humanistic psychology from a Marxist position.
Unfortunately for him, there is no Marxist psychology – it
keeps on turning into sociology, because of the extreme
Marxist reliance on social determinism. He tries to show
that Vygotski, Leontyev and Lucien Sève have a valid
alternative, but in my opinion fails completely. Leontyev is
quoted as saying – 'individual consciousness can exist only
in the presence of social consciousness and language, which
is its real substratum.' This again makes the error of Geller,
of making too much of language. If language were so
important, all the body therapies and all the regressive
therapies would be impossible – they could not possibly
work. It is only because experience is prior to language that
we can have such therapies. Gendlin (1962) put forward
long ago the basic story of how experience turns into
language, and this account has never been bettered.

There has never been an attack on humanistic psychology
which has really shown it to be either untenable or unscientific. Those who accuse humanistic psychology of being
Cartesian are usually much more Cartesian themselves.

One of the more vague and general criticisms, which
attracted a good deal of attention in its day, was the theme
that humanistic psychology was narcissistic. Obviously the
amount of time spent on discussing the self, and self-
actualization, lends itself to this suspicion, but when we

come to look at it closely, the plausibility of it departs. It is
not about egotism or selfishness, and not much even about
self-improvement in the sense of rational self-management.
It is about the sort of movement towards a fuller sense of
self which is very broad and unselfish and all-inclusive. As
the very precise and hard-headed Mahrer (1978) says:

> It involves the commitment to whatever there is within to
> be. This is the leap of faith, the tearing of one's self from
> what one is and the falling into whatever is there within.

This produces what he calls the 'integrating person' – the
person who has taken up the challenge of self-actualization
and has started moving in the direction of greater self-
awareness and greater authenticity. He goes on to say:

> The ordinary person may be said to be engaged in a per-
> petual agonizing struggle to preserve the self, whereas, in
> stark and utter contrast, the integrating person is willingly
> engaged in suicidal self-destruction. These two persons
> are proceeding in opposite directions. The integrating
> person knows that the way to liberation, to integration, to
> metamorphosis, is through the eye of the nameless horror
> which the ordinary person desperately struggles to avoid.

With integration and actualization, a person is able to relate
fully to another person. One of the crucial mistakes made
by critics is to see the stress on autonomy as excluding
relationship with another. But the whole point made by
humanistic psychology is that it is only the autonomous
person who can have real relationships. As Mahrer (1978)
says in his discussion of actualization:

> The highest levels of interpersonal relationships are those
> characterised by integration *and actualization*. This kind
> of relationship exceeds one of integrative love, mutual
> integrative oneness, and mutual integrative being-one-
> with. Because of the nature of actualization, these highest
> levels of interpersonal relationships are *also* characterized
> by mutual contexts enabling each participant toward
> increasing depth and breadth of experiencing. When
> relationships are of this order, they define the highest and

most valued interpersonal relations available to human beings.

From this we can see that the various critiques of humanistic psychology are not such as to cause us any great misgivings about the basic direction of the enterprise. Of course we have a lot to learn still about the details.

JOURNALS AND MAGAZINES

Bulletin of the Group Relations Training Association, 11 Cheverton Road, London N19 3BB. Quarterly.

Changes, Lawrence Erlbaum Associates, 319 City Road, London EC1V 1LJ. Quarterly.

Energy & Character, BCM – CHESIL, London WC1N 3XX. Quarterly.

Green Line, 34 Cowley Road, Oxford, Monthly.

Group & Organization Studies, University Associates, 8517 Production Avenue, San Diego, California 92121, USA. Quarterly.

Human Potential Resources, 35 Station Road, London NW4. Quarterly.

Journal of Applied Behavioural Science, NTL Institute for Applied Behavioural Science, PO Box 9155, Rosslyn Station, Arlington, Virginia 22209, USA. Quarterly.

Journal of Humanistic Psychology, 325 Ninth Street, San Francisco, California 94103, USA. Quarterly.

Journal of Transpersonal Psychology, PO Box 4437, Stanford, California 94305, USA. Twice yearly.

Resurgence (incorporating *Undercurrents*), Ford House, Hartland, Bideford, Devon. Bi-monthly.

Self & Society: The European Journal of Humanistic Psychology, 62 Southwark Bridge Road, London SE1 0AS. Bi-monthly.

SOME USEFUL ADDRESSES

Association for Humanistic Psychology, 325 Ninth Street, San Francisco, California 94103, USA.

Association for Humanistic Psychology in Britain, 12 Southcote Road, London N19 5BJ.

Association for Humanistic Psychology Practitioners, 7 Jackson Tor Road, Matlock, Derbyshire, DE4 3JS.

Group Relations Training Association, 10 Devon Drive, Diggle, Oldham, Lancs, OL3 5PP.

Human Potential Research Project, Department of Educational Studies, University of Surrey, Guildford, Surrey, GU2 5XH.

BIBLIOGRAPHY

Adler, M. (1979), *Drawing Down the Moon*, Boston, Beacon Press.

Adzema, M.V. (1985), 'A primal perspective on spirituality', *Journal of Humanistic Psychology*, 25/3, 83–116.

Alderfer, C. (1972), *Existence, Relatedness, Growth*, New York, The Free Press.

Allen, R.F. (1980), *Beat the System! A way to create more human environments*, New York, McGraw-Hill.

Anderson, W.T. (1973), *Politics and the New Humanism*, Pacific Palisades, Goodyear.

Anderson, W.T. (1983), *The Upstart Spring*, Reading, Addison-Wesley.

Anderson, W.T. (ed.) (1983a), *Rethinking Liberalism*, New York, Avon.

Arendt, H. (1958), *The Human Condition*, Chicago, University of Chicago Press.

Argyris, C. (1970), *Intervention Theory and Method*, Reading, Addison-Wesley.

Ashby, W.R. (1952), *Design for a Brain*, London, Chapman & Hall.

Aspy, D.N. (1965), 'A study of three facilitative conditions and their relationship to the achievement of third grade students', Unpublished doctoral dissertation, University of Kentucky.

Aspy, D.N. (1969), 'The effect of teacher-offered conditions of empathy, positive regard and congruence upon student achievement', *Florida Journal of Educational Research*, 11/1, 39-48.

Aspy, D.N. (1972), *Toward a Technology for Humanizing Education*, Champaign, Research Press.

Aspy, D.N. & Hadlock, W. (1967), 'The effect of empathy, warmth and genuineness on elementary students' reading achievement', Reviewed in C.B. Truax & R.R. Carkhuff, *Toward Effective Counselling and Psychotherapy*, Chicago, Aldine.

Aspy, D.N. & Roebuck, F.N. (1977), *Kids Don't Learn from People They Don't Like*, Amherst, Human Resource Development Press.

Assagioli, R. (1975), *Psychosynthesis: A manual of principles and techniques*, London, Turnstone Press.

Bach, G.R. & Wyden, P. (1969), *The Intimate Enemy*, New York, William Morrow.

Bakalar, J.B. (1985), 'Social and intellectual attitudes toward drug-induced religious experience', *Journal of Humanistic Psychology*, 25/4, 45-66.

Bales, R.F. (1958), 'Task roles and social roles in problem-solving groups' in E.E. Maccoby et al. (eds), *Readings in Social Psychology*, New York, Holt.

Balint, M. (1968), *The Basic Fault*, London, Tavistock Publications.

Bay, C. (1965), 'Politics and pseudopolitics: A critical evaluation of some behavioural literature', *American Political Science Review*, 59, 37–57.

Bay, C. (1967), 'Needs, wants and political legitimacy', *Canadian Journal of Political Science*, 1, 241–60.

Bay, C. (1968), *The Structure of Freedom*, New York, Doubleday.

Bay, C. (1971), '"Freedom" as a tool of oppression' in Benello & Roussopoulos (eds), *The Case for Participatory Democracy*, New York, Viking.

Baynes, C.F. (1968), *I Ching: or book of changes* (3rd ed), London, Routledge & Kegan Paul.

Beck, J. (1972), *The Life of the Theatre: The Relation of the Artist to the Struggle of the People*, San Francisco, City Lights.

Beckhard, R. (1969), *Organization Development: Strategies and Models*, Reading, Mass., Addison-Wesley.

Bennis, W.G. et al. (eds) (1970), *The Planning of Change* (2nd ed), New York, Holt Rinehart & Winston.

Berg, D.N. & Smith, K.K. (eds) (1985). *Exploring Clinical Methods for Social Research*, Beverley Hills, Sage.

Bergantino, L. (1981), *Psychotherapy, Insight and Style*, Boston, Allyn & Bacon.

Berne, E. (1964), *Games People Play*, Harmondsworth, Penguin.

Biddle, W.W. (with Biddle, L.J.) (1965), *The Community Development Process: The rediscovery of local initiative*, New York, Holt Rinehart & Winston.

Binswanger, L. (1975), *Being in the World*, London, Souvenir Press.

Blake, R.R. & Mouton, J.S. (1964), *The Managerial Grid*, Houston, Gulf Publishing.

Blake, R.R. & Mouton, J.S. (1978), *The New Managerial Grid*, Houston, Gulf Publishing.

Blake, R.R. & Mouton, J.S. (1980), *The Grid for Sales Excellence* (2nd ed), New York, McGraw-Hill.

Blake, R.R. & Mouton, J.S. (1982), 'Theory and research for developing a science of leadership', *The Journal of Applied Behavioral Science*, 18/3, 275–91.

Blake, R.R. et al. (1970), 'The union-management intergroup laboratory: strategy for resolving intergroup conflict' in W.G. Bennis et al. (eds), *The Planning of Change* (2nd ed), New York, Holt Rinehart & Winston.

Blanco, M. (1975), *The Unconscious as Infinite Sets*, London, Duckworth.

Blatner, H.A. (1973), *Acting-in: Practical applications of psychodramatic methods*, New York, Springer.

Boadella, D. (1985), *Wilhelm Reich: The evolution of his work*, London, New York, Arkana.

Boadella, D. (in press) 'Biosynthesis' in J. Rowan & W. Dryden (eds), *Innovative Therapy in Britain*, London, Harper & Row.

Boden, M. (1979), *Artificial Intelligence and Natural Man*, Hassocks, The Harvester Press.

Bolweg, J.F. (1976), *Job Design and Industrial Democracy*, Leiden, Martinus Nijhoff.

Bookchin, M. (1986), *The Modern Crisis*, Philadelphia, New Society Publishers.

Boorstein, S. (ed.) (1980), *Transpersonal Psychotherapy*, Palo Alto, Science & Behaviour.

Borton, T. (1970), *Reach, Touch and Teach*, New York, McGraw-Hill.

Bower, T.G.R. (1977), *A Primer of Infant Development*, San Francisco, W.H. Freeman.

Bradford, L.P. et al. (eds) (1964), *T-group Theory and Laboratory Method*, New York, Wiley.

Brammer, L.M. & Shostrom, E.L. (1982), *Therapeutic Psychology: Fundamentals of Counselling and Psychotherapy* (4th ed), Englewood Cliffs, Prentice-Hall.

Bridges, W. (1973), 'Thoughts on humanistic education, or is teaching a dirty word?', *Journal of Humanistic Psychology*, 13/1, 5–13.

Broder, M. (1976), 'An eclectic approach to primal integration', *Primal Integration Monographs*, 1/1.

Brooks, C.V.W. (1974), *Sensory Awareness*, New York, Viking Press.

Brown, G.I. (1971), *Human Teaching for Human Learning*, New York, Viking.

Brown, G.I. (ed) (1975), *The Live Classroom: Innovation through confluent education and gestalt*, New York, The Viking Press.

Brown, P. (1973), *Radical Psychology*, London, Tavistock Publications.

Brown, R.C. & Tedeschi, C. (1972), 'Graduate education in psychology: A comment on Rogers' passionate statement', *Journal of Humanistic Psychology*, 12/1, 1–15.

Brown, S.D. & Lent, R.W. (eds) (1984), *Handbook of Counselling Psychology*, New York, John Wiley & Sons.

Canfield, J. & Wells, H.C. (1976), *One Hundred Ways to Enhance Self Concept in the Classroom*, Englewood Cliffs, Prentice-Hall.

Capra, F. (1983), *The Turning Point*, New York, Simon & Schuster.

Casriel, D.H. (1971), 'The Daytop story and the Casriel method' in L. Blank et al. (eds), *Confrontation*, New York, Collier-Macmillan.

Castillo, G.A. (1978), *Left-handed Teaching: Lessons in affective education*, New York, Holt Rinehart & Winston.

Chaudhuri, H. (1975), 'Yoga psychology' in C.T. Tart (ed.), *Transpersonal Psychologies*, London, Routledge & Kegan Paul.

Clark, D. (1972), 'Homosexual encounter in all-male groups' in L.N. Solomon & B. Berzon (eds), *New Perspectives on Encounter Groups*, San Francisco, Jossey-Bass.

Cohen, J.M. & Phipps, J.-F. (1979), *The Common Experience*, London, Rider.

Coleman, J.C. (1969), *Psychology and Effective Behaviour*, Glenview, Scott & Foresman.

Cooper, D. (1971), *The Death of the Family*, New York, Vintage.

Coover, V. et al. (1978), *Resource Manual for a Living Revolution*, Philadelphia, New Society Publishers.

Darroch, V. & Silvers, R.J. (1982), *Interpretive human studies: An introduction to phenomenological research*, Washington, University Press of America.

Douglas, T. (1983), *Groups*, London, Tavistock Publications.

Dreyfuss, A. & Feinstein, A.D. (1977), 'My body is me: Body-based approaches to personal enrichment' in McWaters, B. (ed.), *Humanistic Perspectives*, Monterey, Brooks/Cole.

Dunayevskaya, R. (1982), *Rosa Luxemburg, Women's Liberation and Marx's Philosophy of Revolution*, Sussex, Harvester Press.

Duval, S. & Wicklund, R.W. (1972), *A Theory of Objective Self Awareness*, New York, Academic Press.

Eiseman, J.W. (1977), 'A third-party consultation model for resolving recurring conflicts collaboratively', *Journal of Applied Behavioural Science*, 13/3, 303–314.

Emery, F. & Thorsrud, E. (1976), *Democracy at Work*, Leiden, Martinus Nijhoff.

Emmet, D. (1966), *Rules, Roles and Relations*, London, Macmillan.

Enright, J. (1970), 'Awareness training in the mental health professions' in J. Fagan & I.L. Shepherd (eds), *Gestalt Therapy Now*, Palo Alto, Science & Behaviour.

Ernst, S. & Goodison, L. (1981), *In Our Own Hands: A book of self-help therapy*, London, The Women's Press.

Esterson, A. (1972), *The Leaves of Spring: A study in the dialectics of madness*, Harmondsworth, Penguin.

Evison, R. & Horobin, R. (1983), *How to Change Yourself and Your World*, Sheffield, Co-counselling Phoenix.

Eysenck, H.J. (1965), *Fact and Fiction in Psychology*, Harmondsworth, Penguin.

Fagan, J. & Shepherd, I.L. (eds) (1970), *Gestalt Therapy Now*, Palo Alto, Science & Behaviour.

Faraday, A. (1976), *The Dream Game*, New York, Harper & Row.

Farrell, W. (1974), *The Liberated Man: Freeing men and their relationships with women*, New York, Random House.

Ferguson, M. (1982), *The Aquarian Conspiracy*, London, RKP.

Feidler, F.E. (1967), *A Theory of Leadership Effectiveness*, New York, McGraw-Hill.

Fisher, S. (1973), *Body Consciousness: You are what you feel*, Englewood Cliffs, Prentice-Hall.

Fiske, D.W. & Maddi, S.R. (eds) (1961), *Functions of Varied Experience*, Homewood, The Dorsey Press.

Flaherty, F. (1968), quoted in W.R. Coulson & C.R. Rogers (eds), *Man and the Science of Man*, New York, Charles E. Merrill.

Fogarty, M.J. (1957), *Christian Democracy in Western Europe 1820–1953*, London, RKP.

Fordyce, J.K. & Weil, R. (1971), *Managing with People: A manager's handbook of organization development methods*, Reading, Addison-Wesley.

Fransella, F. (1972), *Personal Change and Reconstruction*, New York, Academic Press.

Freud, S. (1975), *The Interpretation of Dreams*, Harmondsworth, Penguin.

Friedan, B. (1965), *The Feminine Mystique*, Harmondsworth, Penguin.

Friedenberg, E.Z. (1973), *Laing*, London, Fontana.

Gaines, J. (1979), *Fritz Perls Here and Now*, Millbrae, Celestial Arts.

Gallwey, W. (1974), *The Inner Game of Tennis*, London, Jonathan Cape.

Garfield, P. (1976), *Creative Dreaming*, London, Futura.

Garfield, S.L. & Bergin, A.E. (eds) (1978), *Handbook of Psychotherapy and Behaviour Change* (2nd ed), New York, John Wiley & Sons.

Gelb, L.A. (1972), 'Mental health in a corrupt society' in H.M. Ruitenbeek (ed.), *Going Crazy*, New York, Bantam.

Geller, L. (1982), 'The failure of self-actualization theory: A critique of Carl Rogers and Abraham Maslow', *Journal of Humanistic Psychology*, 22/2, 56–73.

Geller, L. (1984), 'Another look at self-actualization', *Journal of Humanistic Psychology*, 24/2, 93–106.

Gendlin, E.T. (1962), *Experiencing and the Creation of Meaning*, London, Collier-Macmillan.

Gendlin, E.T. (1979), 'Experiential psychotherapy' in R.J. Corsini (ed.), *Current Psychotherapies* (2nd ed), Itasca, F.E. Peacock Publishers.

Gendlin, E.T. (1981), *Focusing* (2nd ed), New York, Bantam.

Gergen, K.J. (1972), 'Multiple identity: The healthy, happy human being wears many masks', *Psychology Today* (US), May.

Gilligan, C. (1982), *In a Different Voice: Psychological Theory and Women's Development*, Cambridge, Massachusetts, Harvard University Press.

Ginsburg, C. (1984), 'Toward a somatic understanding of self: A reply to Leonard Geller', *Journal of Humanistic Psychology*, 24/2, 66–92.

Giorgi, A. (1975), *Duquesne Studies in Phenomenological Psychology*, Duquesne University Press.

Glass, J.F. & Staude, J.R. (eds) (1972), *Humanistic Society: Today's challenge to sociology*, Pacific Palisades, Goodyear.

Glenn, M. (1971), 'Introduction' in the Radical Therapist Collective (eds), *The Radical Therapist*, New York, Ballantine.

Goffman, E. (1974), *Frame Analysis: An essay on the organization of experience*, New York, Harper Colophon.

Golembiewski, R.T. & Blumberg, A. (eds) (1970), *Sensitivity Training and the Laboratory Approach: Readings about concepts and applications*, New York, Peacock.

Golembiewski, R.T. et al. (1982), 'Estimating the success of OD applications', *Training and Development Journal*, April, 86–95.

Goodman, P. (1962), 'Seating arrangements: An elementary lecture on functional planning' in P. Goodman, *Utopian Essays and Practical Proposals*, New York, Vintage.

Gray, E.D. (1982), *Patriarchy as a Conceptual Trap*, Wellesley, Roundtable Press.

Gray, H. (1985), *Organization Development in Education*, Stoke-on-Trent, Deanhouse.

Green, E.E. & Green, A.M. (1971), 'On the meaning of transpersonal: Some metaphysical perspectives', *Journal of Transpersonal Psychology*, 3/1.

Greenberg, I.A. (ed.) (1974), *Psychodrama: Theory and therapy*, London, Condor.

Grof, S. (1975), *Realms of the Human Unconscious*, New York, Viking Press.

Grof, S. (1980), *LSD Psychotherapy*, Pomona, Hunter House.

Grof, S. (1985), *Beyond the Brain: Birth, death and transcendence in psychotherapy*, Albany, State University of New York Press.

Gunther, B. (1969), *Sense Relaxation: Below your mind*, London Macdonald.

Gunther, B. (1978), *Energy Ecstasy: Your seven vital chakras*, Los Angeles, The Guild of Tutors Press.

Hacker, H. (1951), 'Women as a minority group', *Social Forces*.

Haigh, G.V. (1968), 'The residential basic encounter group' in H.A. Otto & J. Mann (eds), *Ways of Growth*, New York, Grossman.

Hall, B.L. (1981), 'The democratization of research in adult and non-formal education', in P. Reason & J. Rowan (eds), *Human Inquiry*, Chichester, Wiley.

Halpin, A.W. & Winer, B.J. (1952), *The Leadership Behaviour of the Airplane Commander*, Ohio State University Press.

Hamblin, A. (1972), 'Ultimate goals', *Women's Liberation Review*, 1, 23–46 (Reprinted in *Self & Society* (1975), 3/12, 1–6, and (1976), 4/2, 19–24).

Hampden-Turner, C. (1971), *Radical Man: The process of psycho-social development*, London, Duckworth.

Hampden-Turner, C. (1977), *Sane asylum*, New York, William Morrow & Co.

Hampden-Turner, C. (1981), *Maps of the Mind*, London, Mitchell Beazley.

Hampden-Turner, C. (1983), *Gentlemen and Tradesmen: The values of economic catastrophe*, London, RKP.

Haronian, F. (1974), 'The repression of the sublime', *Synthesis*, 1/1, 51–62.

Harré, R. (1979), *Social Being*, Oxford, Blackwell.

Hay, D. (1982), *Exploring Inner Space*, Harmondsworth, Penguin.

Hegel, G.W.F. (1892), *The Lesser Logic* (ed. W. Wallace), Oxford, Clarendon Press.

Hegel, G.W.F. (1895), *Lectures on the Philosophy of Religion* (3 vols), London, Kegan Paul Trench Trubner.

Hegel, G.W.F. (1971), *Philosophy of Mind*, Oxford, Clarendon Press.

Heider, J. (1974), 'Catharsis in human potential encounter', *Journal of Humanistic Psychology*, 14/4, 27–47.

Henderson, H. (1982), *Thinking Globally, Acting Locally: The politics and ethics of the solar age*, Berkeley, University of California.

Hendricks, G. & Wills, R. (1975), *The Centering Book*, Englewood Cliffs, Prentice-Hall.

Hendricks, G. & Fadiman, J. (1976), *Transpersonal Education*, Englewood Cliffs, Prentice-Hall.

Hendricks, G. & Roberts, T.B. (1977), *The Second Centering Book*, Englewood Cliffs, Prentice-Hall.

Henley, N. (1977), *Body Politics*, Englewood Cliffs, Prentice-Hall.

Herbst, P.G. (1976), *Alternatives to Hierarchies*, Leiden, Martinus Nijhoff.

Heron, J. (1972), *Experience and Method*, Guildford, Human Potential Research Project.

Heron, J. (1974), *Reciprocal Counselling*, Guildford, Human Potential Research Project.

Heron, J. (1981), 'Experiential research methodology' in P. Reason & J. Rowan (eds), *Human Inquiry*, Chichester, Wiley.

Hersey, P.G. & Blanchard, K.H. (1977), *Management of Organizational Behaviour: Utilising human resources* (3rd ed), Englewood Cliffs, Prentice-Hall.

Hersey, P. et al. (1979), 'Situational leadership, perception and the impact of power', *Group & Organization Studies*, 4/4, 418–428.

Hillman, J. (1979), *The Dream and the Underworld*, San Francisco, Harper & Row.

Hoffman, B. (1979), *No One is to Blame*, Palo Alto, Science & Behaviour.

Horne, J.R. (1978), *Beyond Mysticism*, Waterloo, Canadian Corporation for Studies in Religion.

Horney, K. (1942), *Self-analysis*, London, RKP.

Houston, J. (1982), *The Possible Human*, Los Angeles, J.P. Tarcher.

Huang, A.C.-l. (1973), *Embrace Tiger, Return to Mountain*, Moab, Real People Press.

Huczynski, A. (1983), *Encyclopedia of Management Development Methods*, Aldershot, Gower.

Hudson, L. (1970), *Frames of Mind*, Harmondsworth, Penguin.

Hunter, E. (1972), *Encounter in the Classroom: New ways of teaching*, New York, Holt Rinehart & Winston.

Huxley, A. (1963), *The Doors of Perception*, New York, Harper & Row.

Inglis, B. (1964), *Fringe Medicine*, London, Faber.

Jackins, H. (1965), *The Human Side of Human Beings*, Seattle, Rational Island.

Jackins, H. (1970), *Fundamentals of Co-counselling manual*, Seattle, Rational Island.

Jackins, H. (1973), *The Human Situation*, Seattle, Rational Island.

James, J. (1985), *Male sexuality: The Atlantis position*, London, Caliban Books.

Janov, A. (1970), *The Primal Scream*, New York, Putnam.

Johnson, D. & R. (1975), *Learning Together and Alone*, Englewood Cliffs, Prentice-Hall.

Jones, F. & Harris, M.W. (1971), 'The development of interracial awareness in small groups' in L. Blank et al. (eds), *Confrontation: Encounters in Self and Interpersonal Awareness*, New York, Collier-Macmillan.

Jourard, S.M. (1964), *The Transparent Self*, New York, Van Nostrand.

Jourard, S.M. (1968), *Disclosing Man to Himself*, New York, Van Nostrand.

Jourard, S.M. (1971), *Self-disclosure: An experimental analysis of the transparent self*, New York, John Wiley & Sons.

Jung, C.G. (1938), *Psychology and Religion in Collected Works*, Vol.2, London, Routledge & Kegan Paul.

Jung, C.G. (1959), *Basic writings of C.G. Jung* (ed. V.S. de Laszlo), New York, Modern Library.

Jung, C.G. (1971), *The Portable Jung* (ed. J. Campbell), New York, The Viking Press.

Kahn, M. (1973), 'The return of the repressed' in E. Aronson (ed.), *Readings about the Social Animal*, New York, W.H. Freeman.

Kanter, R.M. (1985), *The Change Masters*, London, Unwin Paperbacks.

Kapleau, P. (ed.) (1967), *The Three Pillars of Zen: Teaching, practice and enlightenment*, Boston, Beacon Press.

Karp, M. (1980), 'The classical psychodrama of Moreno', *Self & Society*, 8/9, 292–5.

Kelman, H.C. (1968), *A Time to Speak: On human values and social research*, San Francisco, Jossey-Bass.

Kennard, B. (1982), *Nothing can be Done: Everything is possible*, Andover, Rittenhouse Publishing Co.

Kirschenbaum, H. (1978), *Advanced Value Clarification*, Mansfield, University Associates.

Klapp, O.E. (1969), *Collective Search for Identity*, New York, Holt Rinehart & Winston.

Knutson, J.K. (ed.) (1973), *Handbook of political psychology*, San Francisco, Jossey-Bass.

Koberg, D. & Bagnall, J. (1974), *The Universal Traveller*, New York, William Kaufman.

Kohlberg, L. (1969), 'Stage and sequence: The cognitive-developmental approach to socialization' in D. Goslin (ed.), *Handbook of Socialization Theory and Research*, Chicago, Rand McNally.

Kohlberg, L. (1981), *The Philosophy of Moral Development*, San Francisco, Harper & Row.

Kolton, M.S. (1973), 'The humanistic treatment philosophy of innovative drug programmes', *Journal of Humanistic Psychology*, 13/4, 47–56.

Kornegger, P. (1975), 'Anarchism: The feminist connection' in Dark Star (ed.), *Quiet Rumours: An anarcha-feminist anthology*, London, Dark Star.

Kotler, P. (1973), 'The elements of social action' in G. Zaltman (ed.), *Processes and Phenomena of Social Change*, New York, Academic Press.

Krech, D., Crutchfield, R. & Livson, N. (1969), *Elements of Psychology*, New York, Knopf.

Krippner, S. (1972), 'Altered states of consciousness' in J. White (ed.), *The Highest State of Consciousness*, New York, Anchor.

Labov, W. (1972), 'The logic of nonstandard English' in P.P. Giglioli (ed.), *Language and Social Context*, Harmondsworth, Penguin.

Laing, R.D. (1967), *The Politics of Experience*, Harmondsworth, Penguin.

Laing, R.D. (1983), *The Voice of Experience*, Harmondsworth, Penguin.

Laing, R.D. & Cooper, D. (1964), *Reason and Violence*, London, Tavistock.

Lawrence, P.R. & Lorsch, J.W. (1969), *Developing Organizations: Diagnosis and action*, Reading, Addison-Wesley.

Leary, T. (1970), *The Politics of Ecstasy*, London, Paladin.

Leeds, R. (1970), 'The absorption of protest: A working paper' in W.G. Bennis et al. (eds), *The Planning of Change* (2nd ed), New York, Holt Rinehart & Winston.

Leonard, G.B. (1968), *Education and Ecstasy*, New York, Dell.

Leonard, G.B. (1977), *The Ultimate Athlete*, New York, Avon.

Lessing, D. (1970), *The Four-gated City*, New York, Bantam Books.

Lethbridge, D. (1986), 'A marxist theory of self-actualization', *Journal of Humanistic Psychology*, 26/2, 84–103.

Leuner, H. (1984), *Guided Affective Imagery*, New York, Thieme-Stratton.

Lewin, K. (1936), *Principles of Topological Psychology*, New York, McGraw-Hill.

Lewin, K. et al. (1939), 'Patterns of aggressive behaviour in experimentally created social climates', *Journal of Social Psychology*, 10, 271–99.

Lewis, H.R. & Streitfeld, H.B. (1972), *Growth Games*, London, Abacus.

Lieberman, M.A. et al. (1973), *Encounter Groups: First facts*, New York, Basic Books.

Lilly, J.C. (1973), *The Centre of the Cyclone*, London, Paladin.

Lincoln, Y.S. & Guba, E.G. (1985), *Naturalistic Inquiry*, Beverley Hills, Sage.

Lipton, L. (1960), *The Holy Barbarians*, New York, W.H. Allen.

Liss, J. (1974), *Free to Feel: Finding your way through the new therapies*, London, Wildwood House.

Loevinger, J. (1976), *Ego Development*, San Francisco, Jossey-Bass.

Lowen, A. (1970), *Pleasure*, New York, Coward McCann.

Lowen, A. & Lowen, L. (1977), *The Way to Vibrant Health: A manual of bioenergetic exercises*, New York, Harper Colophon.

McAllister, P. (ed.) (1982), *Reweaving the Web of Life: Feminism and nonviolence*, Philadelphia, New Society Publishers.

McCall, G.J. & Simmons, J.L. (eds) (1969), *Issues in Participant Observation*, Reading, Addison-Wesley.

McGregor, D. (1960), *The Human Side of Enterprise*, New York, McGraw-Hill.

McNamara, W. (1975), 'Psychology and the Christian mystical tradition' in C.T. Tart (ed.), *Transpersonal Psychologies*, London, RKP.

Macy, J.R. (1983), *Despair and Personal Power in the Nuclear Age*, Philadelphia, New Society Publishers.

Madison, P. (1969), *Personality Development in College*, Reading, Mass., Addison-Wesley.

Mahler, M.S. et al. (1975), *The Psychological Birth of the Human Infant*, London, Hutchinson.

Mahoney, M. (1972), *The Meaning of Dreams and Dreaming*, New York, Citadel Press.

Mahrer, A.R. (1978), *Experiencing: A humanistic theory of psychology and psychiatry*, New York, Brunner/Mazel.

Mahrer, A.R. (1983), *Experiential Psychotherapy: Basic practices*, New York, Brunner/Mazel.

Mahrer, A.R. (1985), *Psychotherapeutic change: An alternative approach to meaning and measurement*, New York, W.W. Norton & Co.

Mahrer, A.R. (1986), *Therapeutic Experiencing: The process of change*, New York, W.W. Norton & Co.

Maloney, G.A. (1979), *Invaded by God: Mysticism and the indwelling Trinity*, Denville, Dimension Books.

Marcuse, H. (1969), *An Essay on Liberation*, London, Allen Lane.

Marmor, J. (1974), *Psychiatry in Transition*, London, Butterworth.

Marrow, A.J. (1969), *The Practical Theorist*, New York, Basic Books.

Martin, S. (1983), *Managing without Managers*, Beverly Hills, Sage.

Maruyama, M. (1981), 'Endogenous research: Rationale' and 'Endogenous research: The prison project' in P. Reason & J. Rowan (eds), *Human Inquiry*, Chichester, Wiley.

Maslow, A.H. (1965), *Eupsychian management*, New York, Irwin Dorsey.

Maslow, A.H. (1966), *The Psychology of Science: A reconnaissance*, New York, Henry Regnery.

Maslow, A.H. (1968), *Toward a Psychology of Being*, New York, Van Nostrand.

Maslow, A.H. (1969), 'Notes on being-psychology' in A.J. Sutich & M.A. Vich (eds), *Readings in Humanistic Psychology*, London, Collier-Macmillan.

Maslow, A.H. (1970), *Motivation and Personality* (2nd ed), New York, Harper & Row.

Maslow, A.H. (1970a), *Religion, Values and Peak Experiences*, New York, Viking.

273

Maslow, A.H. (1973), *The Farther Reaches of Human Nature*, Harmondsworth, Penguin.

Masters, R. & Houston, J. (1978), *Listening to the Body*, New York, Delacorte Press.

May, R. (1967), *Psychology and the Human Dilemma*, Princeton, Van Nostrand.

May, R. (1974), *Power and Innocence: A search for the sources of violence*, London, Souvenir Press.

May, R. et al. (eds) (1958), *Existence*, New York, Basic Books.

Metcalf, A. & Humphries, M. (eds) (1985), *The Sexuality of Men*, London, Pluto Press.

Metcalf, H.C. & Urwick, L. (1941), *Dynamic Administration: The collected papers of Mary Parker Follett*, London, Pitman.

Middlebrook, P.N. (1974), *Social Psychology and Modern Life*, New York, Alfred A. Knopf.

Miller, C. & Swift, K. (1979), *Words and women*, Harmondsworth, Penguin.

Mitchell, J. (1971), *Woman's Estate*, New York, Vintage Books.

Mitchell, J. (1974), *Psychoanalysis and Feminism*, New York, Pantheon Books.

Mitroff, I.I. & Kilmann, R.H. (1978), *Methodological Approaches to Social Science*, San Francisco, Jossey-Bass.

Moltmann, J. (1981), *The Trinity and the Kingdom of God*, London, SCM Press.

Montagu, A. (1978), *Touching* (2nd ed), New York, Harper & Row.

Moreno, J.L. (1964), *Psychodrama*, Vol.1, New York, Beacon House.

Moreno, J.L. (1966), *Psychodrama*, Vol.2, New York, Beacon House.

Moreno, J.L. (1969), *Psychodrama*, Vol.3, New York, Beacon House.

Murphy, G. (1950), 'Psychical research and personality', *Journal of the American Society for Psychical Research*, 44/1, 3–20.

Murphy, M. (1978), *The Psychic Side of Sports*, Reading, Mass., Addison-Wesley.

Negrin, S. (1972), *Begin at Start: Some thoughts on personal liberation and world change*, Washington, Times Change Press.

Newsome, A. et al. (1973), *Student Counselling in Practice*, London, University of London Press.

Nicholas, J.M. (1982), 'The comparative impact of OD interventions on hard criteria measures', *Academy of Management Review*, 7/4, 531–42.

O'Connor, E. (1971), *Our Many Selves*, San Francisco, Harper & Row.

Ouspensky, P.D. (1949), *In Search of the Miraculous*, New York, Harcourt Brace.

Pahnke, W.N. (1972), 'Drugs and mysticism' in J. White (ed.), *The Highest State of Consciousness*, Garden City, Doubleday/ Anchor.

Paton, K. (1971), *The Great Brain Robbery*, London, Keith Paton.

Pedler, M, & Boydell, T. (1981), 'What is self-development?' in T. Boydell & M. Pedler (eds), *Management Self-development: Concepts and practices*, Farnborough, Gower.

Perls, F.S. (1969), *Gestalt Therapy Verbatim*, Moab, Real People Press.

Perls, F.S. (1970), 'Four lectures' in J. Fagan & I.L. Shepherd (eds), *Gestalt Therapy Now*, Palo Alto, Science & Behaviour.

Pierce, R. (1966), 'An investigation of grade-point average and therapeutic process variables' Unpublished dissertation, University of Massachusetts. Reviewed in R.R. Carkhuff & G.B. Berenson, *Beyond Counselling and Therapy*, New York, Holt Rinehart & Winston.

Pierce, R.A. et al. (1983), *Emotional Expression in Psychotherapy*, New York, Gardner Press.

Pirani, A. (1975), 'Creative relations in secondary education', *Self & Society*, 3.

Pleck, J.H. & Sawyer, J. (eds) (1974), *Men and Masculinity*, Englewood Cliffs, Prentice-Hall.

Powell, A. (1986), 'Object relations in the psychodrama group', Group Analysis, 19/2, 125–38.

Rajneesh, B.S. (1977), *The Book of the Secrets* (vol.1), New York, Harper Colophon.

Rajneesh, B.S. (1979), *Roots and Wings*, London, RKP.

Rat, Myth & Magic (1973), Anonymous, no origin given.

Randall, R. & Southgate, J. (1980), *Cooperative and Community Group Dynamics: or, your meetings needn't be so appalling*, London, Barefoot Books.

Rawson, P. (1973), *Tantra*, London, Thames & Hudson.

Rawson, P. & Legeza, L. (1973), *Tao: The Chinese philosophy of time and change*, London, Thames & Hudson.

Reason, P. & Rowan, J. (eds) (1981), *Human Inquiry: A sourcebook of New Paradigm Research*, Chichester, John Wiley.

Reddin, W.J. (1977), 'An integration of leader-behaviour typologies', *Group & Organization Studies*, 2/3, 282–95.

Reich, C.A. (1972), *The Greening of America*, Harmondsworth, Penguin.

Reps, P. (1961), *Zen Flesh, Zen Bones*, Garden City, Doubleday.

Reynaud, E. (1983), *Holy Virility*, London, Pluto Press.

Richards, B. (1974), 'Against humanistic psychology', *Self & Society*, 2/8, 2–6.

Richards, M.C. (1969), *Centering: In pottery, poetry and the person*, Middletown, Wesleyan University Press.

Ring, K. (1974), 'A transpersonal view of consciousness: A mapping of farther regions of inner space', *Journal of Transpersonal Psychology*, 6.

Rogers, C.R. (1942), *Counselling and psychotherapy*, Boston, Houghton Mifflin.

Rogers, C.R. (1951), *Client-centred therapy*, Boston, Houghton Mifflin.

Rogers, C.R. (1961), *On Becoming a Person*, London, Constable.

Rogers, C.R. (1967), 'The interpersonal relationship: The core of guidance' in B. Stevens & C.R. Rogers (eds), *Person to Person: The problem of being human*, Moab, Real People Press.

Rogers, C.R. (1969), *Freedom to Learn*, New York, Charles E. Merrill.

Rogers, C.R. (1970), *On Encounter Groups*, New York, Harper & Row.

Rogers, C.R. (1970), 'Towards a Theory of Creativity' in P.E. Vernon (ed.), *Creativity*, Harmondsworth, Penguin.

Rogers, C.R. (1972), 'Comments on Brown & Tedeschi's article', *Journal of Humanistic Psychology*, 12/1, 16–21.

Rogers, C.R. (1983), *Freedom to learn for the 80s*, Columbus, Charles E. Merrill.

Rogers, C.R. & Dymond, R.F. (eds) (1954), *Psychotherapy and Personality Change*, Chicago, University of Chicago Press.

Rogers, C.R. & Rybeck, D. (1985), 'A psychological view of the Camp David meeting', *Counselling*, no.54.

Romey, W.D. (1972), *Risk-Trust-Love: Learning in a humane environment*, New York, Charles E. Merrill.

Rowan, J. (1975a), 'The four-way workshop', *Self & Society*, 3/5, 16–19.

Rowan, J. (1975), 'Encounter group research: No joy?', *Journal of Humanistic Psychology*, 15/2, 19–28.

Rowan, J. (1976), *The Power of the Group*, London, Davis-Poynter.

Rowan, J. (1976a), 'Ethical issues in organizational change' in P.B. Warr (ed.), *Personal Goals and Work Design*, Chichester, John Wiley.

Rowan, J. (1978), *The Structured Crowd*, London, Davis-Poynter.

Rowan, J. (1979), 'Hegel and self-actualization', *European Journal of Humanistic Psychology*, 1/5, 129–38 and 149–54.

Rowan, J. (1983), *The Reality Game: A guide to humanistic counselling and therapy*, London, RKP.

Rowan, J. (1983a), 'The real self and mystical experiences', *Journal of Humanistic Psychology*, 23/2, 9–27.

Rowan, J. (1983b), 'Person as group' in H.H. Blumberg et al. (eds), *Small Groups and Social Interaction* (vol.2), Chichester, John Wiley & Sons.

Rowan, J. (1985), 'Listening as a Four-level Activity' in *British Journal of Psychotherapy*, 1/4, 273–285.

Rowan, J. (1987), *The Horned God: Feminism and men as wounding and healing*, London, RKP.

Rowan, J. & Dryden, W. (eds) (1987), *Innovative Therapy in Britain*, London, Harper & Row.

Rowbotham, S. et al. (1979), *Beyond the Fragments*, London, The Merlin Press.

Rubin, J. (1973), *Growing (up) at 37*, New York, Bantam.

Russell, P. (1982), *The Awakening Earth: Our next evolutionary leap*, London, RKP.

Sanford, N. (1981), 'A model for action research', in P. Reason & J. Rowan (eds), *Human Inquiry*, Chichester, Wiley.

Sartre, J.-P. (1963), *Search for a Method*, New York, Alfred A. Knopf.

Sartre, J.-P. (1969), *Being and Nothingness*, London, Methuen.

Schachtel, E.G. (1969), 'Perception as creative experience: Critique of the concept of regression in the service of the ego', in H.-M. Chiang & A.H. Maslow (eds), *The Healthy Personality: Readings*, New York, Van Nostrand.

Scheff, T. (1966), *Being Mentally Ill*, London, Weidenfeld & Nicholson.

Schmuck, R. (1966), 'Some aspects of classroom social climate', *Psychology in the Schools*, 3, 59–65.

Schrank, J. (1972), *Teaching Human Beings: 101 subversive activities for the classroom*, Boston, Beacon Press.

Schuttler, B.L. et al. (1975), 'Community problem solving at the neighbourhood level', *Creativity Network*, 1/3, 13–37.

Schutz, W.C. (1967), *Joy*, New York, Grove Press.

Schutz, W.C. (1971), *Here comes Everybody: Bodymind and encounter culture*, New York, Harper & Row.

Schutz, W.C. (1973), *Elements of Encounter*, Big Sur, Joy Press.

Schutz, W.C. (1975), 'Not encounter and certainly not facts', *Journal of Humanistic Psychology*, 15/2, 7–18.

Schutz, W.C. (1977), 'Bodymind' in C.A. Garfield (ed.), *Rediscovery of the Body*, New York, Laurel/Dell.

Schutz, W.C. (1979), *Profound Simplicity*, London, Turnstone Books.

Segal, J. (1985), *Phantasy in everyday life*, Harmondsworth, Penguin.

Seidenberg, R. (1973), 'Is anatomy destiny?' in J.B. Miller (ed.), *Psychoanalysis and Women*, Harmondsworth, Penguin.

Sermat, V. & Smyth, M. (1974), 'Content analysis of verbal communication in the development of a relationship: conditions influencing self-disclosure', *Journal of Personality and Social Psychology*, 26/4, 332–46.

Shaffer, J.B.P. & Galinsky, M.D. (1974), *Models of Group Therapy and Sensitivity Training*, Englewood Cliffs, Prentice-Hall.

Shapiro, S.B. (1976), *The Selves Inside You*, Berkeley, Explorations Institute.

Shaw, J. (1974), *The Self in Social Work*, London, RKP.

Sherwood, C. (1973), 'Control', *Self & Society*, 1/6, 21–3.

Shohet, R. (1985), *Dream Sharing*, London, Turnstone Books.

Shorr, J.E. (1983), *Psychotherapy through Imagery* (2nd ed), New York, Thieme-Stratton.

Simon, S.B., Howe, L.W. & Kirschenbaum, H. (1972), *Values Clarification*, New York, Hart Publishing Company.

Simpson, E.L. (1971), *Democracy's Stepchildren: A study of need and belief*, San Francisco, Jossey-Bass.

Singer, J.L. (1974), *Imagery and Daydream Methods in Psychotherapy and Behaviour Modification*, New York, Academic Press.

Sjöö, M. & Mor, B. (1980), *The Ancient Religion of the Great Cosmic Mother of All*, Trondheim, Rainbow Press.

Skinner, B.F. (1974), *About Behaviorism*, London, Jonathan Cape.

Smith, M.B. (1974), *Humanizing Social Psychology*, San Francisco, Jossey-Bass.

Smith, P.B. (1975), 'Are there adverse effects of sensitivity training?', *Journal of Humanistic Psychology*, 15/2, 29–47.

Snodgrass, J. (ed.) (1977), *A Book of Readings for Men against Sexism*, New York, Times Change Press.

Solomon, D. (ed.) (1964), *LSD: The consciousness-expanding drug*, New York, Berkley Medallion.

Southgate, J. & Randall, R. (1978), *The Barefoot Psychoanalyst* (2nd ed), London, AKHPC.

Spender, D. (1980), *Man made language*, London, RKP.

Spino, M. (1976), *Beyond Jogging*, Berkeley, Celestial Arts.

Spretnak, C. (ed.) (1982), *The Politics of Women's Spirituality: Essays on the rise of spiritual power within the feminist movement*, Garden City, Anchor/Doubleday.

Stafford, P.G. & Golightly, B.H. (1967), *LSD: The problem-solving psychedelic*, New York, Award Books.

Starhawk (1979), *The Spiral Dance: A rebirth of the ancient religion of the Great Goddess*, San Fancisco, Harper & Row.

Starhawk (1982), *Dreaming the Dark: Magic, sex and politics*, Boston, Beacon Press.

Stein, M.I. (1974), *Stimulating Creativity* (2 vols), New York, Academic Press.

Stein, M.R. (1972), 'On the limits of professional thought' in J.F. Glass & J.R. Staude (eds), *Humanistic Society*, Pacific Palisades, Goodyear.

Steiner, C, et al. (1975), *Readings in radical psychiatry*, New York, Grove Press.

Stevens, B. (1970), *Don't Push the River*, Moab, Real People Press.

Stevens, B. (1984), *Burst out Laughing*, Berkeley, Celestial Arts.

Stevens, B. & Rogers, C.R. (eds) (1967), *Person to Person*, Moab, Real People Press.

Stevens, J.O. (1971), *Awareness: Exploring, experimenting, experiencing*, Moab, Real People Press.

Sturgess, D. (1972), 'Happenings in a primary school' in D. Rubinstein & C. Stoneman (eds), *Education for Democracy* (2nd ed), Harmondsworth, Penguin.

Szasz, T. (1961), *The Myth of Mental Illness*, London, Secker & Warburg.

Tart, C.T. (ed.) (1969), *Altered States of Consciousness*, New York, John Wiley .

Tart, C.T. (ed.) (1975), *Transpersonal Psychologies*, London, RKP.

Thomas, H.F. (1970), 'Encounter – the game of no game' in A. Burton (ed.), *Encounter*, San Francisco, Jossey-Bass.

Tichy, N.M. (1977), 'Demise, absorption or renewal for the future of organization development' in W.W. Burke (ed.), *The Cutting Edge: Current theory and practice in organization development*, La Jolla, University Associates.

Torbert, W. (1972), *Learning from Experience: Toward consciousness*, New York, Columbia University Press.

Turner, R. (ed.) (1974), *Ethnomethodology: Selected readings*, Harmondsworth, Penguin.

Varela, J.A. (1971), *Psychological Solutions to Social Problems*, New York, Academic Press.

Vargiu, R. (1974), 'Psychosynthesis workbook: Subpersonalities', Synthesis, 1/1, 74-page section.

Vaughan, F. (1986), *The Inward Arc*, Boston, New Science Library.

Verny, T. (1982), *The Secret Life of the Unborn Child*, London, Sphere.

von Eckartsberg, R. (1981), 'Maps of the mind: The cartography of consciousness' in R.S. Valle & R. von Eckartsberg (eds), *The Metaphors of Consciousness*, New York, Plenum Press.

von Franz, M.-L. (1964), 'The process of individuation' in C.G. Jung (ed.), *Man and His Symbols*, London, Aldus Books.

Walker, B.G. (1983), *The Woman's Encyclopaedia of Myths and Secrets*, San Francisco, Harper & Row.

Walker, R. (ed.) (1985), *Applied Qualitative Research*, Aldershot, Gower.

Wallis, R. (1985), 'Betwixt therapy and salvation: The changing form of the Human Potential Movement' in R.K. Jones (ed.), *Sickness and Sectarianism*, Aldershot, Gower.

Warnock, D. (1982), 'Patriarchy is a killer: What people concerned about peace and justice should know' in P. McAllister (ed.), *Reweaving the Web of Life*, Philadelphia, New Society Publishers.

Watkins, J.G. (1978), *The Therapeutic Self*, New York, Human Sciences Press.

Watts, A.W. (1951), *Psychotherapy East and West*, New York, Pantheon Books.

Watts, A.W. (1957), *The Way of Zen*, London, Thames & Hudson.

Weiner, B. (1985), *Human Motivation*, New York, Springer-Verlag.

Wells, B. (1973), *Psychedelic Drugs: Psychological, medical and social issues*, Harmondsworth, Penguin.

Wheelis, A. (1972), 'How people change' in J.F. Glass & J.R. Staude (eds) (1972), *Humanistic Society*, Pacific Palisades, Goodyear.

Wilber, K. (1977), *The Spectrum of Consciousness*, Wheaton, Quest.

Wilber, K (1980), *The Atman Project*, Wheaton, Quest.

Wilber, K. (1981), *Up from Eden: A transpersonal view of human evolution*, Garden City, Anchor/Doubleday.

Wilber, K. (1982), 'Reflections on the New Age paradigm' in K. Wilber (ed.), *The Holographic Paradigm and Other Paradoxes*, Boulder, Shambhala.

Wilber, K. (1983), *Eye to Eye*, Garden City, Anchor/Doubleday.

Wilber, K. (1986), 'The spectrum of development' and 'The spectrum of psychopathology' in K. Wilber et al. (eds), *Transformations of Consciousness*, Boston, New Science Library.

Willis, E. (1981), *Beginning to See the Light*, New York, Alfred A Knopf.

Winnicott, D.W. (1975), *Through Paediatrics to Psychoanalysis*, London, Hogarth Press.

Wood, D. (1971), 'Strategies' in S. & R. Godlovitch & J. Harris (eds), *Animals, Men and Morals*, London, Gollancz.

Woodcock, M. (1979), *Team Development Manual*, Aldershot, Gower.

Woodworth, R.S. (1958), *Dynamics of Behaviour*, New York, Henry Holt.

Wright, B. (1982), 'Sunpower/Moonpower/Transformation' in P. McAllister (ed.), *Reweaving the Web of Life*, Philadelphia, New Society Publishers.

Wright, D.L. (1973), 'Images of human nature underlying sociological theory: A review and synthesis', Annual Meeting of the American Sociological Association.

Wright, D.L. (1974), 'On the bases of social order: Indoctrinated control versus voluntary cooperation', Annual Meeting of the American Sociological Association.

Wyckoff, H. (1975), 'Problem-solving groups for women' in C. Steiner et al. (eds), *Readings in Radical Psychiatry*, New York, Grove Press.

Yablonsky, L. (1965), *Synanon: The tunnel back*, London, Macmillan.

Zaltman, G. (1973), *Processes and Phenomena of Social Change*, New York, Academic Press.

INDEX

INDEX

Ginsburg, C., 257
Giorgi, A., 254
Glass, J.F., 227
Glenn, M., 217
Glouberman, D., 196
Godfrey, E., 187, 191
Goffman, E., 96
Goldstein, K., 243
Golembiewski, R.T., 121, 134
Golightly, B.H., 16
Goodison, L., 63, 104
Goodman, P., 102
Gouldner, A., 227
Graham, S., 188
Gray, E.D., 228
Gray, H., 117
Green, A.M., 150, 214
Green, E.E., 150, 214
Greenberg, I.A., 101
Groddeck, G., 240
Grof, S., 89, 91, 92, 142, 144, 254
Grusky, O., 126
Guba, E.G., 256
Gunther, B., 30, 39, 68
Guntrip, H., 96
Gurdjieff, 204

Hacker, H., 163
Hadlock, W., 106
Hage, J., 126
Haigh, G.V., 63
Hall, B.L., 255
Halpin, A.W., 131
Hamblin, A., 160, 162, 166
Hampden–Turner, C., 42–6, 47, 49, 50, 64, 77, 212, 222, 224, 226, 255
Harari, C., 188, 192
Harman, W., 38
Haronian, F., 142
Harré, R., 253
Harris, M.W., 163
Harrison, R., 187, 191
Hay, D., 145
Hegel, G.W.F., 27, 32, 46, 84
Heider, J., 67, 68, 145
Henderson, H., 230

Hendricks, G., 114
Henley, N., 68
Herbst, P.G., 130
Heron, J., 79, 83, 84, 85, 188, 190, 192, 195, 199, 210, 212, 255
Hersey, P.G., 133, 134, 231
Higgin, G., 191
Hillman, J., 86
Hoffman, B., 90
Holme, K., 194
Honti, L., 201
Horne, J.R., 31, 144
Horney, K., 80, 84
Horobin, R., 83
Houston, J., 69–70, 196, 210, 211
Huang, A.C–L., 27, 28
Huczynski, A., 121
Hudson, L., 99, 181
Humphries, M., 157, 230
Hunter, E., 109, 110
Huxley, A., 145

Inglis, B., 24
Inkson, J., 126

Jackins, H., 71, 79–85
James, J., 157
Janov, A., 83, 84
Johnson, D., 113
Johnson, R., 113
Jones, F., 163
Jones, G.S., 80
Jourard, S.M., 47–50, 79, 190, 191
Jung, C.G., 86, 93, 95, 96, 143, 206, 208, 212

Kahn, M., 38
Kanter, R.M., 127, 129
Kapleau, P., 25, 65
Karp, M., 101
Kelly, G.A., 255
Kelman, H.C., 256
Kennard, B., 180
Kent, C., 187
Kerouac, J., 21

285